Putting Higher Education to Work
Skills and Research for Growth in East Asia

WORLD BANK EAST ASIA AND PACIFIC REGIONAL REPORT

Well known for their economic success and dynamism, countries in the East Asia and Pacific region must tackle an increasingly complex set of challenges to continue on a path of sustainable development. Learning from others within the region and beyond can help identify what works, what doesn't, and why, in the search for practical solutions to these challenges. This regional report series presents analyses of issues relevant to the region, drawing on the global knowledge and experience of the World Bank and its partners. The series aims to inform public discussion, policy formulation, and development practitioners' actions to turn challenges into opportunities.

World Bank East Asia and Pacific Regional Report

Putting Higher Education to Work

Skills and Research for Growth in East Asia

THE WORLD BANK
Washington, D.C.

© 2012 The International Bank for Reconstruction and Development / The World Bank
1818 H Street NW
Washington, DC 20433
Telephone: 202-473-1000
Internet: www.worldbank.org
All rights reserved

1 2 3 4 14 13 12 11

ISBN: 978-0-8213-8490-9
eISBN: 978-0-8213-8911-9
DOI: 10.1596/978-0-8213-8490-9

Library of Congress Cataloging-in-Publication data has been requested.

Cover photo: Graduates attend the 2009 bachelor's degree commencement ceremony at the Huazhong University of Science and Technology, Wuhan, Hubei province, China. © Feature China / European Pressphoto Agency.

Cover design: Naylor Design, Inc.

Contents

Boxes

Figures

Tables

Foreword

Expanding employment and increasing productivity are at the top of the agenda for policy makers across the globe. For countries seeking to spur growth, creating jobs and raising productivity are primary concerns. For young people, too, these issues are a priority. Students and graduates everywhere are asking for more and better opportunities—to study and work, and to learn and create new knowledge and enterprises.

With skilled labor and technological capability increasingly becoming the touchstones of competitiveness in an open and integrated world environment, the role of higher education in economic growth is thus taking on a greater significance. Not only do higher education institutions help impart the behavioral, cognitive, and technical skills that make workers effective in the labor market, they are increasingly valued as the engines of research that can drive innovation, entrepreneurship, and productivity.

Realizing the potential of higher education to spur growth is a priority for East Asia. *Putting Higher Education to Work: Skills and Research for Growth in East Asia* is a comprehensive look at higher education in East Asia—how it has changed, how it will continue to evolve, and how it can be improved to become more responsive and relevant to the needs of the labor market and the economy as a whole. Using innovative firm surveys and the latest available evidence from the region, the authors shed light on the functional skills that workers must possess to be employable and to support firms' competitiveness and productivity. They also examine how higher education systems can produce the commercially applicable research that will help countries apply, assimilate, adapt, and develop the new technologies that will drive growth.

Though this volume focuses specifically on the developing countries of East Asia, its methodologies, messages, and analysis will be important resources for students, researchers, and policy makers who study and shape the delivery of higher education and training in other regions around the world. The authors offer valuable and succinct guidance on some of the most effective policy measures being deployed by national and regional governments, by firms, and by universities themselves to enhance the contribution that higher education systems can make to economic change.

Higher education will continue to be a core issue for the World Bank and its client countries, and it will also constitute a central pillar of the labor and educational agenda for years to come. I am confident that this volume, the first in the East Asia and Pacific Regional Report Series, will help the region's economies embrace the challenge of achieving rapid growth led by gains in productivity. The measures proposed in this volume should help East Asia reach this objective in an increasingly competitive global environment.

James W. Adams
Vice President
East Asia and Pacific Region
World Bank

Acknowledgments

The preparation of this study was led by Emanuela di Gropello under the guidance of Emmanuel Jimenez and Eduardo Velez Bustillo. The volume was written by Emanuela di Gropello (lead author), Prateek Tandon, and Shahid Yusuf, with significant contributions from many others. Sonali Ballal and Eleanor Wang provided outstanding research inputs. The volume benefited from many commissioned background papers written by international and regional experts outside the core team. The core team is grateful for analytical work done by David Chapman, Dandan Chen, Richard Doner, Hal Hill, HRInc., Patarapong Intarakumnerd, Daniel Levy, Vu Hoang Linh, Giang Thanh Long, Wanhua Ma, Bagyo Moeliodihardjo, Ka Ho Mok, Hena Mukherjee, Kaoru Nabeshima, Reehana Raza, Omporn Regel, Bryan Ritchie, Chris Sakellariou, Edita Tan, Le Viet Thuy, Kin Bing Wu, Weiping Wu, and Yesim Yilmaz. These background papers are available at http://www.worldbank.org/eap/highered.

The World Bank internal peer reviewers were Andreas Blom, Alberto Rodriguez, Jamil Salmi, and Jee-Peng Tan. Excellent comments were also received from Luc Weber (Rector Emeritus, University of Geneva), Mike Luz (former Undersecretary of Education for the Philippines), Vicharn Panich (former Chairman of the Thai Higher Education Commission), Annie Koh (Dean, Office of Executive and Professional Education, and Academic Director, Singapore Management University), and Phonephet Boupha (Director General of Higher Education, Lao People's Democratic Republic). The study was edited by Bruce Ross-Larson.

Finally, this volume incorporates the valuable comments received by policy makers, academics, and international donors during several regional and country consultation events that took place from June 2010 to July 2011. A Global Development Learning Network virtual consultation took place in June 2010 to discuss the initial findings of the study with 180 participants from the region. Other regional consultations occurred in Seoul, Korea, at the Global Human Resource Forum (October 2010); in Phuket, Thailand, at the Conference on Governance and Financing of Higher Education in East Asia (October 2010); in Jakarta, Indonesia, at the Regional Skill Conference (March 2011); and in Bali, Indonesia, at the East Asia Summit Education Ministers' Meeting (July 2011). The task team is grateful for the reactions and comments of the delegations at these and other country events.

Abbreviations

ABD	Asian Development Bank
ALL	Adult Literacy and Life Skills Survey
DGHE	Directorate General of Higher Education
EU	European Union
GDP	gross domestic product
GER	gross enrollment ratio
GPA	grade point average
HECS	Higher Education Contribution Scheme
HEI	higher education institution
ICS	investment climate survey
ICT	information communication technology
ILO	International Labour Organization
IMF	International Monetary Fund
ISCED	International Standard Classification of Education
IT	information technology
KIC	Knowledge-Integrating Community
MIT	Massachusetts Institute of Technology
MNC	multinational corporations
NQF	national qualifications framework
NSB	National Science Board
NUS	National University of Singapore
OECD	Organisation for Economic Co-operation and Development
PHE	private higher education
PHEI	private higher education institution
PISA	Programme for International Student Assessment
POSTECH	Pohang University of Science and Technology
PPP	purchasing power parity
PROPHE	Program for Research on Private Higher Education
S&E	science and engineering
SAR	Special Administrative Regions

SJTU	Shanghai Jiao Tong University
SLF	Student Loan Fund
SME	small and medium enterprise
SMK	*sekolah menengah kejuruan* (vocational secondary schools), Indonesia
SMU	*sekolah menengah umum* (general secondary schools), Indonesia
SOE	state-owned enterprises
STEM	science, technology, engineering, and math
STF	State Training Fund
TAMA	Technology Advanced Metropolitan Area
THES	Times Higher Education Supplement
TIMSS	Trends in International Mathematics and Science Study
TLO	technology licensing office
TTI	Technology Transfer Initiative
TVET	Technical and vocational education and training
UIL	university-industry link
UIS	UNESCO Institute for Statistics
USPTO	U.S. Patent and Trademark Office
VHLSS	Vietnam Household Living Standards Survey
WB	World Bank
WDR	World Development Report
WIPO	World Intellectual Property Organization

Country abbreviations used in figures

ARG	Argentina
AUS	Australia
AUT	Austria
BEL	Belgium
BRA	Brazil
CAN	Canada
CHE	Switzerland
CHL	Chile
CHN	China
DEU	Germany
DNK	Denmark
ESP	Spain
FIN	Finland
FRA	France
GBR	United Kingdom
GIB	Gibraltar
HKG	Hong Kong SAR, China
IDN	Indonesia
IND	India
ISR	Israel
ITA	Italy
JPN	Japan
KHM	Cambodia
KOR	Korea, Republic of
LAO	Lao People's Democratic Republic
MEX	Mexico

MYS	Malaysia
NLD	Netherlands
NOR	Norway
NZL	New Zealand
PHL	Philippines
RUS	Russian Federation
SGP	Singapore
SWE	Sweden
THA	Thailand
TUR	Turkey
VNM	Vietnam
ZAF	South Africa

Note: These three-letter country codes are part of the International Organization for Standardization (ISO) 3166 standard to represent countries.

Currency equivalents

(rates effective April 20, 2011)

Thai Baht

US$ 1 = 29.960 THB
THB 1 = US$ 0.334

Chinese Yuan

US$ 1 = 6.525 CNY
CNY 1 = US$ 0.153

Vietnamese Dong

US$ 1 = VND 2092
VND = US$ 0.0048

Indonesian Rupiah

US$ 1 = IDR 8654.5
IDR 1 = US$ 0.0001

Philippine Pesos

US$ 1 = PHP 43.279
PHP 1 = US$ 0.023

Cambodian Riels

US$ 1 = KHR 3998
KHR 3998 = US$ 0.0002

Singapore Dollars

US$ 1 = SGD 1.24
SGD 1 = US$ 0.8

Mongolian Tugriks

US$ 1 = MNT 1226.5
MNT 1 = US$ 0.0008

Lao Kip

US$ 1 = LAK 8045
LAK 1 = US$ 0.0001

Special Drawing Rights

1XDR = US$ 1.602

Fiscal year

January 1–December 31

Summary

Despite impressive gains, higher education could contribute even more to East Asia's development agenda

East Asia is a model region that has grown rapidly, but its low- and middle-income countries face the challenges of maintaining growth and climbing the income ladder, both requiring improvements in productivity. Higher education is critical in this effort because it provides the high-level skills and research to apply current technologies and to assimilate, adapt, and develop new technologies, two drivers of productivity.[1] It can thus be a key driver of growth. Individuals with more years of higher education score higher on measures of skill competencies than do individuals with few or no years of higher education. And academic, technical, thinking, and behavioral skills and productivity are shown to be positively related. Several indicators of innovation also support the need for higher education. An innovative firm is associated with an increase of about 25 percentage points in its share of workers with more than 12 years of schooling. And countries that have more science and engineering graduates and that engage in more higher education research tend to have better innovation outcomes.

Access has increased dramatically in low- and middle-income East Asia, but higher education is not yet fulfilling its potential. Low- and middle-income East Asia has been expanding access to higher education over the past 20 to 30 years, going in many cases from very low enrollment rates to enrollment rates of 20 percent or more. Fluctuating between 10 and 50 percent, tertiary gross enrollment rates of low- and middle-income East Asian countries are on par with those of countries of similar income levels but are still below those of upper-income countries. A key vulnerability to sustained growth of low- and middle-income East Asia is in developing and deploying enough of the right types of skills and research for a more competitive global economy. Higher education can reduce this vulnerability by sufficiently providing the skills and research to increase productivity and innovation.

But higher education today does not sufficiently provide its graduates with the skills that firms need to increase their productivity. The quantity of higher education graduates is still too low for the labor market in countries like Cambodia, China, and Vietnam. More important than quantity, however, is quality. Across low- and middle-income East Asia, employers expect workers—particularly those with higher education—to possess the technical, behavioral, and thinking skills to increase their productivity and growth. They need science, technology, engineering, and math (STEM) skills. They also need the problem-solving and creative skills to support a higher-value-added manufacturing sector and the business, thinking, and behavioral skills for a higher-productivity service sector. Employer perceptions and wage skill premiums point to gaps in all these groups of skills in newly hired professionals across the region.

Compounding the quality issues is higher education's exclusion of capable and talented students because of their socioeconomic status, ethnicity, and rural residence. Across the region, ethnic minorities, in particular, appear to exhibit shortfalls in both tertiary enrollment and completion.

Higher education also fails to provide the type of research needed to boost technological upgrading in firms. Governments are urging universities to go beyond simply providing skills to support innovation through research and technology. Research enables universities to produce ideas for the business community, thereby contributing to knowledge and technological innovation through basic and applied research and technology transfer. But international rankings and research output indicate that low- and middle-income East Asian higher education systems are not providing research of adequate quality. Even mere university involvement in technology adaptation and upgrading is limited in lower- and middle-income East Asia, with the possible exception of China. In Malaysia, Mongolia, and Thailand, for instance, universities are mentioned as leading in acquiring technological innovations (in a broad sense) by only 1–2 percent of firms.

Five disconnects

A major reason higher education fails to do its job is that its institutions have been managed as disconnected individual institutions. Higher education needs to be seen as a "system" including both institutions and the stakeholders that interact with them. Such a system includes firms, research institutes,

earlier education institutions, and other skill providers. Higher education outcomes are the product of the interactions between all these actors, and failing to consider the links between higher education institutions and the wider world around them leads to poor performance and poor outcomes.

At least five disconnects are evident in East Asia's higher education systems, roughly ranked for their impact on higher education outcomes:

- A gap between higher education institutions and the skill needs of employers
- A weak research and technology nexus between higher education institutions and companies
- A separation between teaching and research institutions (or more generally teaching and research functions)
- A disconnect among higher education institutions themselves and between these institutions and training providers
- A separation between higher education institutions and earlier education institutions (schools)

These disconnects are pervasive throughout low- and middle-income East Asia, but their intensity varies across income and technology cluster groups, tending to be most severe in low-income–lower-technology cluster countries. The intensity of the various disconnects within each country will also vary, giving rise to diversified diagnostics by country.

Public policy and its three pillars

Most disconnects are due to information, capacity, and incentive constraints that have been poorly addressed, suggesting market and policy failures. Public policy has the potential to address them (although not all the policies are strictly related to higher education, and not all actors and interactions at the core of higher education systems will be equally amenable to policies). Reforms in the following areas should have the highest priority in low- and middle-income East Asia:

- Financing adequately the aspects of higher education that correct for externalities and market failures, such as research, science, technology, engineering, math, and scholarships and loans for the poor and disadvantaged—all within a coherent financing framework

- Managing public higher institutions by supporting more autonomous and accountable institutions
- Providing better stewardship for the higher education system, especially by putting in place the right incentives for the private sector to thrive, ensuring links between industry and providers, and handling the interaction between domestic and international higher education

More efficient spending and financing of higher education

In most countries, public spending goes to institutions regardless of whether they are addressing public goods (such as research), externalities (as in STEM), or equity concerns. Too often it is not allocated in a way that is performance based. This lack of prioritization and these inefficiencies contribute to many of the disconnects by underfunding of research, STEM skills, scholarships, and other equity-related measures. Improved public spending can address many of these issues. For instance, it can help tackle the disconnect with earlier education by supporting student transitions from secondary to tertiary education through scholarships and loans. It can also help tackle the disconnects between universities and firms in research and technology by supporting higher funding for research in universities combined with performance-based funding.

The precise challenges vary across the individual countries, but all countries face some common imperatives. First, countries need to be selective in deciding their priorities for funding. Second, they need to identify priorities for public spending (research, inclusiveness, and so forth). Because public resources are scarce, countries should be as efficient as possible in allocating these resources and be more innovative in raising funds. Greater efficiency means being more selective and performance based in the way public funds

for teaching and research are allocated across institutions and targeting scholarships and loans better. Being innovative in raising resources means attracting more private funds. Variable fee policies, combined with effective loan schemes, are one effective way to mobilize private resources while protecting access for the poor and disadvantaged. Public-private matching grant schemes are other options successfully applied in some upper-income East Asian countries.[2]

Better management of public institutions

Public tertiary institutions are critical in East Asia because 70 percent of all students are enrolled in them. Yet decision-making autonomy in public sector institutions remains underdeveloped. Academic and procedural autonomy are particularly misaligned, with greater autonomy in academic than procedural issues. Accountability structures fall particularly short in developing relationships with nongovernment stakeholders (employers, faculty members, students). Having insufficient autonomy to select the staff members they want and to decide on their academic programs makes it difficult for tertiary institutions to deliver what firms need—perpetuating the disconnect between skill providers and users. And the lack of accountability of university management to representative university boards makes it less compelling for institutions to fulfill the needs of skill or research users.

By setting the right incentives for public institutions through appropriate autonomy and accountability, governments can address many disconnects. Although autonomy is most urgent for middle-income countries, the beneficial effects of autonomy are valid at all income levels. It is also essential for all countries to complete their accountability frameworks by delegating greater power and responsibilities to institution boards and by providing students the information to choose and the opportunity to move across institutions, while ensuring continuous accountability to governments.

Exercising stewardship of the higher education system

Beyond managing the public sector, higher education departments need to coordinate actors and connections not under their full control but critical to the performance of the sector. Exercising stewardship requires the capacity to coordinate higher education departments with other departments and ministries, steer private higher education institutions, support links between higher education institutions and firms in skills and research, and handle the interaction between the domestic and international higher education markets. The lack of interaction between higher education institutions and firms to some extent reflects a lack of information on what works and a lack of legal and financial incentives to connect. Disconnects between skill providers and users are also related to a private sector not fulfilling its potential because of poor policy, regulatory, and information incentives. Both issues point to stewardship failures.

Governments can improve their stewardship by ensuring that private and public providers complement each other, especially in meeting the skill needs of employers. They can ensure favorable policies, clear and efficient regulation and information, and better access of both public and private providers to student loans (and competitive funding for research). Governments can also connect firms and providers of skills and research by sharing best practices—from collaborating in curriculum development to setting up university incubators—and by offering the incentives to make these university-industry links work (bringing in intermediaries and providing matching funds).

Country priorities, policies, and reform

The final goals of higher education are much the same across countries. But the challenges, disconnects, and constraints—which are related not just to higher education—vary, leading to different intermediate goals and thus to different immediate priorities. Addressing skill gaps through higher-quality graduates and greater inclusiveness should be the first immediate goal of lower-income countries, followed by gradually increasing the quantity of graduates and starting to build research capacity in some university departments relevant to the economy's needs. For middle-income countries, it will be critical to have both a solid skill base and a stronger capacity for innovation through skills and research. The priorities will differ across countries. Indonesia and the Philippines, for instance, should focus on improving graduate quality and inclusiveness, while building research capacity in a few universities. China should continue developing its skill base (both quality and quantity) and further scale up its research effort and impact.

The underlying disconnects, constraints, and priorities will dictate the policy pillars, levers, and specific policy measures for each country and country group. The report illustrates the policy priorities overall and by income group and technology cluster. With this suggested set of priorities as a start, individual country diagnostics of disconnects (including better assessments of the intensity of the various disconnects in each country) and their causes are then needed to inform more refined policy measures. Moving from policy to reform will require careful consideration of the political economy and the broader economic policies affecting higher education to decide on the appropriate content, sequencing, and pace of reform.

Notes

1. *Higher education* is defined broadly to include all public and private formal institutions of learning that take place beyond upper-secondary education.
2. Under a coherent financing framework, private funding would not only complement public funding in financing some of these activities but also support system expansion and diversification (targeting some of the other country priorities, such as increasing enrollment or service-related disciplines).

Higher Education for Growth through Skills and Research | 1

A fundamental question facing East Asia, especially its low- and middle-income economies, is how to sustain or even accelerate the growth of recent decades. From 1950 to 2005, for example, the region's real income per head rose sevenfold. With aging populations, these economies will need to derive an increasing share of growth from productivity improvements rather than from physical factor accumulation to drive growth.[1]

The recent global economic and financial crisis has served only to lend urgency to East Asia's search for avenues to higher productivity and competitiveness in an increasingly global market, ultimately leading to growth. Investment in human capital, physical investment in research and development (R&D), technological progress, and the increase in total factor productivity arising from scale economies and agglomeration effects are all elements of the search. These investments will help East Asia reap the rewards of globalization and rapid technological development, promote within-sector productivity growth, and provide the necessary incentives for further labor reallocation toward high-productivity sectors.

Investing in education—particularly higher education—is a crucial part of East Asia's drive toward greater productivity, growth, and technological development. This book introduces a conceptual framework for the analysis of higher education in lower- and middle-income countries in East Asia (the target country group).[2] The book takes a broad definition of higher education to include all public and private formal institutions of learning beyond the upper-secondary level. These institutions award formal academic degrees, diplomas, or professional certification and include, but are not limited to, universities, two- and four-year colleges, institutes of technology, religious-based educational institutions, online and distance learning, foreign branch campuses, and other collegiate-level institutions (such as vocational, trade, or career) (see appendix A for a detailed list of higher education institutions in East Asia).

At the very core of the conceptual framework is the idea that higher education in low- and middle-income East Asia has the potential to lift productivity and competitiveness by providing the high-level skills demanded by the labor market and by launching or expanding robust research needed for innovation and growth. As important is the need to consider higher education as a system composed of the higher education institutions themselves; the other skill and research users and providers that interact with them; the underlying policies that support higher education institutions; and the interactions among higher education institutions, users, and providers. While it is important to note that higher education provides several non-economic benefits such as nation building and socialization, this book focuses on the economic benefits of higher education as they relate to skills and research.

The book argues that higher education is failing to deliver skills for growth and research for innovation because of widespread disconnects between higher education institutions and other skill and research users and providers. These disconnects undermine the very functioning of the higher education system. The main assumption of the report is that to deliver labor market skills to higher education graduates, these institutions (a) must have characteristics that are aligned with what employers and employees need and (b) must be well connected among themselves and other skills providers. Similarly, to deliver research that can enhance innovation and productivity, higher education institutions need to have a strong role in research provision and have strong links with firms and other research providers.

Getting the system to work well requires adequate information, capacity, and incentives that are closely related to financial resources, public higher education management, and stewardship for higher education systems. Government and households have a critical role to play at the policy stage, including holding institutions accountable for results and providing public and private resources. The disconnects are ultimately illustrative of weaknesses and failures in the way financial resources and institutions are managed. Prompt public intervention is required because no country in East Asia has reached high-income status without a strong higher education system.

Figure 1.1 illustrates this conceptual framework as presented throughout the chapters of this report. This first chapter presents the economic landscape in East Asia,

showing the vast differences of productivity and growth across countries in the region. To show how low- and middle-income countries can advance, this chapter then introduces the role of higher education in equipping individuals with skills and producing research that can lead to greater productivity and growth. Chapter 2 continues with a diagnostic of higher education in skills and research in low-, middle-, and upper-income economies in East Asia. Chapter 3 shows how failures to deliver on skills and research in lower- and middle-income countries are related to critical disconnects between (a) higher education and (b) users and providers of skills and research. It demonstrates how these disconnects are related to problems with poor information, low capacity, and weak incentives. Given these challenges, chapters 4–6 provide policy recommendations to address these problems and mitigate the disconnects through better financing of higher education (chapter 4), better management of public higher education institutions (chapter 5), and better stewardship for the higher education system (chapter 6).

East Asia's economic landscape

The economies of East Asia can be divided into three income groups, which beyond a certain income per capita tend to share some common characteristics in terms of economic structure, human development, and business climate. The first income group is made up of Hong Kong SAR, China; Japan; the Republic of Korea; Singapore; and Taiwan, China. These economies also have a sophisticated economic structure and advanced human development indicators. China, Indonesia, Malaysia, Mongolia, the Philippines, and Thailand[3] represent the second middle-income group of East Asia. More precisely, according to the income classification adopted by the *World Development Report*,[4] five of these countries are lower-middle-income economies, and Malaysia is an upper-middle-income economy. This group is fairly heterogeneous, but countries in it generally share more developed

FIGURE 1.1   Conceptual framework

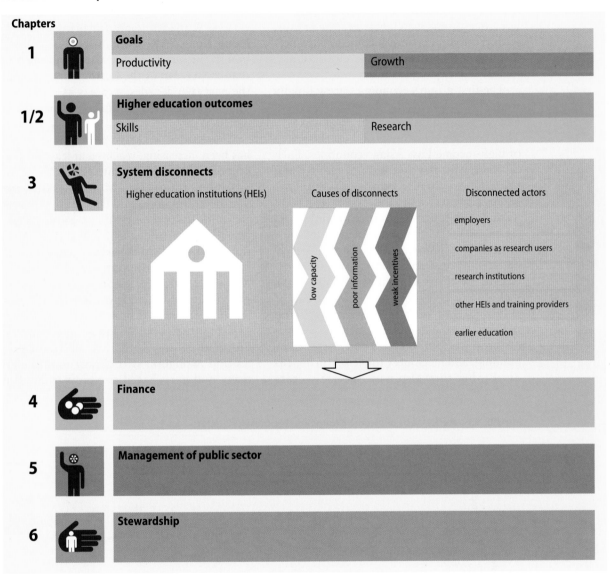

Source: Authors' elaboration.

economic structures, human development indicators, and business climate than the lower-income economies have. Finally, the lower-income group comprises Cambodia, the Lao People's Democratic Republic, and Vietnam.[5] These countries are late starters, as is apparent from their per capita gross domestic products (GDPs) and development levels.

In addition to the three income groups, the East Asian economies can be divided into three technology clusters on the basis of the skill and high-tech intensity of their products and exports.[6] Together, these metrics serve as a proxy for measuring an economy's level of innovation in supporting productivity and its development of science and technology. As a result, this proxy provides an assessment of an economy's productivity and ability to move up the value chain within the service, manufacturing, non-manufacturing industry, and agricultural sectors. Although the relationship between income and technology is similar, there is not a one-to-one match between the groups, with economies within income groups performing at slightly different levels of technological capacity (figure 1.2).[7]

The first group's economies grew rapidly from the mid-1960s to the mid-1990s and have achieved high income levels (table 1.1). They coincide therefore now with the group of high-income East Asian economies. Each of them, with the exception of Hong Kong SAR, China, focused on manufacturing, which accounts for around a quarter of GDP (table 1.2). Growth was sourced mainly from capital accumulation, supplemented by gains in factor productivity, with investment largely financed by domestic savings.

Overall, these economies are East Asia's technological leaders in a wide range of medium- and high-tech manufacturing industries, including electronics and electrical products, automobiles and parts, shipbuilding, and machinery (table B.4 in appendix B), but they also have service sectors

with high levels of innovation and productivity and thus form part of the top technology cluster. While less manufacturing oriented, Hong Kong SAR, China's level of innovation in the service sector also positions it in that cluster, but at the bottom. Throughout the past two decades, exports as a share of GDP have grown significantly (table B.3 in appendix B).

The share of services is also significant and has been increasing, reaching at least 60 percent of GDP in 2007 (figure 1.3).

China, Indonesia, Malaysia, Mongolia, the Philippines, and Thailand compose the middle-income country group. They are all in the under-US$7,000 per capita range (table 1.3) in constant nominal GDP. Indonesia, the Philippines, and especially Mongolia trail in manufacturing value added (table 1.4) and investment. Electronics and electrical products are the leading export subsectors in China, Malaysia, the Philippines, and Thailand, while Indonesia and Mongolia still export mainly primary and agro-based products (table B.8

FIGURE 1.2   A schematic of income groups and technology clusters

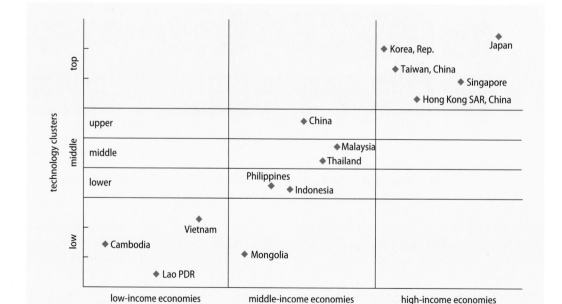

Source: Authors' elaboration.
Note: Income level is given by GDP per capita in 2009. Economies' position in the figure reflects their ranking by income and technology.

TABLE 1.1   Per capita GDP averages, upper-income economies

Economy	Nominal (constant 2000 US$)		PPP (constant 2005 international $)		Change (%)
	1990–99	2000–09	1990–99	2000–09	
Japan	35,310	38,368	27,462	29,841	9
Singapore	18,269	26,500	29,201	42,358	45
Hong Kong SAR, China	23,115	29,188[a]	27,133	34,262[a]	26
Taiwan, China	11,102.2	16,044[a]	17,476	25,255[a]	45
Korea, Rep.	8,974	13,593	14,813	22,439	51

Source: World Development Indicators (WDI) database.
Note: PPP = purchasing power parity.
a. Hong Kong SAR, China, and Taiwan, China, average for 2000–08.

in appendix B). Unlike those economies in the upper-income group, when they produce or export electronics, this group's countries are mainly assemblers and processors of electronic products, operating at a far lower level of technological competency and at lower points in the value chain. Services account for about 35–55 percent of GDP, and their share has been increasing in most of these countries. This sector (as well as agriculture) is also working at lower levels of productivity. From that perspective, and because they cannot yet be classified as innovative, although China,[8] Malaysia, and to a lesser degree Thailand began encouraging investment in R&D in the 1990s, they are part of another technology cluster.

Within this lower cluster there are, however, substantial differences between countries and countries' subgroups. China, Indonesia, Malaysia, the Philippines, and Thailand started climbing the technological ladder in the 1970s and have facilitated technology assimilation by becoming increasingly open and following the example of the East Asian frontrunners by promoting industrialization and infrastructure development through high levels of investment (table B.7 in appendix B). In contrast, Mongolia is much more of a late starter and, as such, part of an even lower cluster together with lower-income countries. As will be further illustrated below, even within the five countries with some developing innovative capacity, there are significant differences between China, clearly ahead, and countries such as Indonesia and the Philippines, trailing behind.

TABLE 1.2   Manufacturing value added, upper-income economies

Economy	1990–99 (average % of GDP)	2000–09 (average % of GDP)	Change (%)
Korea, Rep.	27.1	27.2	0
Singapore	26.0	24.4	−6
Taiwan, China	27.1	23.3[a]	−14
Japan	24.0	21.1[a]	−12
Hong Kong SAR, China	9.4	3.9[b]	−59

Source: WDI database.
a. Japan and Taiwan, China, average for 2000–08.
b. Hong Kong SAR, China, average for 2000–07.

Cambodia, Lao PDR, and Vietnam are the lower-income East Asian countries, but they have moved onto a rapid-growth trajectory (table 1.5). Although Lao PDR's and Cambodia's investment rates remain below 20 percent (table B.11 in appendix B), Vietnam's are similar to those of its neighbors at earlier stages of development. Vietnam and Cambodia are building manufacturing capacity (table 1.6) but have yet to rise beyond the low-tech, labor-intensive stage of manufacturing, as clearly reflected in their exports (table B.12 in appendix B). Lao PDR is further behind in terms of manufacturing capacity. Services represent about 40 percent of GDP in all countries, and they are still working at low productivity levels. These three countries, together with Mongolia, are part of the lower technology cluster, with Vietnam sitting in front, but with generally smaller differences in technological capability across countries.

FIGURE 1.3   Sectoral value added as a share of GDP, 1997 and 2007

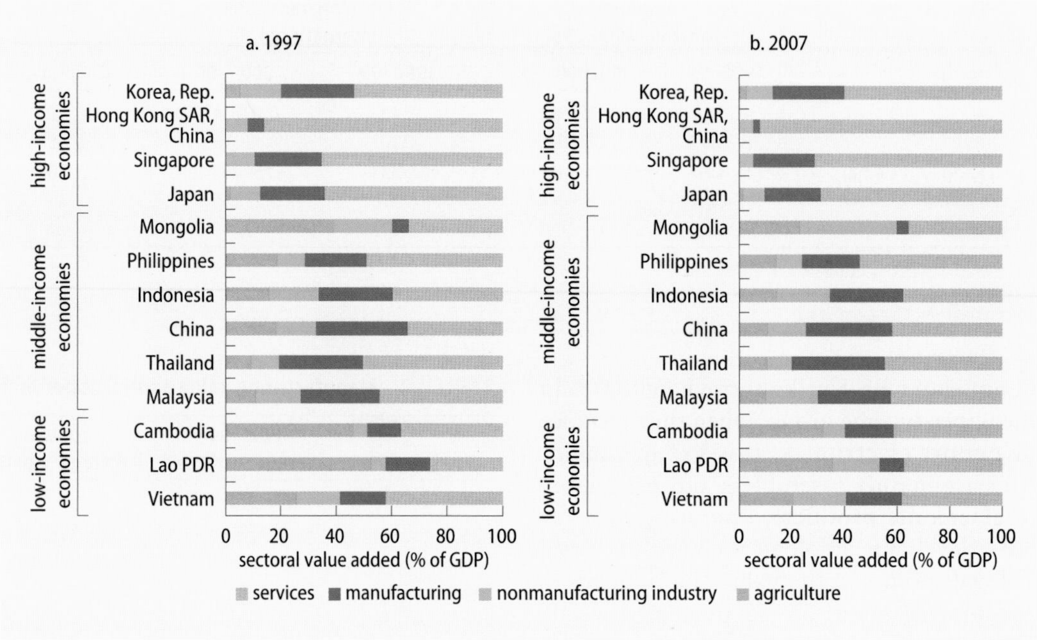

Sources: WDI database.

TABLE 1.3   Per capita GDP averages, middle-income economies

Economy	Nominal (constant 2000 US$)		PPP (constant 2005 international $)		Change (%)
	1990–99	2000–09	1990–99	2000–09	
Malaysia	3,382	4,539	8,619	11,567	34
Thailand	1,792	2,320	5,070	6,563	29
China	628	1,482	1,766	4,164	136
Philippines	901	1,094	2,385	2,897	21
Indonesia	767	945	2,602	3,204	23
Mongolia	432	580	1,930	2,593	34

Source: WDI database.
Note: PPP = purchasing power parity.

TABLE 1.4   Manufacturing value added, middle-income economies

Economy	1990–99 (average % of GDP)	2000–09 (average % of GDP)	Change (%)
Thailand	29.5	34.4	17
China	32.9	32.6	−1
Malaysia	27.0	28.8	7
Indonesia	23.7	28.1	19
Philippines	23.3	22.5	−3
Mongolia	18.5	4.6	−75

Source: WDI database.

This picture conveys the main challenges facing East Asian low- and middle-income economies. The members of the East Asian technology clusters are competing in export markets—often fiercely with each other—to enlarge the gains from industrialization and trade, seeking to move up the value chain in manufacturing while increasing the productivity of their growing service sectors.

Japan leads the top technology cluster (and upper-income group), followed by Hong Kong SAR, China; Korea; Singapore; and Taiwan,

TABLE 1.5   Per capita GDP averages, lower-income economies

Economy	Nominal (constant 2000 US$)		PPP (constant 2005 international $)		
	1990–99	2000–09	1990–99	2000–09	Change (%)
Vietnam	299	530	1,187	2,109	78
Cambodia	239[a]	407	823[a]	1,400	70
Lao PDR	263	399	1,088	1,648	51

Source: WDI database.
Note: PPP = purchasing power parity.
a. Cambodia average for 1993–99.

China. These last four have some way to go before they achieve per capita income parity with Japan. Korea most closely approximates Japan in manufacturing breadth, while Hong Kong SAR, China, and Singapore are the furthest removed. All have one thing in common: they are at the technological frontiers in their respective industries. Moreover, Japan, Korea, and Taiwan, China, are among the most innovative industrial economies, pushing the technological frontiers in electronics, petrochemical, metallurgical, automotive, and other fields, such as services and agriculture. Singapore is attempting to join the other members of the cluster through research in biotechnology and electronics, with some success. Its innovations are more conspicuous in services (such as managing hotels and industrial parks, and urban planning), water purification, logistics, and use of information and communication technology. All five economies are exemplars for the rest of East Asia.

Middle-income countries of the middle technology cluster range in size from China with more than 1.3 billion people to Malaysia with 28 million. With China comfortably in the forefront of the technology cluster, all these nations have acquired significant manufacturing capabilities. China is the world's second-ranked industrial nation and the largest exporter. In less than two decades it has emerged as the leading producer of products ranging from steel, glass, and cement to electronics, photovoltaic cells, and household appliances. China's export competitiveness speaks to its rapidly maturing manufacturing capabilities and strengthening grasp of production technologies across several sectors.

TABLE 1.6   Manufacturing value added, lower-income economies

Economy	1990–99 (average % of GDP)	2000–09 (average % of GDP)	Change (%)
Vietnam	15.2	20.3	34
Cambodia	11.1[a]	18.0	62
Lao PDR	14.2	14.6[b]	3

Source: WDI database.
a. Cambodia average for 1993–99.
b. Lao PDR average for 2000–08.

Malaysia, Thailand, the Philippines, and Indonesia, in that order, have also built up competitive manufacturing industries, with electronics, textiles, automotive, and resource-based industries the most important. Electronics and electrical engineering are the most important for the first three countries, whereas light manufacturing and processing activities are of greater significance to Indonesia. All these countries have relied extensively on foreign direct investment to build manufacturing capacity and to master production technology. Multinational corporations and their joint ventures account for a sizable share of production for export (the most advanced and competitive segment of industry),[9] though production skills are now widely diffused, with domestic manufacturers often able to compete with multinationals.

Nevertheless, members of the middle technology cluster are still some years and, in the case of Indonesia and the Philippines, decades away from acquiring the technological capabilities of the leading industrial nations. Except China (which is more diversified and has greater industrial depth), the other countries are largely focused on assembly, processing, testing, and relatively low-value-adding operations, and their indigenous technological capabilities are limited to simpler downstream activities. Their service sectors are also still low productivity. And although they are achieving high levels of efficiency in production, their indigenous technological capabilities are limited to simpler downstream activities. Even China, whose exports overlap with those of countries in the Organisation for Economic Co-operation and Development (OECD), still operates in the lower-quality and value-adding ends of manufacturing.[10] While China is closing the technology gap in virtually all fields of manufacturing—and in some areas is approaching the point where it can become an innovator—its domestic capability still lags behind that of leading industrial nations,[11] leaving substantial room for catch-up in some areas.

Some countries in Southeast Asia (four are in the middle cluster) began taking a serious interest in innovation as a new growth driver after the crisis of 1997–98, because of lost growth momentum and declining private investment. Innovation captured the imagination of policy makers in Malaysia, and to a lesser degree in Thailand and even China (which did not experience a comparable growth slowdown). Countries clearly show differences, though, because while firms in China are beginning to experiment with real innovation, firms in Indonesia and the Philippines see it as a more distant prospect.

Most middle-income countries' biggest gains at this stage are from applying, assimilating, and adapting new technology. Businesses have rationally shown little interest in developing new technologies when there is so much low-hanging fruit to be picked. For most companies, the demand for innovation is the same as learning technologies already developed (in country or outside) and adding to production and technological capabilities.

The lower-income and low technology cluster includes the latecomers, countries that began industrializing in the 1990s and that have not progressed much beyond light manufacturing and simple assembly operations. They are likely to remain in the learning mode for some time. The primary challenge

for these economies is to increase productivity in all sectors and break into manufacturing. Climbing the technology ladder is another immediate objective.

Given this economic context, how can low- and middle-income East Asia develop higher levels of productivity in the short run? And how can economies develop the technological capacity they need to increase productivity in the medium run, which has shown to be so important in determining the higher productivity levels of upper-income East Asia? Skills, which enhance capacity to apply, adapt, and create new technology, and research, which enhances capacity to develop new technology, will be two key drivers. And higher education can supply both.

Role and impact of higher education

Skills are positively related to innovation and productivity (and so growth), as discussed below. This is one reason why in low- and middle-income East Asia—whether playing technological catch-up or moving from catch-up to creation (both parts of a broad definition of innovation in this report)—the importance of higher education as a source of scientific, technical, and analytical skills is increasing. A well-trained and highly educated workforce underpins growth: skilled labor can deploy flexibly, achieve high levels of productivity, apply existing technologies, and engage in innovation as a means to increase a nation's competitiveness and growth. At the same time, East Asian markets are absorbing a larger share of exports from the region itself; thus, adapting technologies while customizing products, processes, and design will be of greater significance and will call for the kind of support higher education can provide.[12]

As economies move up the technology ladder and the gap between some of them and the leading industrial economies narrows, their need for education and skills at all levels grows, particularly at the tertiary level.[13] Thus a range of tertiary institutions take on larger responsibilities—and they can help accelerate industrial change—because they are the source of an increasing share of entrepreneurs, managers, and skilled workers. Additionally, a few research universities begin contributing to innovation through basic research that generates ideas or upstream applied research and technology transfer (or both) that initiates the process of transmuting knowledge and ideas into applications with potential commercial relevance.

Higher education provides several noneconomic benefits, such as nation building and socialization (box 1.1). But this report focuses on the contribution of higher education to the productivity that allows economies to remain competitive in a global market.

Whether tertiary education is a more significant predictor of growth than primary education in developing countries continues to be debated.[14] There is, however, some consensus that tertiary education is positively associated with economic growth and GDP regardless of a country's development level. Very crudely, this relationship is apparent from figure 1.4, which shows a positive correlation between GDP and enrollments in higher education. While causality cannot be established (given the many other factors that matter, including the composition and quality of higher education itself), no country or region has achieved, in the long term, high-income status without first crossing

BOX 1.1 Private and public benefits of higher education

As a proponent of liberal education, the Oxford scholar Cardinal Newman advocated for higher education as a place for cultivating universal knowledge rather than developing vocational training and research. He believed students should study the classics and philosophy because these courses had the ability to "strengthen, refine, and enrich the intellectual powers." With this "habit of mind," individuals would be equipped to think clearly and articulate their thoughts in any profession.[a] While Cardinal Newman's view is an important mission of higher education, the benefits of higher education extend from individuals to society and from economic to social benefits.

There is much evidence of the economic benefits of investing in higher education. Individuals who attend higher education have higher average earnings, are more likely to be employed, and are less likely to experience poverty than individuals without higher education. Data on lifetime earnings of U.S. workers by education level show that relative to high school graduates, individuals with some college education have on average 17 percent higher earnings, and those with a professional degree have more than three times the earnings. Thus, individuals who invest in higher education can expect their future economic returns to exceed the costs of tuition, fees, and forgone earnings from not working.

Higher education also generates economic benefits to society. Countries with a large labor force of individuals with higher education have higher productivity and higher tax payments. This also lowers dependence on public welfare programs. The United States spends US$800–2,700 less per year on social programs for graduates of higher education than for high school graduates. All these factors contribute to a country's economic growth.

In addition to economic benefits, higher education provides several social benefits. Higher education institutions are good settings for individuals to socialize with peers. Individuals with higher education tend to have higher standards of living and better well-being. They also tend to be in better health, are less likely to smoke, and are less likely to engage in criminal activities. The benefits of higher education also extend across generations: children of parents with higher education are more exposed to reading, have higher cognitive skills, and are better able to concentrate. Finally, higher education promotes nation building, because citizens with higher education are more likely to vote, to donate blood, and to participate in community service. These benefits show how higher education can enhance the quality of life for individuals and countries.

Source: Baum and Payea 2005.
a. Newman 1976.

FIGURE 1.4   **Tertiary enrollment and per capita GDP, 2008**

Source: EdStats database.

FIGURE 1.5   **Tertiary enrollment and labor productivity, 2005**

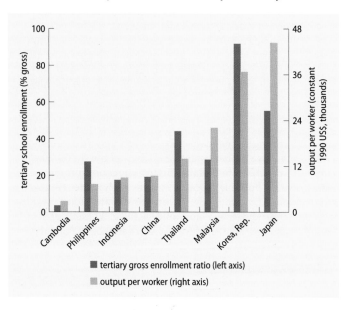

Sources: International Labour Organization data; WDI database.

a "respectable" higher education threshold. And figure 1.5 reports a positive relation between labor productivity and higher education.

The relation between higher education and skills is well documented. Results of seven participating countries of the Adult Literacy and Life Skills Survey undertaken by the OECD show a strong positive correlation between cognitive skills (generally considered a combination of academic and thinking skills—see box 1.2) and educational attainment, with individuals having more years of higher education consistently scoring at higher skill levels than individuals having fewer or no years of higher education (figure 1.6). This finding is consistent with those of past studies that educational attainment is a leading contributor of cognitive skills such as literacy and numeracy.[15]

BOX 1.2   Defining skills

At least three main categories of skills can be identified: academic skills, generic (or life) skills, and technical skills. *Academic skills* are directly measured and are generally associated with subject areas (math, literacy, English). They are typically taught in schools and measured through standardized tests. *Generic (or life) skills* refer to a broader set of skills transferable across jobs and from education to employment. They generally include thinking (critical and creative thinking, and problem solving), behavioral (communication, organization, teamwork, time management, ability to negotiate conflict and manage risks, and leadership), and computing skills. *Technical skills* are those associated with one's profession. They are generally considered a mix of specific knowledge and skills to perform specific jobs. Cognitive skills are often used as a further categorization and typically include a combination of academic and thinking skills.

These three skill categories can also be divided internally: there are both threshold-level academic, generic, and technical skills, and higher-order academic, generic, and technical skills. The level and combination of required skills vary by firm and job function. The nature of the skill acquisition process implies that a comprehensive approach to skill development is needed. Formal education is one critical actor. High-quality and relevant school-based formal education has a strong role in providing all three types of skills discussed. Primary education systems can provide basic academic and generic skills. Secondary education systems can provide more advanced academic and generic skills, as well as some technical skills. And tertiary education systems can provide all three types, of a higher order.

In turn, skills are positively related to productivity, labor market outcomes, and growth. Earlier research on the contribution of human capital to economic growth using regression analysis yielded equivocal results on the relation between education and growth. More recent analysis that factors in the quality of education and moves beyond the criticized measures of educational achievement (which largely relied on years of schooling) has been, however, more successful in establishing a relationship running from the level of education to the level of output and from the quality of education to growth of GDP.[16] Along these lines, recent evidence confirms that there is a direct relation between cognitive skills, on the one hand, and productivity and growth, on the other.[17] An emerging literature has also demonstrated the link between cognitive ability and labor market outcomes.[18] Beyond cognitive skills, noncognitive skills (intended mostly as behavioral skills) are increasingly shown to have a positive impact on labor market outcomes.[19]

Beyond supporting the application of current technology, higher education can foster innovation (in this report defined broadly as the ability of economies to both create and adapt new knowledge) through the skills that it provides. Those individuals with more education of better quality have a higher probability of starting a technology-intensive business, hiring skilled workers, and engaging in innovation.[20] This is also illustrated by the positive relation at the firm level between technological innovation, defined in a broad sense,[21] and ratio of workers with higher education found in a sample of firm surveys of the region (figure 1.7).[22] The correlation would be stronger if one were able to control for the quality of higher education graduates, considering their skill sets. Unfortunately, that cannot be done. Nevertheless, it is known that there is a positive relation between professionals with management skills, innovation, and productivity,[23] or that a higher share of graduates with science, technology, engineering, and math (STEM) skills is generally correlated with higher

FIGURE 1.6   Educational attainment and skills proficiency

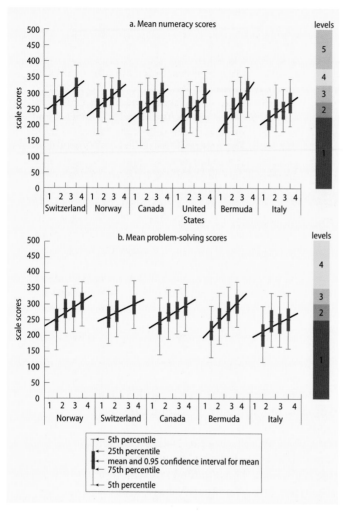

Source: OECD 2005.
Note: The numbers on the x axis denote: 1 = Less than upper secondary; 2 = Upper secondary; 3 = Post-secondary, non-tertiary; 4 = Tertiary type B or higher.

innovation outcomes (figure 1.8). Firm innovation surveys undertaken for this report in Indonesia, the Philippines, and Thailand showed that the active innovators are those with higher levels of R&D expenditures, more highly qualified staff, and located in more R&D-intensive industries.[24]

The top technology cluster in East Asia can also readily illustrate the relation between higher education, innovation, and growth through both skills and research. High-income economies in East Asia are among the world's most innovative. No member of this group has attained high innovation and income status without making considerable strategic investments in higher education. Korea, for example, has invested aggressively in government research institutes and university-affiliated science parks, as well as pursued policies leading to high enrollment in higher education (particularly in science and engineering) since the 1970s.[25] Similarly, Singapore has devoted much capital to developing world-class scientific and technological capabilities through higher education.[26] Hong Kong SAR, China, has pursued an agenda to develop itself as a hub for higher education, pouring resources into improving quality, developing staff, fostering greater links between academia and industry, and incentivizing research. And Taiwan, China, has attributed investment in science, engineering, and higher education as a key driver of its economic growth.[27] Long-term trends in R&D undertaken by higher education compared with long-term trends in some innovation outcome indicators, while not perfectly aligned, point to a positive correlation between higher education and innovation outcomes in upper-income East Asia (and other advanced economies) (figures 1.9–1.12).

The relation between higher education and innovation is also widely illustrated in several studies that show the positive relationship between economic growth and higher levels of education as measured by variables such as tertiary gross enrollment ratio (GER), science test scores, R&D, and number of scientists and engineers per capita.[28]

This evidence suggests that low- and middle-income economies will need to start prioritizing higher education if they want to grow. As a matter of example, while coverage of higher education has been rising fairly steadily since the 1970s in most economies (figure 1.13), the GER still remains below par in developing East Asia (figure 1.14). Korea possesses one of the highest tertiary GERs in the world: almost 100 percent of the adult school-age population is enrolled. Japan's tertiary GER has reached 60 percent. The tertiary GERs of Hong Kong SAR, China;

Japan; and Korea are on par with (or even higher than) those of several high-income countries in Europe and North America. But the relatively poor performance of most low- and middle-income East Asian economies has kept the developing-Asia region's average tertiary GER significantly below the OECD average, at a paltry 20 percent.

Quantity, however, is not necessarily a goal in itself. Indeed, as seen above, similar GDP and innovation outcomes are related to very different quantity levels. And as shown in figure 1.6, the variation in skills and attainment indicates that other factors may influence skill proficiency (besides attainment).[29] What matters is the capacity of higher education to provide labor market skills and research for productivity and innovation. On both counts, lower- and middle-income countries have a long way to go, as will be seen.

From higher education to growth: Skills and research

As a provider of high-quality skills relevant to current and future labor market needs, effective higher education systems improve human capital formation and allow entrepreneurs, managers, and skilled workers to perform well, thus supporting technological mastery, productivity, and competitiveness. These systems also help develop countries' technological capability by undertaking research, supporting technology transfer, and providing workers with (and upgrading) the skills for innovation.

Skills and research support longer-run productivity and competitiveness by reorienting, upgrading, and diversifying national economic structures. Cross-country regressions have shown that a college degree is associated with higher individual earnings, higher productivity, and higher wages.[30] One commentator has written, "Tertiary education helps countries build globally competitive economies by developing a skilled, productive, and flexible labor force and by creating, applying and spreading new ideas and technologies."[31]

FIGURE 1.7 **Share of tertiary-educated workers in technologically and nontechnologically innovative firms**

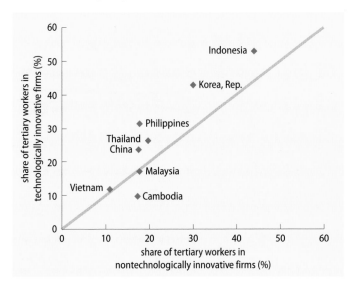

Source: Almeida 2009b, on the basis of World Bank Investment Climate Surveys (ICSs), various years.

FIGURE 1.8 **Correlation between STEM supply and patents, 2004–09**

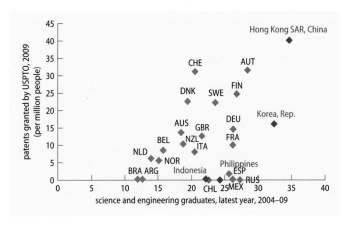

Sources: U.S. Patent and Trademark Office data; WDI database.

In pursuing these twin tracks, countries need to consider opportunities of access to and inclusiveness of higher education. Whatever higher education coverage targets they choose, they must be able to draw from the widest talent pool possible, ensuring that the most able students are not excluded

FIGURE 1.9   Trends in higher education R&D, 1996–2007

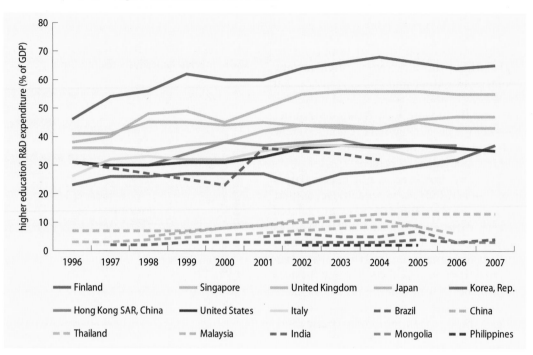

Sources: UNESCO Institute for Statistics (UIS) Data Centre; WDI database.

FIGURE 1.10   Trends in patents, 1996–2007

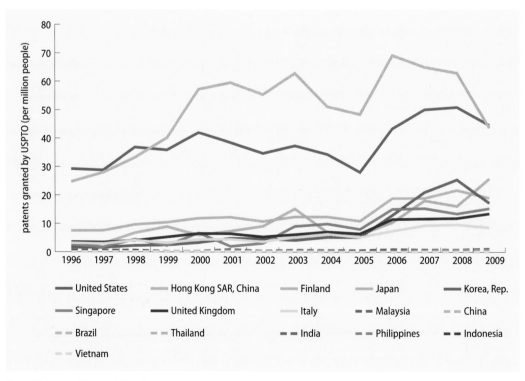

Source: U.S. Patent and Trademark Office data.

FIGURE 1.11   Trends in journal articles, 1995–2007

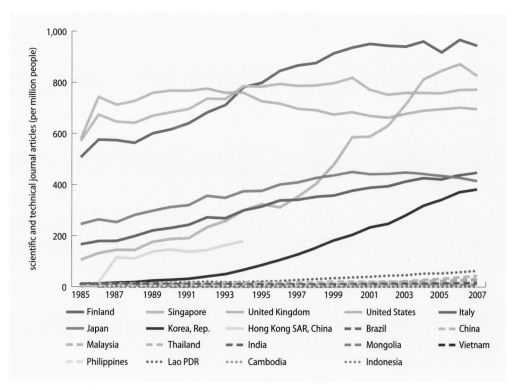

Source: WDI database.

FIGURE 1.12   Trends in technology licensing, 1975–2007

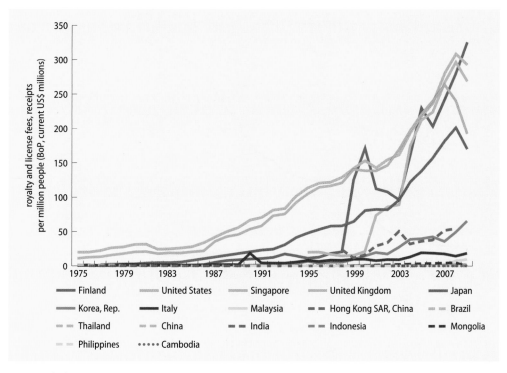

Source: WDI database.

FIGURE 1.13 Tertiary GERs in East Asia and some comparator economies, 1970–2010

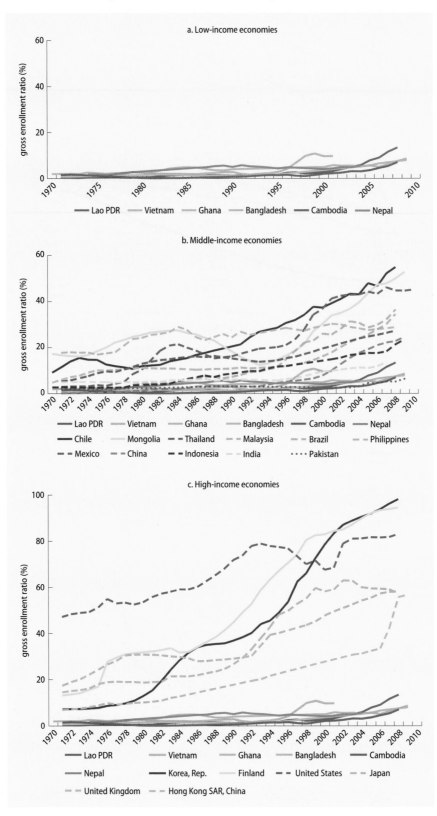

Source: EdStats database.

from higher education because of inequities of access or long-term disadvantage. This is not only an ethical choice but also an economic one.

Countries will not find a one-size-fits-all target for access. For example, to support a more focused innovation agenda, they may assume a strong focus on developing centers of excellence and very highly skilled graduates, a strategy that may contrast with the idea of more widely available higher education. Others looking to improve their higher education system's labor market relevance may make investments and assign priorities in ways that are more compatible with broader access. Still, the critical economic criteria guiding the system's expansion are the current and future labor market absorption capacity, the need for a critical mass to support innovation, and budget constraints. The next two sections delve deeper into the roles of skills and research.

Higher education as a provider of skills

As suggested by the definitions of skill categories (box 1.2), skills are produced in many different ways, dynamically, and through multiple actors. Preemployment education and training, on-the-job training, work and life experience, and peer learning all contribute to skill development that could be useful on the job.[32] Whereas academic skills are normally acquired through formal and nonformal educational institutions, generic or life skills are acquired in various ways. Early-childhood parental education, specifically targeted curricular and pedagogical approaches, on-the-job training, and work experience all develop and enrich these types of skills. Technical skills are generally provided through targeted upper-secondary and tertiary training programs, on-the-job training, and learning-by-doing.

Skill acquisition is thus a cumulative and dynamic process that occurs throughout the life cycle. It starts at birth with parental education and continues through the course of school education, training, and experience. And just as these skills can grow over time,

FIGURE 1.14 **Tertiary GERs in East Asia and OECD average, latest available year**

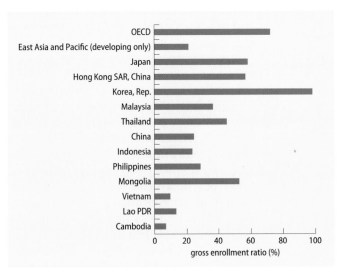

Sources: EdStats database; UIS Data Centre.
Note: The East Asia and the Pacific average also includes the Democratic People's Republic of Korea, Papua New Guinea, and Timor-Leste.

they can deteriorate if the possibilities for lifelong learning are not well developed.

Actors outside the formal education system also have a large role. Quality nonformal education and training can provide academic, generic, and technical skills to out-of-school populations and can complement formal education with additional generic or technical skill instruction. It can also provide opportunities to update academic and technical skills over time, particularly for the non-school-age population. Firm and on-the-job training can complement both formal and nonformal education and training by providing additional job-relevant technical and generic skills. This type of training can also provide opportunities to maintain the existing generic and technical skills of workers.

Within this broad skill framework, higher education plays a crucial role—perhaps no more clearly than in skill provision. Higher education institutions provide the basis for the range of skills needed for both mature and developing economies. Tertiary graduates enter the workforce with cognitive, technical, social, and behavioral skills honed at university that allow them to bring advanced knowledge to bear on complex problems, use that knowledge to work toward their solution, perform research, and develop ideas of more productive ways of performing. It is during higher education that more mature students have the capacity, ability, and time to learn sophisticated client orientation, communication, problem solving, and creativity skills, not only through close links with particular careers (for example, business and communication), but also across careers through the use of well-crafted teaching-learning methodologies. While many practical skills will be acquired on the job, higher education also offers a critical opportunity to its students to apply academic skills to more concrete and practical cases through case studies and other methodologies, with wider breadth than more specific on-the-job training would provide. Other research indicates that higher education instructors can teach students relevant technical and behavioral skills that they will need to know and use as industrial actors, without actually doing industrial research themselves.[33]

These points reflect in some part a changing concept of the role of higher education. As technological structures and the nature of industry evolve, academic qualifications are increasingly taken as indicators of a particular level of academic competence and of the skills to deal with the demands of a fast-changing work environment. Employers expect tertiary graduates to possess the academic, generic, and technical skills to increase their productivity and growth.[34] Increasingly, employers also expect a smaller group of workers to possess the ability to think, to be creative, and to have the capacity to spur innovation. This is consistent with emerging research on academic knowledge transfer, which has found that skilled graduates bring to industry attitudes and abilities for acquiring knowledge and using it in novel ways.[35]

Keen to bolster their productivity, East Asian economies are giving new consideration to the knowledge and skills of their workers, and consequently the education and training systems that shape them. Policy makers in East Asia are reexamining how higher education systems should prepare graduates to take their places in the labor force. They are also asking how graduates should be equipped to deal with changing labor force structures and demands from employers in ways that can meet both the current and future needs of the economy.

A better perspective of higher education's potential for delivering skills requires knowing the skills—particularly tertiary—that low- and middle-income East Asian labor markets need, as seen in demand both for tertiary graduates and for specific functional skills.

Trends in demand for tertiary graduates

In the long term, demand for tertiary graduates has been generally on the rise in the region, as seen in the steep increase in wage premiums for completing a tertiary education in Cambodia, China, Mongolia, and Vietnam, as well as gradually increasing ratios of tertiary education workers in Cambodia, China,[36] and Vietnam (figure 1.15). In Mongolia, the decreasing trend of a tertiary-educated workforce clearly indicates quantity gaps. Alongside sharper increases in the number of workers with a tertiary education, the slightly increasing or flat premiums in the Philippines, Indonesia, and Thailand indicate sustained demand for such graduates.[37]

Demand is particularly dynamic in the service sector. Trends in tertiary education premiums and the tertiary-educated workforce by sector reported in appendixes C and D[38] show that demand for tertiary graduates has been generally stronger in services, though often sluggish in manufacturing (but with differences across countries). The evolution of tertiary education premiums has been rather sector specific in Indonesia, the Philippines, and Thailand, with generally decreasing returns in agriculture, mixed performance in manufacturing (decreasing in Indonesia and the Philippines, flat in Thailand), and increasing in services (at least in Indonesia[39] and the Philippines). The evolution of education premiums has been broad-based in Cambodia,

FIGURE 1.15   Trends in wage education premiums and educated workforce in selected East Asian economies

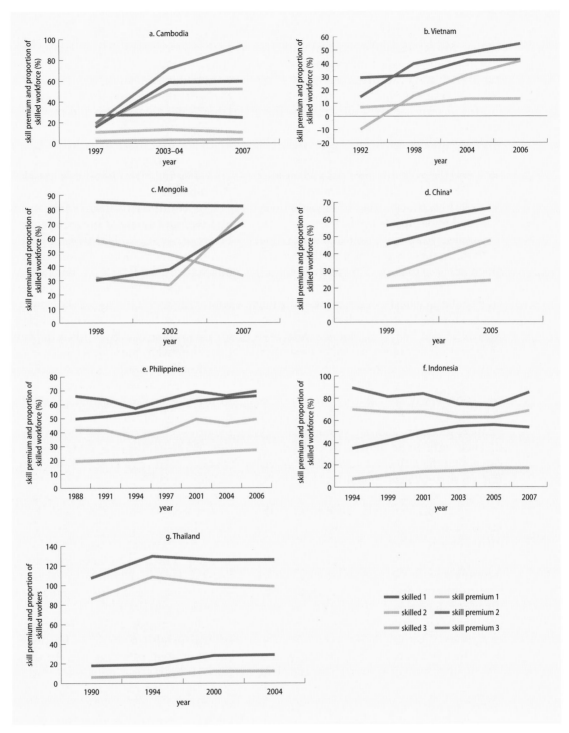

Source: di Gropello and Sakellariou 2010, on the basis of labor and household surveys (various years).

Note: For Cambodia, skilled 1 = workforce with at least lower-secondary education; skilled 2 = workforce with at least upper-secondary education; skilled 3 = workforce with tertiary education and above; skill premium 1 = wage premium for workforce with at least lower-secondary education compared to workforce with less education; skill premium 2 = wage premium for workforce with at least upper-secondary education compared to workforce with less education; skill premium 3 = wage premium for workforce with at least tertiary education compared with workforce with less education. For other countries, skilled 1 = workforce with at least upper-secondary education (secondary education for the Philippines); skilled 2 = workforce with at least tertiary education; and skill premium 1 = wage premium for workforce with at least upper-secondary education (secondary education for the Philippines) compared to workforce with less education; skill premium 2 = wage premium for workforce with at least tertiary education compared to workforce with less education.
a. One needs to interpret the trends carefully in the Chinese case, given the much shorter time covered by the data and the less updated information.

China, Mongolia, and Vietnam (with services showing an edge, particularly if compared with the upward trends in educated workers in this sector). Apart from Mongolia, the share of tertiary-educated workers has increased in all sectors across countries, with a generally faster increase in services. Tertiary education premiums have generally increased the most in subsectors such as business, finance, and information technology (IT) services, transport and telecommunication, and trade (appendix D).

Given services' significant employment and GDP share, these trends indicate that tertiary graduates need to possess the skills demanded by the sector. To the extent that services' GDP and employment shares grow—aligning more with the East Asian high-income (see figure 1.2) and OECD economic structure—and the trend continues toward more skill-intensive subsectors,[40] services will increasingly drive demand for graduates with a tertiary education. It will be important to ensure the delivery of service-related careers in business, finance, transport and telecommunications, or even only some generic social science careers (at the university and college levels) that support workers' mobility and flexibility among service-related jobs.

Tertiary graduates also need to meet the needs of technologically intensive and open manufacturing: within the sector, foreign-owned enterprises, more technologically intensive firms, and to some extent, more export-oriented firms employ a greater number of tertiary graduates. Beyond sector composition effects, firm surveys[41] offer evidence of a robust positive correlation among foreign direct investment, measures of technological adaptation and innovation, and share of tertiary-educated workers at the firm level, confirming the presence of skill-biased technical change; the role of exports in driving demand for tertiary-educated workers is less clear-cut (figure 1.16).[42]

More sophisticated cross-section regression analysis (appendix E) confirms these results.[43] Although this type of analysis can imply only association,[44] it suggests two initial points: (a) that foreign investors bring to their overseas subsidiaries various managerial, organizational, and technical innovations that would not otherwise be diffused to the host country, and (b) that highly skilled labor is needed to adapt and further diffuse these innovations. This second point is particularly the case in Vietnam (table 1.7), where foreign firms employ more highly skilled graduates and play a larger role in technology development.

The results also underscore the broad and well-documented positive relationship between technological development, also including technological assimilation and adaptation, and tertiary education (this relation goes both ways, from the tertiary-educated workforce to technological innovation, and vice versa), which is clearer in middle-income countries (likely explained by their somewhat more developed innovation systems). By contrast, the net effect of exports on the employment of tertiary graduates heavily depends on the relative importance of the pressures of international competition and the drive to specialize and within specialization on the importance of low-skill-intensity products relative to high-skill-intensity ones. In China and Vietnam, the net effect is negative (fewer tertiary graduates employed in export sectors), but in Cambodia, Indonesia, and Thailand, the effect is clearly positive (more tertiary graduates employed in export sectors). The pressure exerted by Chinese exports largely accounts for the negative overall outcomes in low- and middle-income countries in table 1.7.

Manufacturing demand for tertiary graduates depends on trends in openness indicators, among other factors. To the extent that globalization continues and stimulates higher foreign direct investment[45] and import penetration—in turn related to higher access to technology and new working practices—demand for tertiary graduates in manufacturing may increase (despite the sector's slower value-added upgrading in most of the region).[46]

The association among foreign direct investment, technology, and tertiary education in East Asian manufacturing is also important when looking forward, particularly because it has the potential to shape future growth and development patterns.[47] In a context in which low-income countries need to break into manufacturing and engender a technological capability, and middle-income countries need to move further up the manufacturing value chain (while continuing to develop their technological capability), governments must achieve an alignment of foreign direct investment, technology, and higher-level skills.

Doctoral graduates may therefore be important, because they are key contributors in conducting research, fostering innovation, and sharing knowledge. Furthermore, the experience of the leading East Asian economies suggests that developing indigenous technological capabilities requires a steady increase in the stock of scientists and engineers who help in assimilating and adapting foreign technology. The experience of Japan, Korea, and Taiwan, China, suggests that if an economy is to rapidly assimilate technology, one-third or more of its university graduates must have studied science and engineering. The positive relation between STEM skills and innovation has been illustrated above.

Trends in demand for functional skills
Recent employer and employee surveys provide a benchmark of the generic and technical skills the region needs (box 1.2). To the extent that these apply to professionals and managers (expected to be educated at

FIGURE 1.16   Share of tertiary-educated workers by foreign ownership and export status of firms

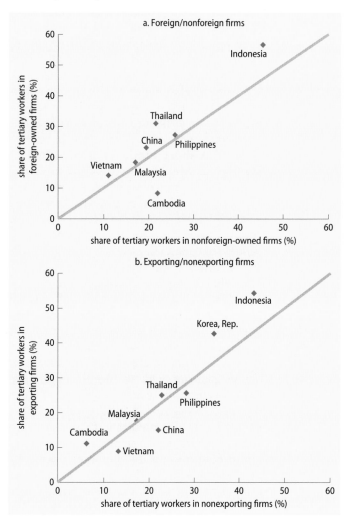

Source: Almeida 2009b, based on World Bank ICSs, various years.

TABLE 1.7   Regression coefficients of technological and openness variables in a sample of East Asian economies

Variable	Cambodia	Vietnam	Philippines	Indonesia	China	Thailand	Malaysia	Korea, Rep.	Low income	Middle income[a]	Middle income[b]
Foreign ownership	0.628	0.400***	−0.231	−0.118	0.191***	0.0121	0.131	0.419***	0.459***	0.0721	0.0785
Technology innovation	−0.161	0.0549	0.497***	0.247*	0.342***	0.134**	0.00724	0.0509	0.015	0.297***	0.280***
Exports	1.531***	−0.0503	−0.0276	0.388**	−0.406***	0.142**	0.336	0.015	0.002	−0.115**	−0.0958**

Source: Appendix E.
Note: Dependent variable is the share of workers with more than 12 years of schooling.
a. All East Asian economies except low-income countries, Malaysia, and Republic of Korea.
b. All East Asian economies except low-income countries and Republic of Korea.
Significance level: * = 10 percent; ** = 5 percent; *** = 1 percent.

the tertiary level), these surveys reveal the skills expected from tertiary graduates.[48] A share of skilled production and nonproduction workers is also educated at the tertiary education level (particularly college education and technical and vocational education and training), making these other categories of workers also relevant. (Charts by country derived from employer and employee surveys—Investment Climate Surveys, and firm skill surveys—are included in appendix F.) A short summary is provided in table 1.8, which ranks (from 0 to 7) the relative importance of each skill within each country, largely for professionals. Differences between professionals and other relevant workers' categories are alluded to in a couple of countries.

According to the surveys and as illustrated in table 1.8, employers and employees in East Asia are giving particular emphasis to some job-specific skills and several thinking and behavioral skills, reflecting a change in skill demand. Job-specific technical skills—both theoretical and practical—are important in most countries, with an edge for experience and practical job-related knowledge. Thinking and behavioral skills, and to a lesser extent IT skills, are also important. Problem solving and creativity receive significant emphasis in most countries, as do communication and leadership skills. English skills are subject to significant fluctuations in importance across

countries but are becoming a priority in countries such as Cambodia, Mongolia, Thailand, and Vietnam. While there are no obvious differences across countries, creativity and IT skills tend to have a higher relative importance within upper-middle-income countries. A further analysis of data for Indonesia and the Philippines shows that skill demands are lower overall for skilled production and nonproduction workers—and that most of the relative priorities in terms of skills are maintained for the Philippines, while changing more substantially in Indonesia. Overall, basic academic skills, practical knowledge of the job, IT, teamwork, and ability to work independently become particularly relevant, whereas English, leadership, and creativity decrease in importance.

The relative importance of generic skills varies by sector, trade orientation, and foreign ownership. Behavioral skills appear to be more important in services. (Further disaggregation of skill demand[49] in other studies shows that behavioral skills, such as ability to work independently, initiative and leadership skills, communication skills, and teamwork skills, tend to have higher importance in services than in manufacturing in Indonesia, Malaysia, the Philippines, and Vietnam, particularly communication skills.) Several generic skills are, however, also critical in manufacturing. Problem-solving skills and creativity (at least for a few workers in the

TABLE 1.8 Importance of technical, thinking, and behavioral skills for professionals

Skill	Vietnam[a]	Cambodia	Indonesia	Malaysia[b]	Philippines	Thailand[b]	Mongolia	Average
Technical	7	4	5	7	7	5	5	5.7
Communication	6	5	7	5	5	4	4	5.1
English	5	5	3	4	3	7	7	4.9
Problem solving	—	7	5	4	6	4	3	4.8
Leadership	—	6	4	4	6	4	4	4.7
Information technology	—	3	4	6	3	6	6	4.7
Creativity	—	—	6	5	4	4	4	4.6
Work attitude	7	5	6	4	4	3	3	4.6

Source: Appendix F.
Note: Ranking from 0 to 7 of the relative importance of each skill for employers.
a. Relates to college graduates.
b. Relates to professionals and other skilled workers.
— = not available.

case of creativity) appear to be much more important in the exporting than nonexporting sector in Indonesia (figure 1.17) and the Philippines, as well as negotiation and leadership skills for professionals and managers in both countries, highlighting the pressure of international competition. Foreign-language and communication skills are also particularly important in Vietnamese foreign-owned enterprises.

Leading firms that attach importance to innovation look for several attributes in their new hires. They value industry experience and a "big picture mindset," and, in a small but important group of workers, creativity and the ability to "think outside the box."[50] Similar opinions were reflected in the firm surveys undertaken in Indonesia, the Philippines, and Thailand (box 1.3).

Across sectors, practical knowledge also appears crucial, particularly so for low- and lower-middle-income countries. This comes out clearly from firm surveys in Indonesia, the Philippines, and Vietnam (appendix F), which emphasized the practical knowledge of the job (even more than theory) and general experience in the field.

As a further illustration of the importance of practical orientation, labor force surveys suggest that firms often prefer workers with technical and vocational education and training (TVET) skills. High shares of such graduates are, for instance, employed as professionals in Indonesia and Mongolia (the share is even higher than for university graduates in Indonesia). Managers and professionals with TVET command, relative to unskilled workers, similar or even higher salary premiums (especially in Mongolia, because of its lower technology demands) than managers and professionals with a university education (figure 1.18). In Mongolia skilled workers with TVET are also paid much more than skilled workers with university degrees. The situation is different in Thailand where the much higher share of university graduates in professional occupations may indicate a combination of better university education, poor primary and secondary education, and

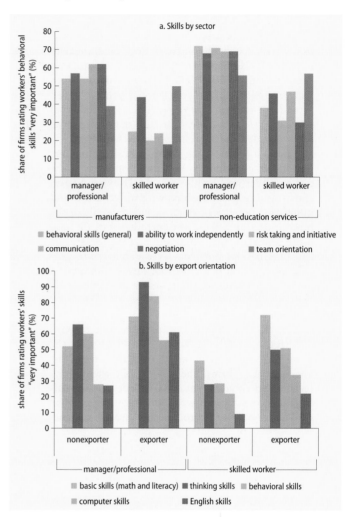

FIGURE 1.17   **Importance of generic skills by sector and export orientation, Indonesia, 2008**

Source: di Gropello, Kruse, and Tandon 2011.

the need for certain skills that only university graduates can offer.

The data in figure 1.18 also show that a significant share of tertiary education graduates, particularly those educated at TVET and college level, find employment as skilled production and nonproduction workers—and that therefore demand for skills at these levels is also one of the benchmarks.

In sum, employers expect professionals and other skilled workers to have some key technical and generic skills, and

---

BOX 1.3   A snapshot of skills for innovation in Indonesia, the Philippines, and Thailand

To understand how much Indonesia's higher education system is contributing to innovation at the firm level, the World Bank interviewed 12 Jakarta-based firms in October 2009. The firms were drawn from services and manufacturing. Service firms included providers of mining services, education, financial services, research, and logistics; manufacturing firms included pharmaceutical, wireless technology, and palm oil–processing companies. Respondents were asked questions on the education levels of the top manager and employees, R&D expenditure, staff training, relationships with universities, and innovation activities (which included details of the innovation, the person who introduced it, the requisite education and skill levels, and the constraints encountered). Respondents were also asked to provide any general recommendations on innovation policy as it relates to Indonesia's higher education system.

Responses varied about the importance of education levels in the innovation process. Two respondents regarded PhDs as required: unsurprisingly, the wireless technology manufacturer and one of the pharmaceutical firms. The majority of the remaining respondents thought that a master's degree was sufficient. Two of the firms reported that the requisite skills were obtained through outsourcing. On-the-

job experience was mentioned and was presumably relevant in most cases.

As to the skill levels required, all firms (except one nonrespondent) emphasized the importance of relevant industry-specific technical knowledge and a broad understanding of the company's general operations. Several referred to the importance of understanding international best practice. Some respondents stressed the importance of generic skills such as "curiosity," "proactivity," and "creativity"; significantly, these remarks originated from firms with a general commitment to R&D and education.

Similar surveys were carried out in the Philippines and Thailand. Philippine respondents emphasized the importance of a strong base of core skills in all new employees, and firms in IT and manufacturing underscored the importance of job-specific technical skills as well. In Thailand, surveyed managers, particularly for exporting firms, complained of weak language skills (English), lack of creativity (workers seemed to do only what they were told by their managers), and lack of teamwork skills. As a result, most new employees of surveyed firms underwent some form of in-house training.

Sources: Doner, Intarakumnerd, and Ritchie 2010; Hill and Tandon 2010; Tan 2010.

---

requirements for some of these skills are even higher in services and open sectors. This clearly has implications for higher education, which, beyond providing the training needed for some careers, will also need to inculcate the functional skills for workplace requirements.[51]

The dynamism of demand for tertiary graduates in services emphasizes the importance of tailoring curriculum design and pedagogical approaches of tertiary education to labor-market needs. Service-related careers in business, finance, transport, and telecommunications will remain important, as well as some broader social science tracks, gained at both university and college levels. Skills more typically applicable to services include higher-order behavioral skills such as client

orientation, communication, and initiative skills, as well as knowing a foreign language. At the same time, technology and engineering careers, as well as problem solving, some command of foreign language, and IT skills, among other things, will help manufacturing firms respond to the requirements of foreign direct investment and competitive export markets and therefore need to be possessed by tertiary educated workers. And there is evidence that critical and creative thinking and management skills are already requested by employers from a group of employees to move their technology frontier forward. Finally, possessing practical knowledge is a plus in all countries, particularly in low- and lower-middle-income countries that need to develop higher technological capability.

FIGURE 1.18   Labor market outcome indicators of TVET and university graduates, Mongolia, Indonesia, and Thailand

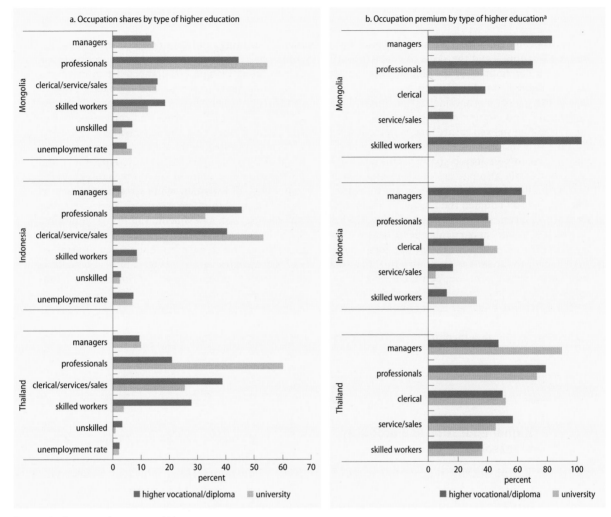

Sources: Labor force surveys, latest years available.
a. Excluded category is unskilled workers.

The demand for skills will continue changing in East Asia. As countries move up the value-added chain, the types of skills needed will continue evolving to a greater focus on more sophisticated technical skills and on the high-level generic skills that are increasingly driving labor productivity (such as analysis, problem solving, and communication). The experience in the United States shows that as countries' demand for interactive and analytical skills increases, demand for manual and routine cognitive skills falls. The European Union (EU) is tackling this problem (box 1.4) in its own way. As in industrial countries, greater client orientation and teamwork, new ways of working, and greater computer use are likely to accelerate demand for new skills in East Asia.[52] Moving forward, higher education sectors will need to provide the skills relevant to the labor markets of today with a vision of tomorrow—they cannot stand still. Skills for the service sector, high-order generic skills, and skills for innovation not only are needed now but also will be in increasing demand moving forward.

BOX 1.4   Skills for the future

The European Union has formally recognized that lifelong learning—and the skills to enable it—will be a major determinant of the bloc's future innovation, productivity, and competitiveness. In the context of increasing internationalization and regional integration, and continuous technological upgrading, it is taking steps to ensure that its education and training systems develop a workforce that will not only be able to keep its job-specific skills up to date and relevant but also possess certain generic skills that will allow workers to better adapt to change. The EU in 2006 adopted the European Framework for Key Competences for Lifelong Learning, the aim of which is to inform curricular development at all levels of education. It identifies the key competences that European citizens will require for "personal fulfillment, social inclusion, active citizenship, and employability in [the] knowledge-based economy."

The framework defines eight competences that young people should possess by the end of their formal education to equip them for their working life,

further learning, and skill development. These are communication in the mother tongue, communication in foreign languages, competence in math and basic competence in science and technology, digital competence, learning to learn, social and civic competence, a sense of initiative and entrepreneurship, and cultural awareness and expression.

The framework emphasizes competence in the basic skills of language, literacy, numeracy, and information and communication technology as the foundation of learning, while stressing the importance of critical thinking, creativity, initiative, problem solving, risk assessment, and decision making. With the framework, the EU aims to develop a workforce better able to adapt to changing circumstances and technologies, innovate, create jobs, and make its education and training systems more relevant to productivity and growth.

Source: The Expert Group on New Skills for New Jobs 2010.

Higher education as a producer of research

The most critical growth-oriented objective of higher education is producing enough proficient and innovative graduates for the labor market, but the importance of higher education in directly supporting technological development and innovation is also growing. The presence of a few research universities also becomes a key priority for growth.

There is a close positive relation between R&D and innovation. Expenditure on R&D (usually as a share of GDP) is a common metric that provides a reading on a country's acquisition of technological capacity, and it is much higher in the East Asia upper-income innovative economies. By this yardstick, Japan was the largest spender in East Asia in 2006 (3.4 percent of GDP), followed closely by Korea with 3.2 percent (table 1.9). The position of these two countries switched

in 2007. Singapore had been increasing its spending on R&D, at 2.6 percent that year. By comparison, R&D in Southeast Asia amounted to less than 1 percent of GDP. The fastest rate of growth was in China, rising from 0.6 percent in 1996 to 1.5 percent in 2007 (and 1.7 percent in 2009). Given its rapid economic growth during this period, the increase in the volume of resources committed was huge.

The low R&D spending rate by low- and middle-income countries (lower and middle technology cluster) is also much lower than the OECD average (figure 1.19), which only Japan, Korea, and Singapore exceed.

Mirroring the overall pattern in OECD countries, firms account for two-thirds or more of R&D spending in a majority of East Asian economies (table 1.10).

Private and public funding have a complementary role in R&D. As the technological gap narrows, increasing attention to process

TABLE 1.9   R&D expenditure, 1996–2007
percent of GDP

Economy	1996	2000	2002	2004	2005	2006	2007
Vietnam	—	0.1	0.2	—	0.3	—	—
Philippines	—	—	0.2	—	0.1	—	—
Indonesia	—	0.1	—	0.1	0.1	—	—
China	0.6	0.9	1.1	1.2	1.3	1.4	1.5
Thailand	0.1	0.3	0.2	0.3	—	0.2	—
Malaysia	0.2	0.5	0.7	0.6	—	0.6	—
Korea, Rep.	2.4	2.4	2.5	2.9	3	3.2	3.5
Singapore	1.4	1.9	2.2	2.2	2.4	2.3	2.6
Japan	2.8	3	3.2	3.2	3.3	3.4	3.4

Source: WDI database.
— = not available.

innovation by firms prepares the ground for competition strategies alive to the need for continuous innovation, because improved processes can be integrated more readily into the operations of a firm and because the returns accrue quickly. Once process innovation, which is generally incremental, gathers momentum and its utility is widely perceived, R&D gains stronger adherence (most importantly from management) both inside the firm and outside. It also becomes better integrated into the operations of an entire industry. Firms can and should then start to play a larger role and support university research. Thus, encouraging firms to improve existing processes and products through systematic research must be a major strand of government policy aimed at stoking interest in innovation. Such encouragement can complement efforts to augment research in universities and public research institutions with the help of public financing. In particular, in lower- and middle-income countries the public sector can have an important role in financing basic early-stage applied research and technology transfer through universities and research institutions, when private initiative is still limited, but positive externalities are clear.[53] R&D spending during the beginning stage of development can be thought of as part of the effort to assimilate and internalize foreign technology as well as to build the foundations of a national innovation system. It supplements the technological

FIGURE 1.19   R&D expenditure, East Asia and OECD

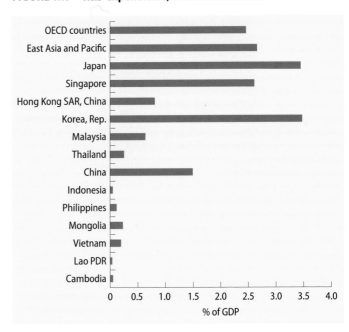

Source: WDI database (latest year, 2002–07).

upgrading achieved through technological change embodied in equipment and through interaction with overseas buyers and suppliers. During the rapid-growth phase of Japan, more than 30 percent of R&D was devoted to learning.[54] The role of public financing continues even later with the continuous contribution of universities and research centers to basic research and their potential role in high-tech R&D, often too costly to be undertaken by firms. Indeed, government and higher education research maintain a significant share of overall R&D in the economies of the top technology cluster (table 1.10), even more so in Hong Kong SAR, China, and Singapore. And in Singapore, the role of higher education was even larger 15 years ago, illustrating its importance in leading R&D effort and economic development.[55]

Firms and universities have a complementary role. Research universities not only add to the fund of knowledge, but universities and other tertiary institutions can also help countries of the lower technology cluster raise their technological capabilities and countries of the middle technology cluster go beyond technology assimilation to innovation by assisting firms in assimilating and upgrading technology through providing consulting services, hosting incubation facilities, and customizing foreign technologies for local requirements, among other approaches. Because most small and medium enterprises in the lower and middle technology cluster carry out very little R&D (and even large firms only do a modest amount of applied research), universities can step in to help narrow the technology gaps between technology clusters by enhancing technological capabilities.

Among the region's high-income countries, several research universities are sources of ideas and engage in applied research (see, among other indicators, the higher-ranked universities in table 2.7, chapter 2). But universities cannot substitute for firms, and several challenges exist in setting up effective university-industry links (reviewed in the rest of this report). Research by universities and even the R&D by firms themselves will yield meager returns if businesses have limited faith in the usefulness of innovating and are not persuaded of the value of making innovation into a routine. The type of university-industry link will also change across country groups.

Economies of scope and scale provide further justification for research universities. An important assumption of this study is that there are economies of scope between teaching and research, and economies of scale in research,[56] making support to research in at least a few higher education teaching institutions an effective option (and more effective than using only research centers). Although the link between teaching and research has been hotly debated, results from three meta-analyses find a positive correlation suggesting that teaching and research are not mutually exclusive goals in education.[57] A comparison of the world's highest-ranked universities reveals several similar characteristics, such as conducting research, teaching innovative curricula, and integrating research into undergraduate teaching.[58]

TABLE 1.10   Composition of R&D expenditure
percent

Economy	Business enterprises	Government	Higher education	Private nonprofit
Vietnam	14.5	66.4	17.9	1.1
Philippines	68.0	19.1	11.1	1.8
Indonesia	14.3	81.1	4.6	0.0
China	71.1	19.7	9.2	0.0
Thailand	43.9	22.5	31.0	2.6
Malaysia	71.5	10.4	18.1	0.0
Korea, Rep.	77.3	11.6	10.0	1.2
Hong Kong SAR, China	48.3	2.2	49.5	0.0
Singapore	65.7	10.4	23.9	0.0
Japan	77.2	8.3	12.7	1.9

Source: UIS Data Centre.
Note: Hong Kong SAR, China, and Malaysia (2004); the Philippines and Thailand (2003); Vietnam (2002); Indonesia (2001); other countries (2005–08).

There are certainly several arguments that research facilitates teaching, with benefits to both students and professors. Students who are actively engaged in research acquire knowledge and experience in their fields. They gain exposure to research methodology, data analysis, critical analyses, and presentation of the findings. All these are greatly needed skills (as seen above). Research also provides students with credibility and concrete evidence of what their professors teach. In developing countries, professors can often relay more current research to students than textbooks.[59]

Indeed, other findings suggest that teaching receives larger beneficial effects from research than research does from teaching and that these benefits are greater at the graduate than the undergraduate level.[60] There is, however, also evidence of the benefits that research receives from teaching, and studies suggest three factors are important: (a) teaching provides young researchers with opportunities to present their ideas; (b) teaching and students can stimulate ideas for new research; and (c) classrooms can act as a forum for academics to clarify and close gaps in their research.[61] In addition, a U.S. study found that teaching has a positive effect on research up to eight hours of teaching per week, indicating that previous inconclusive results could be because teaching and research have a curvilinear relationship, rather than the previously accepted linear relationship.[62]

Institutions that provide teaching and research gain several benefits. Research increases an institution's image and reputation, and thus attracts high-quality students and faculty. Teaching and research share similar skills such as creativity, critical thinking, and diligence. Students exposed to research are more likely to conduct research, including in areas that have few researchers. Students and faculty engaged in research can foster collaboration and learning of research. Finally, presenting research results not only reinforces the research but also generates ideas for further investigation.[63]

Results of several empirical studies of the costs of conducting research in universities in the United States and Japan provide further evidence of product-specific economies of scale. A study of more than 300 comprehensive universities in the United States finds product-specific economies of scale for conducting research in undergraduate and graduate public and private universities. Similarly, the study also finds product-specific economies of scope in these institutions.[64] Another study of nearly 1,900 U.S. higher education institutions further illustrates that institutions that combine undergraduate teaching, graduate teaching, and research are more efficient than single-output institutions. In this study, product-specific economies of scale for research are most apparent in public graduate institutions.[65] Finally, a study of 94 private universities in Japan finds product-specific economies of scale for conducting research in large universities.[66]

Innovation is clearly not fully captured by patents, journals, or even technology licensing since mere technological upgrading may be an even more important objective. But a simple relation between science and technology journals and R&D undertaken at the university level on the one side, and patents and R&D undertaken at the university on the other, indicates that there is a positive correlation between university research and innovation (figures 1.20 and 1.21), pointing to (at least potential) beneficial effects of R&D carried out at the university level.

Conclusion

Higher education has the potential to deliver skills and research for productivity and innovation. While the final goals of higher education are the same across countries, the different conditions faced by income and technology cluster groups dictate slightly different immediate broad priorities. Low-income and low-technology-cluster countries striving toward middle-income status must focus their immediate attention on higher education as skill producers and develop their human capital

FIGURE 1.20   Correlation between higher education R&D and scientific and technical journals

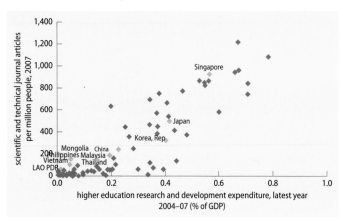

Sources: UIS Data Centre; WDI database.

FIGURE 1.21   Correlation between higher education R&D and patents

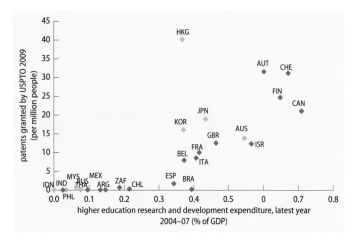

Sources: UIS Data Centre; U.S. Patent and Trademark Office data; WDI database.

base. To further enhance innovation, as a second goal they must start building some research capacity in higher education. Middle-income countries aspiring toward high-income status must focus urgently on both further developing the skills of their labor force and fostering research through higher education as a research provider. How much they should aim to do in relation to technology and innovation will very much

depend on their position within the technology cluster. For instance, developing the technological and engineering capacity of workers and building some limited research capacity for technology upgrading may be sufficient for countries such as Indonesia and the Philippines at their stage of technological development but would not be sufficient for China. The bottom line is that all countries need to start moving up within their income and cluster group and beyond, and higher education can help them to do so. But does it?

Notes

1. The earlier performance was driven primarily by rapid accumulation of physical capital, gains in labor and total factor productivity, and generally favorable institutional and policy environments (IMF 2006).
2. The terms *higher education* and *tertiary education* are used interchangeably in this book.
3. Thailand very recently transited to upper-middle-income status but was still a middle-middle-income economy according to the gross national income per capita Atlas method applied to 2009 data. Hence, it is considered a middle-middle-income economy in this book. This classification is also justifiable from the fact that all available higher education indicators are for 2009 or earlier.
4. The *World Development Report* uses the gross national income per capita Atlas method applied to 2009 data (latest available update).
5. Vietnam very recently transited to lower-middle-income status but was still a lower-income economy according to the gross national income per capita Atlas method applied to 2009 data. Hence, it is considered a lower-income economy in this book. This classification is also justifiable from the fact that all available higher education indicators are for 2009 or earlier.
6. See Castellacci and Archibugi (2008) for an adaptation of the concept from the convergence club literature and an attempt at grouping countries.
7. While the income group is the main classification followed in the book, reference is often made to technology clusters when technological capacity is a critical variable for the understanding of some issue or when technological

clusters are more closely aligned to economy performance.

8. China's technological prowess in biotechnology and nanotechnology might enable it to cross this threshold in the next decade.

9. Because of this technical advancement, exporting firms and multinational corporations tend to hire more educated workers than nonexporting or domestic firms (Yilmaz 2009).

10. Schott 2006.

11. China still lacks core technologies in most advanced areas of electronics and transport equipment, for example.

12. Kapur and Crowley 2008.

13. Vandenbussche, Aghion, and Meghir (2006) draw attention to the greater returns from investment in skills and research as a country approaches the technological frontier.

14. Gittleman and Wolff 1993; Sianesi and Van Reenen 2003.

15. Boudard 2001; Kirsh and others 1993.

16. Dowrick 2003; Permani 2009.

17. Hanushek and Wößmann 2007.

18. In Canada, for instance, higher reading scores at age 15 lead to higher future wages (OECD 2010b). Improving the quality of education improves test scores in the short term (Jakubowski and others 2010) and labor market success in the medium term (Bertschy, Cattaneo, and Wolter 2009).

19. Borghans and others (2008) and Heckman, Stixrud, and Urzua (2006) highlight the importance of noncognitive and cognitive abilities on social and economic success.

20. Entrepreneurial performance is associated with the quality of formal schooling (Berry and Glaeser 2005; Glaeser 2007; van der Sluis, van Praag, and Vijverberg 2008).

21. The technology variable refers to firms having "introduced a new technology that substantially changed the way the main product was produced in the three years prior to the survey" (definition adopted in the World Bank's Investment Climate Surveys). This definition, which is related to process innovation, leaves room for both adaptation of an existing technology (developed domestically or imported from abroad) and innovation within the firm.

22. Almeida (2009b) gives details on methodology and sample. The different samples are not directly comparable, however. The Indonesia sample, for instance, covers a greater number of large and foreign-owned firms than some other samples. It is the comparisons between technologically and nontechnologically innovative firms within countries that are relevant. By the same token, the firm sample of Indonesia distorts somewhat the results by including more firms close to the technology frontier.

23. Yusuf 2003.

24. These surveys, undertaken in 2009–10, sought to understand the extent to which higher education systems in these countries contribute to innovation at the firm level. The firms, which were in services and manufacturing, included providers of mining services, financial services, research and logistics, pharmaceuticals, and wireless technology as well as rubber processors and palm oil processors. Respondents were asked questions on the education levels of the top manager and employees, R&D expenditure and staff training, relationships with universities, and innovation activities. The last included details of the innovation, the person who introduced it, requisite education and skill levels, and the constraints encountered when introducing the innovation. Respondents were also asked for general recommendations on innovation policy as it related to their national higher education system.

25. Mok 2010.

26. Mok 2010.

27. T.-C. Lin 2004.

28. Barro and Sala-i-Martin 1995; Gittleman and Wolff 1993; Lederman and Maloney 2003.

29. OECD 2005.

30. Bloom, Hartley, and Rosovsky 2004; Macerinskiene and Vaiksnoraite 2006.

31. Salmi 2009.

32. Indeed, school is considered only the fourth source of skills for college-level workers in Vietnam, after on-the-job experience, training, and previous experience (World Bank 2008); whereas in Indonesia, school is still considered the most important source of skills for managers and professionals, but it comes after on-the-job exposure and previous experience for nonproduction and skilled production workers (di Gropello, Kruse, and Tandon 2010).

33. Nelson 1987.

34. Computerization has increased the demand for college preparation to undertake nonroutine cognitive tasks as machines take over routine tasks (Autor, Levy, and Murnane 2001). The scarcity of skilled and technical workers and of R&D facilities is a major reason for the slow pace of industrial upgrading in Southeast Asia (Tan 2010).

35. Senker 1995.

36. One needs to interpret the trends carefully in the Chinese case, however, given the much shorter time covered by the data and the less updated status of the information.

37. They also indicate some emerging constraints in the overall absorption capacity for new tertiary-educated graduates.

38. The regression framework for estimating education (and industry) wage premiums follows the approach used by Goldberg and Pavcnik (2005) and other researchers. Specifically, for each year the log of worker i's wage ($\ln(w_{ijt})$) is regressed on worker i's characteristics (H'_{ijt}) such as gender and age; on whether, based on his or her education, the worker is skilled or unskilled (S_{ijt}); and on a set of industry j indicators (I_{ijt}) reflecting worker i's industry affiliation:

$$\ln(w_{ijt}) = H'_{ijt}\beta_H + S_{ijt} \cdot I_{ijt}\, sp_{jt} + I_{ijt}\, wp_{jt} + \varepsilon_{ijt}$$

where sp_{jt} represents the sectoral return to education (or education premium) of sector j at time t, and wp_{jt} represents the industry premium.

39. In Indonesia about 65 percent of service firms confirm to having seen skill requirements increase over these past 10 years (compared with about 50 percent of manufacturing firms), and 95 percent of firms (in both manufacturing and services) think skill requirements will continue to rise over the next 10 years (di Gropello, Kruse, and Tandon 2010).

40. Increases in value added within services, though only gradual, are visible in Cambodia, Indonesia, the Philippines, and Vietnam and where the public administration and other services subsector has been generally decreasing, with corresponding increases in the more skill-intensive finance and business, transport and communication, and trade and tourism subsectors. In these cases the public administration and other services subsector includes a mix of services with both higher-educated workers (health, education) and lower-educated workers (private household services, lower public administration levels, nonformal). Further, despite the recent global economic downturn, finance and banking subsectors in Singapore; trade and tourism subsectors in Cambodia, Lao PDR, and Vietnam; and the communication subsector in the Philippines are seen as emerging or quickly recovering, implying that these sectors will need increasingly skilled workers (Asia Business Council 2009).

41. The main data set used here is a large firm-level database collected by the World Bank, Investment Climate Surveys, covering eight developing countries in East Asia. The surveys were conducted in 2002–05, and the samples were designed to be representative of the population of firms according to their industry and location within each country. The final sample has 9,776 firms distributed across a wide range of sectors (manufacturing 77 percent, construction 1.37 percent, services 20 percent, and agro-industry 0.8 percent). Manufacturing covers a range of industries, such as auto and auto components, beverages, chemicals, electronics, food, garments, leather, metals and machinery, nonmetallic and plastic materials, paper, textiles, and wood and furniture.

42. The relationship with technological innovation was shown in figure 1.4.

43. The model, fully detailed in Almeida (2009b), is related to a vast literature linking foreign investment, trade, and technology with skills. See, among others, Berman, Bound, and Machin (1998); Fajnzylber and Fernandes (2004); Feenstra and Hanson (1997); and Tybout (2000).

44. This limitation is despite the effort to control for as many observable and unobservable variables as possible.

45. Such investment would continue the upward trend experienced in some countries. In Thailand, for example, foreign direct investment as a share of GDP increased from only 1 percent in 1990 to 5 percent in 2008. Concurrently in Indonesia, foreign ownership in manufacturing rose from 22 percent to 37 percent (*WDI* database various years).

46. The evidence suggests that the generally low-value-added food, textile, timber, and furniture subsectors employ most workers in Indonesia and Vietnam, while other subsectors that add higher value are developing only slowly (mainly chemicals in Indonesia and machinery and equipment in Vietnam). The Philippines focused more on other, higher-value-added, manufacturing subsectors, but the direction of change is not clear, with an increase in the employment share of other manufacturing but a decrease of the machinery and transport subsector.

47. As mentioned previously, one can look at the relation both ways: from technology and foreign direct investment to demand for tertiary education, or from tertiary education to

technological innovation and attraction of foreign capital.

48. This book uses Investment Climate Surveys, related skill modules, and two employer and employee skill surveys carried out in Indonesia and the Philippines. This book analyzes how employers (and employees where possible) rate the importance of generic (thinking, behavioral, IT), technical (job-specific), and in a few cases subject-based (academic) skills for doing their jobs. The analysis is carried out for Cambodia, Indonesia, Malaysia, Mongolia, the Philippines, Thailand, and Vietnam. Some results are not strictly comparable across countries because of different samples' compositions and sizes, occasionally different skill definitions (which have been kept as comparable as possible), and in some cases slightly different units of measure. Even so, it is possible to derive some main findings.

49. See di Gropello, Kruse, and Tandon 2011; di Gropello, Tan, and Tandon 2010; Malaysia Investment Climate Surveys 2002, 2007; World Bank 2008.

50. Wadhwa and others 2007.

51. Learning such skills will be coordinated with other education and training levels and types, since, as illustrated previously, skill acquisition is cumulative and diverse.

52. And they are likely to create demand for new skills related to higher education workers, as illustrated by the results of alternative specifications checking robustness of the tertiary education determinants to different technological variables (see appendix E), which show a positive association among R&D, use of computers, use of the Internet, and share of workers with more than 12 years of schooling.

53. Although without the existence of at least some proactively innovating firms (or firms demanding innovation), increasing the supply of ideas alone will rarely bear any fruit.

54. Mok 2010.

55. Mok 2010.

56. Cohn, Rhine, and Santos 1989; Hashimoto and Cohn 1997; Koshal and Koshal 1999.

57. Allen 1996; Feldman 1987; Hattie and Marsh 1996.

58. Salmi 2009.

59. Jenkins and others 1998.

60. Smeby 1998.

61. Zaman 2004.

62. Mitchell and Rebne 1995.

63. Zaman 2004.

64. Koshal and Koshal 1999.

65. Cohn, Rhine, and Santos 1989.

66. Hashimoto and Cohn 1997.

Is Higher Education Meeting Its Promises? | 2

The previous chapter noted that higher education has the potential to lift productivity and competitiveness. This chapter analyzes how much higher education is fulfilling that potential in low- and middle-income East Asia, delivering to its students sufficient skills for growth while fostering innovation through research. Disentangling education's impact from other factors, however, is sometimes hard, as will be seen from survey and other data used in this chapter.

The main broad conclusion of this chapter is that higher education in low- and middle-income East Asia is not delivering the skills and producing the research that is required to address labor market and innovation needs.

With skills, the challenges are multiple. Some countries urgently need to grow their higher education systems in terms of enrollment. In most countries there is scope to enhance equitable access to widen the talent pool, and the share of graduates in science, technology, engineering, and mathematics (STEM) remains too low to support much technological capability. At the same time, beyond pervasive gaps in technical skills in most countries (including the capacity to apply knowledge), both employers and employees are increasingly recognizing the significance of gaps in other types of skills—thinking and behavioral—which tertiary education is not providing well enough. And the importance of most of these generic skills will keep on growing as the share of the service sector grows and international competition intensifies. As the share of the service sector continues to grow and the importance of practical knowledge persists, countries will also most likely have to maintain a balanced tertiary education sector among technical and vocational education and training (TVET) institutions, social sciences, and STEM fields.

Moreover, beyond weaknesses in delivering high-level skills, universities are also shown to be weak in terms of quality rankings and research and technology development outputs in all low- and middle-income countries, thus increasing the magnitude of the higher education challenge.

Higher education and skills for growth: The main issues

Investment Climate Surveys (ICSs)—which provide large national samples of firm-level data across the industrial, manufacturing, and to a lesser extent, service sectors of the region—point to macroeconomic instability, regulatory economic and policy uncertainty, and corruption, as well as the skills and education of workers, as the main obstacles to operating in a country (figure 2.1). East Asia as a region is second only to North Africa—and at the level of Latin America and Africa—for the importance of skills as an obstacle.[1]

Time to fill professional and skilled vacancies is a standard indicator to measure difficulties in matching skill demand and supply. It takes about six weeks to fill professional vacancies in both Malaysia and Thailand, and more than four weeks in China and Mongolia (figure 2.2a), which is high relative to a high-income country such as the Republic of Korea and a low-income country such as India (but still lower than Brazil). These figures are also higher than for the United States, where recent data from the 2010 Job Opening and Labor Turnover Survey indicated that 3.5 weeks are needed to fill a skilled vacancy. An update of the vacancy data for the countries for which updated ICSs or other surveys (figure 2.2b) are available indicates a slight improvement in Malaysia but the contrary in Indonesia, the Philippines, and Thailand. For Indonesia and the Philippines, which use more extensive employer skill surveys, this result reveals possibly higher skill inadequacies in services.

Skill gaps have also increased in lower-income countries—as illustrated by the fact that even in the Lao People's Democratic Republic and Cambodia, where skills were initially a lesser obstacle (figure 2.1), the latest ICS data confirm that in both countries about 40 percent of firms considered skills to be at least a moderate obstacle for their business (with almost 20 percent considering them at least a major obstacle). These results show that lower- and middle-income countries have been unable to raise skill supply and quality, though demand has strengthened and wage premiums are overall attractive.

In a worrisome trend, finding the right skills becomes harder the greater the export orientation and technological intensity of manufacturing firms, where many tertiary graduates work. In manufacturing, skill gaps grow with the firms' degree of openness and

technology adoption, a fact already apparent from simple correlations (figure 2.3) and from more sophisticated multivariate regressions (appendix G).[2] The regression analysis confirms that both (a) technology innovation or adoption and (b) openness (measured by export orientation) are positively correlated with measures of skill gaps, even with the inclusion of such control variables as firm size and firm ownership and alternative specifications including location, manager education, access to finance, and several indicators of technological intensity and firm performance.[3] Notwithstanding the small size of the country samples, which requires particular care in interpretation, the effects of technology on gaps are particularly evident in Indonesia, Malaysia, the Philippines, Thailand, and Vietnam (table 2.1). Overall, the relation between skill gaps and technology is apparent in all income groups but somewhat stronger for middle-income countries.[4]

The export sector faces skill gaps, particularly in China, Indonesia, the Philippines, and Thailand.[5] These gaps may already be reflected in some of these countries' export performances, particularly the declining share of relatively high-value-added products (though direct connections cannot be made).[6] These results also illustrate that skill gaps in the export sector are more of an issue for middle-income countries than low-income ones. An upper-income country like Korea experiences both lower skill gaps and a weaker relation among skill gaps, technology, and openness.

Skill constraints may have become an issue in many parts of East Asia when measured as obstacles to business and time to fill skilled vacancies, but to what extent is it the fault of education in general and higher education in particular?

Of course, higher education has a key role to play in skill supply. As economies and demand for skills grow, the quantity and the quality of tertiary graduates generally adjust to the rising needs of the region's labor markets and innovation systems—coverage of higher education is higher in upper-middle-income and upper-income

FIGURE 2.2   Time to fill professional vacancies

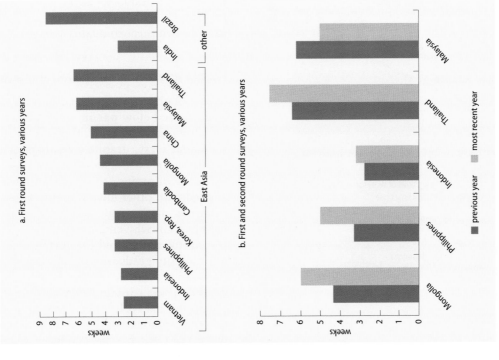

a. First round surveys, various years

b. First and second round surveys, various years

Sources: World Bank IC Surveys (various years), di Gropello, Kruse, and Tandon (2011), and di Gropello, Tan, and Tandon (2010).

FIGURE 2.1   Business climate obstacles and skill bottlenecks

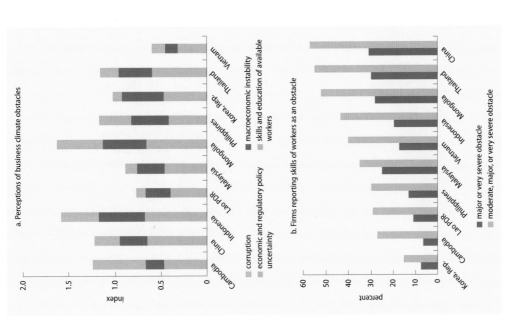

a. Perceptions of business climate obstacles

- corruption
- economic and regulatory policy uncertainty
- macroeconomic instability
- skills and education of available workers

b. Firms reporting skills of workers as an obstacle

- major or very severe obstacle
- moderate, major, or very severe obstacle

Source: Almeida 2009a, based on World Bank Investment Climate Surveys (ICSs), various years.

FIGURE 2.3 **Skill bottlenecks, technology, and openness**

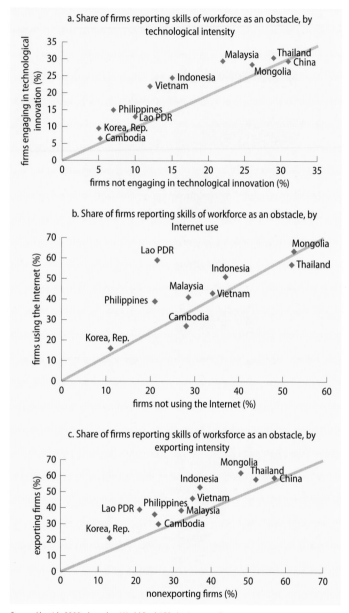

Source: Almeida 2009a, based on World Bank ICSs (various years).

Quantity of higher education graduates

This first section looks at the issue of quantity of higher education graduates. The next section then turns to quality issues.

Higher education for the labor market

Even though tertiary gross enrollment ratios (GERs) are below par in several countries (as shown in chapter 1), three points must be made. First, despite overall poor performance in East Asia's low- and middle-income countries, they are nonetheless aligned with other low- and middle-income countries in other regions. These results may help explain why employers in most countries in the region find the current quantity of university graduates, or quantity of education in general, much less of an issue than quality in skill gaps (appendix H).

Second, the GER and current proportion of tertiary graduates may not be fully aligned when the GER has been subject to recent changes (such as recent growth). The proportion of adults in low- and middle-income East Asia with a university degree tends to be proportional to the country's GER. For example, as a result of its longer-term increases in the GER, the Philippines also has a higher ratio of workers with university qualifications (figure 2.4). In contrast, the gaps between GERs and the ratio of university graduates in Mongolia and Thailand suggest that enrollment growth has been more recent.

Third, "below par" does not mean that the lack of supply of tertiary graduates is an immediate cause of skill gaps in all countries. While demand for higher education is rising in all countries in East Asia, the trends in education premiums in Indonesia and the Philippines, for example, point to a very different labor market than in Vietnam. In the longer run, higher education coverage will likely continue growing (all the more if services continue to grow), but the growth imperative is not the same for all countries—an important factor when one assesses the key country-level issues of higher education.

East Asian economies. But to what extent can the skill gap in low- and lower-middle-income East Asia be explained by too few tertiary graduates? And looking beyond head counts to quality, is higher education delivering to its graduates the skills that allow them to be productive and innovative?

TABLE 2.1 Regression coefficients of technological and openness variables in a sample of East Asian economies

Variable	Lao PDR	Cambodia	Vietnam	Mongolia	Philippines	Indonesia	China	Thailand	Malaysia	Korea, Rep.	Low-income economies	Middle-income economies[a]	Middle-income economies[b]
Technological innovation[c]	0.013	−0.001	0.046**	−0.008	0.062**	0.066**	0.003	0.017	0.063*	0.025	0.032**	0.031**	0.035**
Technological innovation[d]			0.050			0.457**	−0.006	0.081*	0.018	−0.040	0.050	0.131***	0.104***
Openness[c]	−0.01	−0.017	0.026	−0.008	0.089**	0.026	0.042	0.048*	−0.005	0.045	0.012	0.044***	0.037***
Openness[d]			0.091			0.284**	0.121**	0.065	−0.082	−0.096	0.091	0.144**	0.105***

Source: Appendix G.
a. All East Asian economies except low-income economies, Malaysia, and the Republic of Korea.
b. All East Asian economies except low-income economies and the Republic of Korea.
c. Dependent variable is perceptions on skill bottlenecks.
d. Dependent variable is time to fill skilled vacancies.
Significance level: * = 10 percent; ** = 5 percent; *** = 1 percent.

These points call for an analysis of demand-side and supply-side factors in each country when assessing how much the number of tertiary graduates may be a constraint, which follows here.

Several critical indicators are reviewed for each country. The main demand-side (labor market) indicators include the level and trend of the tertiary education premium (for the overall adult population and specific generations), the time required to fill professional vacancies, the unemployment rate of tertiary graduates, and the proportion of tertiary graduates working in professional occupations (the "professionalization" rate). Education premiums, employment, and vacancy indicators can be used to measure the capacity of absorption of the surrounding economy and, related to that, the scarcity or abundance of tertiary graduates. For instance, high unemployment rates, low professionalization rates, and short required times to fill skilled vacancies, combined with decreasing or low education premiums, may suggest the presence of constraints on the labor market side (limited demand for tertiary graduates), and vice versa.

The main supply-side indicators include the level and trends in the ratio of the tertiary-educated workforce and the tertiary GER. (The values of all the demand-side and supply-side indicators mentioned in the text are reported in appendix I, and their main

FIGURE 2.4 **Proportion of adult population with university qualifications**

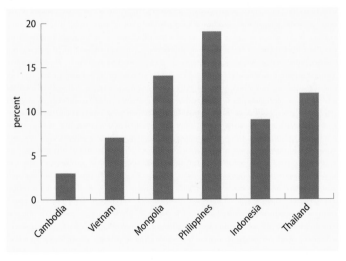

Source: Sakellariou 2010b.
Note: Cambodia and Indonesia data are for 2009; Vietnam data are from 2008; Mongolia data are from 2007; Philippines and Thailand data are from 2006. Adult population is 22–65 years of age.

trends by country group experiencing similar trends are reported in table 2.2.) Combined, these indicators allow assessment of both the situation of tertiary graduates in the labor market and the magnitude of their supply to identify possible pressure points. This analysis is undertaken with the understanding that it is a simplified exercise and that the trends in some labor market indicators may also indicate the presence of other issues beyond

TABLE 2.2 Tertiary education quantity analysis by country groups

Country group	Indicators	Severity of quantity gaps	Suggested response
Cambodia, China, Vietnam	High[a] or quite sharply increasing education premium across sectors[b] High tertiary professionalization rate[c] and low unemployment rate[d] Significant time required to fill professional vacancies[e] Education premium for youth stable or increasing[f] Low ratios of tertiary educated workers Low tertiary GER	Overall quantity gaps (including new graduates) confirmed by demand and supply indicators Quantity gaps particularly strong in Cambodian manufacturing	Supply push to increase number of graduates
Mongolia, Thailand	High (quite sharply increasing in Mongolia) education premium Low unemployment rate and high professionalization rate Significant time required to fill professional vacancies Education premium for youth stable (Mongolia) or decreasing (Thailand) Low (in relation to GER) or decreasing ratio of tertiary-educated workers (particularly in Mongolian manufacturing) Tertiary GER high regionally	Overall quantity gap in current tertiary-educated workers (but sufficient new graduates for labor market) confirmed by demand and supply indicators	Focus on tertiary-educated workers (rather than supply push)
Indonesia, Philippines	Decreasing or flat education premium, but higher and increasing education premiums on tertiary graduates in Indonesian manufacturing and Philippine services Significant unemployment and low professionalization rates Education premium for Philippine youth decreasing Short time required to fill professional vacancies Relatively high ratio of tertiary-educated workers in the Philippines (though remaining flat in services); a lower ratio in Indonesia (even decreasing in manufacturing)[g] GER relatively high regionally in the Philippines but low internationally; low GER in Indonesia	Quantity gaps (including new graduates) in specific sectors (Indonesian manufacturing; Philippine services) confirmed by demand and supply data, but no overall quantity gap In Indonesia lack of overall quantity gap illustrated by demand data coexisting with supply data on the low side	Reallocation across sectors Policies to enhance demand for tertiary workers
Malaysia[h]	Fairly high but decreasing time to fill professional vacancies University graduates marginal and decreasing cause of vacancies GER relatively high regionally but low internationally	No clear quantity gaps according to demand indicators (at least for new graduates), although current GER might be higher	

Sources: Appendixes C and I.
Note: Magnitude is assessed in relation to regional and international levels.
a. The education premiums are lower in China and Vietnam because of their much lower starting point (because of later market liberalization).
b. The increase is even more marked in Cambodian manufacturing.
c. This relies on the proportion of tertiary graduates working as professionals (admittedly an imprecise indicator of local absorption potential because it is normal to have a share of tertiary graduates working as skilled production or nonproduction workers).
d. The professionalization rate is somewhat lower in Cambodia because of a more basic economic structure and because of insufficient diversification of tertiary graduates.
e. Apart from Vietnam possibly, but the time required there is likely to be higher for managerial positions and certain professional categories (according to more recent evidence).
f. This indicates that rewards to higher education are not decreasing as supply increases.
g. A high and increasing premium, combined with a decreasing ratio of tertiary workers in manufacturing in Indonesia, is evidence of quantity gaps in the sector. The same reasoning is valid, though the evidence is a bit less clear-cut, for Philippine services.
h. Data for Malaysia are too scarce to perform a complete analysis.

quantity-related ones (such as labor market distortions and poor quality).

Figures 2.5–2.7 provide a visualization for each country using several key indicators from the table 2.2. From these data, one can broadly distinguish four main groups of countries. In the first group (Cambodia, China, and Vietnam), most of the demand-side and supply-side indicators suggest that the overall quantity of tertiary graduates is still insufficient to respond to the needs of the economy and a supply push is thus warranted to increase the number of graduates. While not all indicators are consistent (some of the caveats are explained in table 2.2), these countries are generally characterized by levels and trends in the demand-side and supply-side indicators that indicate a situation of quantity gaps (supply-side constraints). As a result, for all three countries, the right side of the graphs tends to be more developed visually than the left.

Quantity gaps are particularly strong in Cambodia's manufacturing sector, judging from the particularly steep increase in the tertiary education premium in that sector combined with a very low and stagnant tertiary-educated workforce (appendix C). This finding suggests the need for Cambodia to widen its very low curriculum diversification (discussed in chapter 3). Otherwise the system faces a strong risk of persisting in producing unemployed or poorly employed graduates and in failing to meet manufacturing demand for graduates.

One needs to be careful when interpreting trends in rates of return in China, given the short period under discussion and the lack of more recent evidence. Anecdotal evidence (for instance, in newspapers) suggests that over the past few years tertiary graduates may have seen stagnating returns and increasing rates. The recent postcrisis recovery should, however, have put things back on track.

In the case of Vietnam, the evidence confirms the perception of employers about the lack of sufficient tertiary graduates as a key reason for skill gaps (appendix H).

FIGURE 2.5 **Benchmarking quantity gaps in tertiary education, Cambodia, China, and Vietnam**

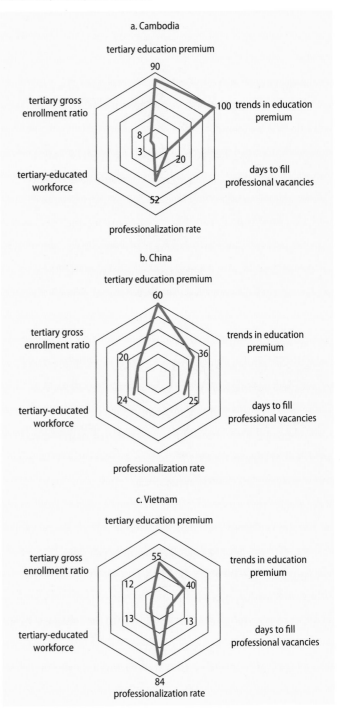

Source: Appendix I.

FIGURE 2.6   **Benchmarking quantity gaps in tertiary education, Mongolia and Thailand**

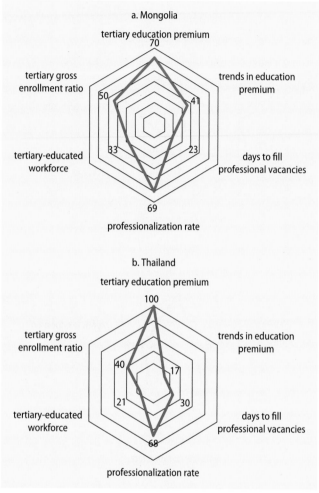

Source: Appendix I.

In the second group, Mongolia and Thailand have gaps in the current quantity of tertiary-educated workers but not in the tertiary GER. The relevant figures are demand-side indicators suggesting the need for more tertiary graduates in the labor market, combined with relatively low or decreasing ratios of tertiary-educated workers on the one side, but quite high tertiary GER on the other (and decreasing returns for tertiary-educated youth in Thailand). In both cases, sufficient GERs are also confirmed by the employers' perception that universities are producing enough graduates (appendix H). The gap in

tertiary-educated workers is stronger in Thailand, but the decrease in tertiary-educated workers is more notable in Mongolia (particularly in manufacturing), likely because of emigration.[7]

These findings highlight a need to focus on the number of tertiary-educated workers in these two countries rather than on a supply push for new graduates (beyond sustaining the current GER). In Thailand the problem appears to be how to provide tertiary education to the current adult population to cover the transition period; in Mongolia much of the problem is how to retain current tertiary workers in the country. The charts for both countries are relatively more symmetric than the charts for the other countries.

The third group of countries—Indonesia and the Philippines—experience some tertiary education quantity gaps limited to critical sectors such as services (the Philippines) and manufacturing (Indonesia), but no immediate overall quantity gap.

The Philippines seems to experience an insufficient supply of tertiary graduates in services. This is because of higher and increasing education premiums on such graduates in services (appendix C), combined with quantity being a bit more of an issue in this sector (according to employers), as well as a flat ratio of tertiary-educated workers in services.

More evident is the supply gap of tertiary graduates in Indonesian manufacturing, according to high and increasing rates of return in that sector (appendix C), combined with the higher importance of quantity constraints (according to employers) and a low and even decreasing ratio of tertiary-educated workers in that sector.

But in both countries, at least for the time being, reallocation across sectors would be sufficient. For overall labor market indicators (the demand side) for tertiary-educated workers, neither country apparently has an overall immediate tertiary education quantity gap. To illustrate this point, the charts for the two countries have a somewhat more developed left-hand side. Beyond this bump, they differ. While the quantity issue is confirmed by supply-side indicators for the Philippines (relatively high ratio of tertiary-educated workers and tertiary enrollment), a different picture emerges for the same indicators in Indonesia. The relatively low tertiary supply-side indicators suggest that Indonesia would need more of an overall supply push, but it is currently constrained by a sluggish demand for skills, as also illustrated by a longer-term wage compression on tertiary workers.[8] Broader policies to enhance the demand for tertiary workers may also be needed (assuming that demand does not rise drastically in the future). Visually speaking, as a result of both supply and demand constraints, the figure for Indonesia is the narrowest of all.

Data for Malaysia, on its own in the fourth group, are too scarce to perform a complete analysis. The still-significant but decreasing length of time to fill professional vacancies, combined with very low (and decreasing) significance of the shortage of new university graduates as a reason for vacancies, but still relatively low tertiary GERs, points to possible demand constraints in relation to new graduates. However, without data on the current stock of tertiary-educated workers (such as returns, ratio, and employment performance) one cannot conclude if the "likely" relatively low ratio of tertiary-educated workers is demand constrained (as in Indonesia) or supply constrained (as in Thailand).

Even in East Asian countries that seem to need an immediate boost to the number of tertiary graduates, it seems clear that their absorption capacity is lower than that of developed countries or Latin America when one compares return levels with the tertiary education stock. In Indonesia and Thailand, tertiary graduates earn about 100–120 percent more than primary education graduates, which is a substantial gain.[9] Figures are broadly similar in other East Asian economies, though lower for China and Vietnam because of their lower starting points (caused by late liberalization).

A simple equivalence obtained between education premiums as calculated in this book and the more traditional annualized rates of return allows comparison of magnitudes with other countries. For Indonesia the estimate of

FIGURE 2.7   **Benchmarking quantity gaps in tertiary education, Indonesia and the Philippines**

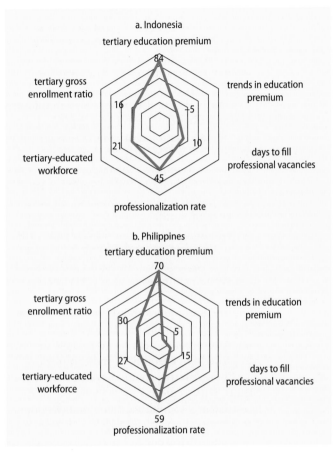

Source: Appendix I.

1.084 for tertiary over primary is the difference in coefficients for tertiary and primary in the estimated earnings equation. Dividing 1.084 by the difference in years of education between tertiary and primary education (10 years) implies an annualized return of about 10.8 percent. Similarly, to derive an estimate of the return to tertiary over senior secondary (instead of primary), one would calculate the difference between 1.084 and 0.508, that is, 0.576; annualized, this implies an average return of 14.4 percent for each year of tertiary education over senior secondary.

These are significant annual rates of return comparable with high-income Asian and most OECD economies,[10] but they are lower than Latin America's returns.[11] When one relates these numbers to the much higher coverage of tertiary education in OECD countries and high-income East Asia, and the equivalent coverage levels in Latin America, these findings also indicate increasing, but still relatively limited, capacity of absorption of tertiary graduates in low- and middle-income East Asia.[12]

Finally, beyond enrollment, completion matters. Regional tertiary completion rates for the International Standard Classification of Education (ISCED) 5A[13] programs suggest room to improve the retention of tertiary students. China and Indonesia have ISCED 5A completion rates of less than 20 percent, lower than middle-income countries outside the region; Malaysia and the Philippines perform a bit better, and Mongolia performs much better (figure 2.8). Rather than increasing enrollment rates (and another reason not to do it), this evidence confirms that Indonesia and the Philippines should focus on enhancing student retention (to allow efficiency improvements). China seems to have scope to improve both enrollment and completion.

These relative trends have persisted over time, with regional high-income countries consistently exhibiting much higher completion rates than others. Although one must compare different cohorts with care, the difference between ISCED 5A enrollment (the largest share of the overall GER) and completion rates suggests weaknesses in how lower- and middle-income countries in the region are retaining and supporting students. This hypothesis is confirmed by a comparison of gross completion rates and income levels: most countries are underperforming in relation to their income per capita (see figure 2.8).

The preceding analysis suggests that the lack of tertiary enrollment opportunities for young people or adults in Cambodia, China, Thailand, and Vietnam may be insufficient for the skills required by the labor market. In Indonesia and the Philippines constraints are more sector-specific. Does this breakdown also hold good for innovation indicators?

Higher education for innovation

While more innovative economies—such as Japan and Korea—also have higher education coverage, in the longer run the relation between higher education coverage and innovation outputs is very loose. Japan, for instance, has better innovation outputs than Korea (see chapter 1) despite lower coverage. And lower development levels also show no such relationship (figure 2.9).[14] Indeed, above a certain threshold level, too high a GER is associated with lower innovation outputs: Mongolia and the Philippines, for example, seem to have prioritized education quantity over quality. Two further points can therefore be made. First, this evidence suggests that while there may be a minimum coverage threshold to spur innovation, the volume of tertiary education graduates matters much less than the composition of the graduates and their skills. Second, this evidence also raises the possibility of a quantity-quality trade-off in higher education.

Because the potential capacity of firms to absorb and develop technology depends upon STEM skills of employees, degrees in science and engineering fields are a better indicator of building capabilities than the overall volume of tertiary education graduates. STEM shares are too low in several countries. As reported

FIGURE 2.8   Tertiary gross completion rates and per capita income

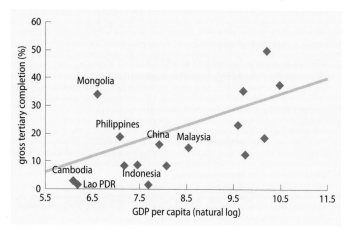

Source: Yilmaz 2009.

in chapter 1, the experience of leading East Asian economies suggests that indigenous technological capabilities require an abundance of scientists and engineers in the earlier stages of industrialization. Indeed, more than half of students earn science and engineering degrees in China, Japan, Singapore, and Thailand. Between half and one-third of students earn science and engineering degrees in Hong Kong SAR, China; Korea; and Taiwan, China; and about one-fourth in Indonesia and the Philippines (table 2.3).[15]

Another source of data (figure 2.10) confirms that less than one-fourth of students earn their degrees in science and engineering in most of East Asia's low- and middle-income countries. While the East Asian average is slightly higher than the G7 average (25 percent compared with 22 percent),[16] these shares remain a challenge in several countries.

Equity in higher education

In addition to issues of quantity of higher education graduates for the labor market and innovation, many of East Asia's low- and middle-income countries are constraining innovation simply by limiting the pool of talent accessing and completing tertiary education. GERs and completion rates mask disparities in access by socioeconomic status, race or ethnicity, and rural and urban location, suggesting inclusiveness issues. Disparities are particularly acute in Cambodia, Indonesia, Vietnam, and, to a lesser extent, the Philippines (figure 2.11). Inasmuch as these disparities are correlated with ability, the potential for innovation is not necessarily affected, but if some capable and talented females or ethnic minority students are excluded, for example, potential for innovation can be seriously affected. And there is evidence that disparities in access and completion are indeed not related to ability but rather to economic, cultural, or yet supply-side factors that have prevented otherwise talented youth from getting access to and thriving in higher education. Box 2.1 makes this case by showing that students of

FIGURE 2.9 **Tertiary gross enrollment ratio and number of journal articles, latest available year**

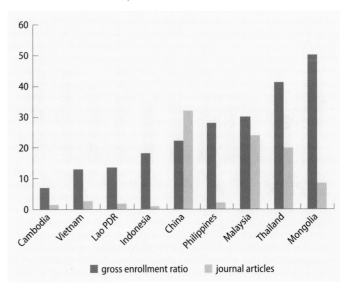

Source: United Nations Educational, Scientific and Cultural Organization (UNESCO) Institute for Statistics (UIS) Data Centre.
Note: Journal articles published per million people.

TABLE 2.3 **Share of first university degrees in science and engineering**
percent

Economy	Percent	Year
Philippines	26	2004
Indonesia	27	2006
China	56	2004
Thailand	69	2001
Korea, Rep.	46	2004
Taiwan, China	41	2005
Hong Kong SAR, China	38	2004
Singapore	59	2004
Japan	63	2005

Sources: National Science Board 2008; data for the Philippines are from the World Bank Knowledge Assessment Methodology data set (http://www.worldbank.org/kam).
Note: The National Science Board's definition of science and engineers contains science, engineering, agriculture, and health (and possibly math) and counts only the completion. The standard UNESCO Institute for Statistics definition picks up only science and engineering and is based on enrollment data.

the poorest quintile and ethnic minority students in Asia and Latin America perform as well as other students after controlling for student and school background variables. The exceptionally high number of resilient

FIGURE 2.10 **Enrollment shares in science and engineering, latest available year**

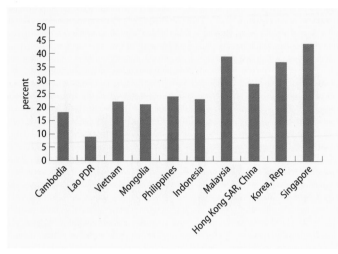

Source: UIS Data Centre.

children in East Asia's high-income economies also shows that even economically and socially disadvantaged children can perform well on international tests of math and reading. These studies show that lower academic ability is not caused by lower innate ability but rather attributable to school factors and student background. While some students in East Asia's high-income economies are able to overcome their disadvantaged backgrounds, lower- and middle-income economies must increase their number of resilient children by providing better educational opportunities to disadvantaged students. In this way, economies will have a better skilled labor force that will lead to increased productivity for the individual and the country.

Ethnic minorities appear to exhibit significant disparities in both tertiary enrollment and completion. This disparity is most apparent in Cambodia where the Khmer majority dominates tertiary enrollment by a ratio of eight to one,[17] and its completion rates are several orders of magnitude higher than among minorities who enroll. Similarly, in Vietnam enrollments by the majority Kinh are almost fourfold higher than enrollments by minority groups, and completions are

nearly fivefold higher. In Thailand, majority Thais are twice as likely to enroll and three times more likely to complete the tertiary cycle than ethnic minorities. Time series data indicate that these differences in these three countries have generally persisted, though in recent years in Vietnam minorities have increased their enrollment—though not completion—rates. Controlling for other variables,[18] the negative correlation between rural location and tertiary access is still quite strong in all countries. And while disparities by gender are less acute, females are still penalized in Cambodia and China, whereas males are lower completers in the Philippines and Thailand. Finally, the poorest quintile still faces lower access to and completion of higher education. In Cambodia, for example, controlling for other socioeconomic factors, students from the top income quintile are more than 50 percent more likely to enroll in higher education than students from the lowest income quintile, thus excluding many talented poor students.

To sum up this section, a few countries such as Cambodia, China, and Vietnam present a case for further expanding tertiary education to address immediate labor market needs. Most low- and middle-income countries, however, prompt an economic efficiency argument for a focus on decreasing dropouts during the tertiary cycle (that is, aiming for higher completion rates), supporting more inclusive access to increase the talent pool accessing higher education, and increasing enrollment in STEM fields.

So much for the quantity side of the analysis. What about quality?

Quality of higher education graduates

The quality (and relevance) of education and training appears to be much more of a binding constraint than the quantity of students in all employers' surveys, except for Vietnam.[19] For example, some 30–40 percent of firms report quality to be an important or very important issue in Indonesia and the Philippines. And 15–35 percent of firms recognize

FIGURE 2.11   Predicted ratios of enrollment and completion in tertiary education, by key characteristics

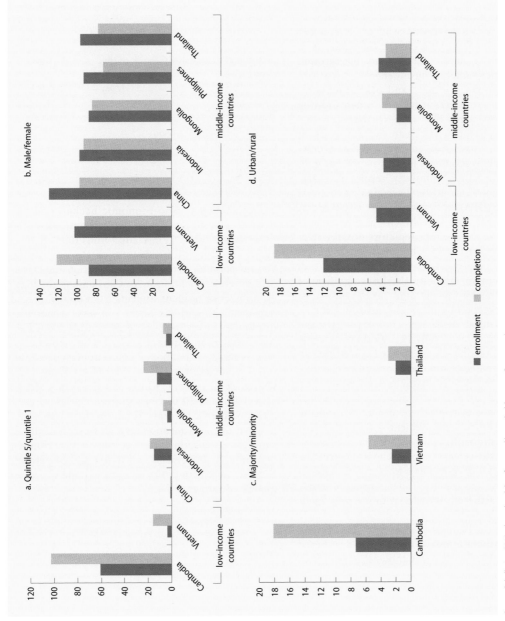

Source: Sakellariou 2010a, based on labor force and household surveys (latest year).

BOX 2.1   Preventing wasted talent in East Asia

Regression analyses provide a useful tool for understanding how different factors contribute to an outcome. In particular, they provide evidence that supporting disadvantaged groups can prevent wasted talent in East Asia. The following table of Programme for International Student Assessment (PISA) 2009 reading achievement for students in Shanghai, China, shows that students' background characteristics—including mother's education, number of books at home, and other measures of wealth—are important factors in determining reading achievement. This suggests that students' background characteristics can explain much of the variation in reading scores, whereas simply being in the poorest quintile is not a significant indicator of performance.[a] Similarly, results of regression analyses looking at the determinants of grade point average (GPA) for first-year university students in Vietnam indicate that ethnicity and household income are not significant predictors of GPA after controlling for parental background, geographical location, and other wealth-related measures.[b] And, always in Vietnam, ethnicity also loses significance after controlling for various family wealth measures, parental background, and quality of education in analyses looking at the determinants of primary and secondary test scores.[c] Similarly, a World Bank study of PISA 2006 reading scores for six Latin American countries and three high-income countries, including Korea, finds that school characteristics rather than wealth contribute to student achievement. Results show a small and generally insignificant relationship between wealth and achievement within schools—but a large and significant relationship between wealth and achievement among schools, suggesting that school quality contributes to cognitive achievement and that low-income students perform worse on cognitive achievement because of the poor quality of their schools.[d]

Results of the PISA 2009 also highlight the prevalence of resilient children among disadvantaged groups. "Resilient students are those who come from

TABLE B2.1   2009 PISA reading achievement for poorest quintile, Shanghai, China

Regression model	(1)	(2)
Poorest quintile	−30.52***	−5.60
	[5.31]	[3.46]
Controlling for student background characteristics	No	Yes
Constant	562.43***	504.69***
	[2.24]	[4.95]
Observations	5,115	5,094
R-squared	0.02	0.23
Reading achievement among poorest quintile	531.91	499.09

Source: World Bank 2010a.
Note: Standard errors are noted in brackets.
Significance level: *** = 1 percent.

a disadvantaged socio-economic background and perform much higher than would be predicted by their background."[e] PISA 2009 finds that on average, 31 percent of disadvantaged students in the Organisation for Economic Co-operation and Development are resilient. East Asia has among the highest number of resilient students from disadvantaged backgrounds, with six of the top seven economies in number of resilient students coming from East Asia. Shanghai, China, has the highest number of all economies, with about 75 percent of its disadvantaged students. It is followed by Hong Kong SAR, China, at 72 percent; Korea at 56 percent; Macao SAR, China, at 50 percent; Singapore at 48 percent; and Japan at 42 percent. Although these economies may have better education systems to support disadvantaged groups, the lower levels of resilient children in Thailand (26 percent) and Indonesia (24 percent) suggest these economies need to expand access to quality education systems.[f]

a. World Bank 2010a.
b. Linh, Thuy, and Long 2010.
c. World Bank 2010g.
d. OECD 2010a.
e. OECD 2010a.
f. OECD 2010a.

---

the lack of required core or technical skills as one of the three main causes of vacancies in Malaysia, Mongolia, and Thailand.

The coexistence of significant demand for professionals, relatively high tertiary unemployment rates, and fairly long times to fill professional positions suggests skill mismatches between the labor market and the tertiary education system in some countries (figure 2.12). These mismatches may show

FIGURE 2.12 **Tertiary unemployment rates and time to fill professional vacancies**

■ unemployment rate of tertiary graduates (percent)
■ weeks to fill professional vacancies

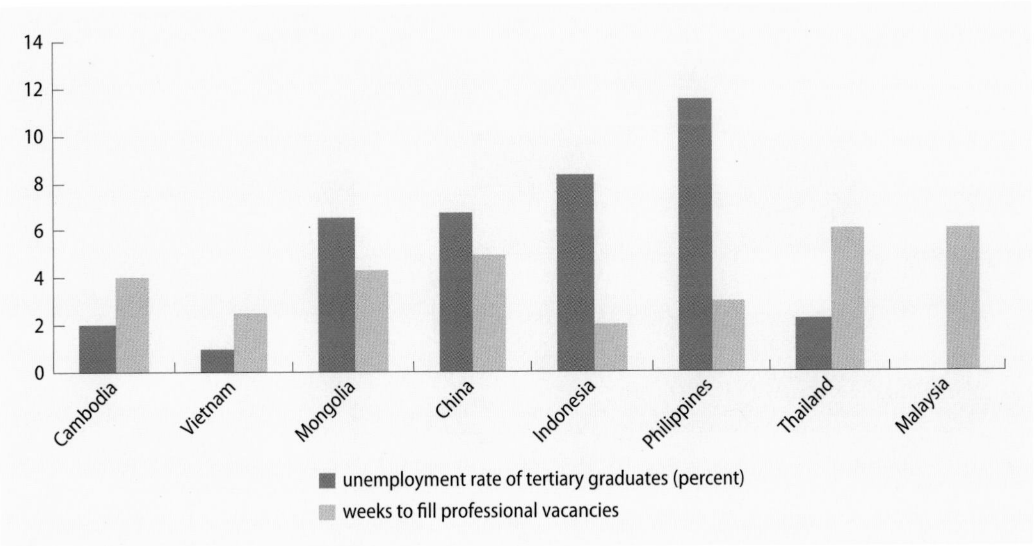

Sources: Sakellariou 2010b; World Bank ICSs (various years).

either that the matching process is not working properly or—what is of greater interest here—that higher education graduates simply do not have the right skills. This latter reason is likely the case in China, Mongolia, and the Philippines, for example.[20]

Gaps in thinking, technical, and behavioral skills

Gaps in generic and technical skills for newly hired professionals[21] (who to a large extent possess tertiary qualifications in East Asia) as reported by employers and employees themselves point to clear skill gaps among tertiary graduates. Such gaps are assessed simply in terms of lack of skills to perform the job. Because all skills are (or will be) relevant in the near future, given the comparison of skill importance across countries, both current and future needs are considered relevant. (Detailed results of skill gaps by country are shown in appendix J.) The main gaps by country, where the intensity of each gap is assessed relative to other gaps in the country, are shown in table 2.4.[22] There is no direct comparison across countries.

The most important and the weakest skills were also compared by country relative to current demand for that skill (see table 2.4). For instance, information technology (IT) gaps in the Philippines, while important in themselves, become less of an issue when compared with current demand for IT skills, but gaps in technical skills in the Philippines become more important.

One limitation is the absence of standardized comparable tertiary testing, which would have allowed objective skill comparisons to be made among countries.

Gaps in thinking skills are multiple. Most countries cite thinking skills as a gap. Looking at employers' and employees' opinions from ICS data and the skill surveys, there is particular emphasis on creative-thinking gaps in Malaysia and Thailand,[23] and on both creativity and problem-solving gaps in Indonesia and the Philippines.[24] Thailand has the largest deficiencies, with 20–30 percent of employers putting creative thinking and problem solving among the three most serious gaps. Basic analytical skills—which include academic and problem-solving skills—are the most important gap in Cambodia. All these skills, already in high demand, will become

TABLE 2.4   Comparative skill gaps among professionals

	Creativity	Information technology	English	Leadership	Communication	Problem solving	Work attitude	Technical skills	Numeracy/literacy
Cambodia	—			Decision making		Lack of analytical skills			
Vietnam	—	—		—		—			
Mongolia									
Philippines									
Indonesia									
Thailand									
Malaysia									

Source: Appendix J (employer and employee surveys).
Note: The darker the shade, the stronger the gap (within each country only). Dotted cells indicate gaps that became less serious, and hashed cells indicate gaps that became more serious, in relation to the current demand for that skill.
— = not available

more so as the push to innovation intensifies in the region.

Gaps in behavioral skills are also pervasive. Gaps in leadership, initiative, and decision-making skills are given particular emphasis in Indonesia, the Philippines, Thailand (where 30 percent of employers put leadership among the three weakest skills), and Cambodia. For Cambodia, Indonesia, and the Philippines this finding may point to a positive relation between countries that are generally considered "more open" politically and the importance of these skills (when one compares the evidence on the most important and weakest skills).[25]

Gaps in communication and negotiation skills are also relevant, particularly in Vietnam, in the employer and employee surveys. But some of the samples cover only manufacturing, where these skills are less important, and so may underestimate these skills' importance and gaps. Indeed, communication and negotiation are particularly important and also present a relatively important gap in Indonesia (all the more in relation to current needs) and the Philippines, which have the most sector-balanced surveys. In Malaysia and Mongolia employees have a worse perception of their professional communication skills than employers. Overall, gaps in behavioral skills are bound to be particularly problematic in services, where they are of importance and where most tertiary graduates work.

Gaps in IT and computer skills come out clearly in most countries.[26] These trends are in line with the finding that gaps are higher in the exporting and technologically intensive sector of the economy. While countries such as Cambodia and Mongolia do not consider IT skills among the most critical, these skills will likely become more important as international and technological integration continues. Employees' opinions on skill gaps are aligned with employers' opinions (except in Mongolia where employees view these gaps as less serious). Gaps in creativity and IT skills are clearer in middle-income and upper-middle-income countries than in low-income ones, reflecting in part their higher importance in this setting. This does not mean, however, that low-income countries should ignore these skills because sooner or later jobs will require them. Moreover, breaking into manufacturing is already requiring higher levels of creativity.

Gaps in technical skills are also evident, particularly in practical job knowledge. While gaps in generic skills are on the rise, gaps in job-specific technical skills (practical and theoretical knowledge of the job) remain pervasive, all the more in relation to current needs. This is particularly the case in Vietnam, where only a small share of college graduates are said to possess good technical knowledge of their job (figure 2.13), and Indonesia, where technical gaps are significant in relative terms (and more so for employers). But even in Malaysia, though it may not be the largest gap, a significant number of employees still feel that they do not have the needed technical or professional skills (figure 2.14), and the problem grows in relation to the importance given to these skills.

In the three countries for which the theory versus practice differentiation exists (Vietnam, Indonesia, and the Philippines, as illustrated in appendix J), practical knowledge is even more of a gap than theoretical knowledge of the job. This gap is stronger for college graduates than for secondary TVET graduates in Vietnam (figure 2.13). The employer skill surveys of Indonesia and the Philippines point to better specific skills (including practical knowledge) acquired in tertiary TVET than in tertiary academic education.

Some surveys focusing on China, such as one on foreign employers by McKinsey (China), find that poor technical skills are a critical issue for engineering graduates.[27] It concluded that only 10 percent of science and engineering graduates had acceptable technical skills. (The same report notes that the quality of university graduates is a serious issue in Vietnam, where firms report that only 10 percent of the graduating class of engineers had the potential to become "effective employees.")

A 2010 study by the American Chamber of Commerce in China found that 28 percent of U.S. companies based in China reported recruiting talented management-level individuals as a top-five business challenge, second only to regulatory problems, but harder than problems in transparency, bureaucracy,

FIGURE 2.13 **Key job-specific skill gaps in Vietnam**

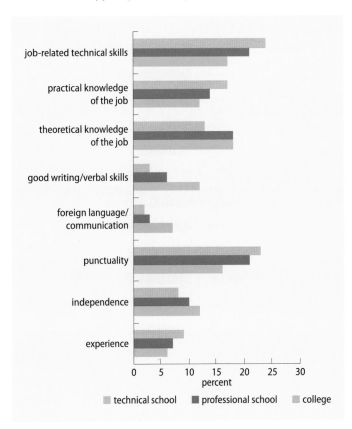

Source: World Bank 2008, based on 2003 MOLISA-ADB survey on labor market.
Note: Characteristics possessed by recruits of different education level (percentage).

and intellectual property.[28] Similarly, a 2008 McKinsey survey of Chinese firms found that 44 percent of executives cited insufficient talent as their main challenge for reaching global ambitions and that China has seen a widening gap in the skills mismatch between firms and employees at all employment levels.[29]

Academic skills

Academic skills appear to be an important constraint, according to employers, more so in low-income countries. Literacy is weak in Vietnam, and literacy and numeracy in Cambodia. But employers (and employees) in more advanced countries such as Malaysia and Thailand also complain about numerical skill gaps: about 20 percent of Thai employers, for example, rank numerical skills among

FIGURE 2.14   **Key job-specific skill gaps in Malaysia**

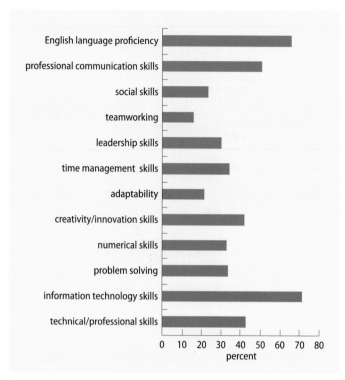

Source: World Bank Malaysia Investment Climate Survey 2007 (employee module).
Note: Skills most lacking among employees (proportion of respondents indicating particular skill "one of the three most lacked"), both professionals and skilled workers.

the three weakest skills—or worse than technical skills.

Malaysian and Thai employers are correct in highlighting these gaps, which are traditionally better measured through standardized international testing. While standardized data are available only up to the secondary level, the following chapters illustrate in detail that education levels are connected and that low preparation in earlier levels translates into deficiencies later on.

English is the weakest academic skill in most lower- and middle-income countries according to employers and employees. Of easier assessment by employers—with the expected exception of the Philippines and Malaysia, both of Anglo-Saxon tradition, and less expected of Cambodia—English appears to be the number one weakness in all countries. According to employees it is also still a critical skill gap in Malaysia. English is bound to continue to gain importance as

international integration continues, particularly in Vietnam because of its recent accession to the World Trade Organization or in Indonesia because of its planned increase in exports. Gaps in English skills are felt particularly strongly in Thailand.

Wage skill premiums

Results from employer and employee skill modules in Thailand (figure 2.15) and Malaysia (figure 2.16) further suggest that employers are willing to pay a premium for certain skills, thereby confirming scarcity. In Thailand skills such as English skills, numerical skills, leadership, and even creativity skills are indeed commanding higher wages. In Malaysia professionals with very good professional communication, technical skills, and IT skills command, as expected, the largest wage premiums in relation to professionals with very poor levels of these skills.[30]

Retraining

Critical skill gaps associated with preemployment education and practical knowledge are also confirmed by the need to retrain, especially younger workers. This need appears significant in the three countries for which this information was gathered in the employer surveys—Indonesia, the Philippines, and Vietnam.[31] In Indonesia, for instance, employers rate that 30 percent of their employees 30–45 years of age need retraining, and the share increases to almost 50 percent in the under-30 employees. (The situation is even worse in the Philippines.)

In Indonesia a significant proportion of professionals (about 20–25 percent), largely trained at the higher education level, need retraining. Most university graduates, regardless of position, need retraining in the Philippines (figure 2.17). Similarly, in Vietnam about 30 percent of those surveyed reported significant need for training college graduates (retraining, new training, or upgrading).

It is important to acknowledge, or remember here, that these skill gaps are not the sole responsibility of higher education. Indeed, skills such as creativity, problem solving, communication, and most academic skills typically start to be taught very early in the education cycle, and others such as practical knowledge are also taught on the job. It is thus a responsibility of the whole skill development system to support better skills. Higher education has, however, a critical responsibility in both the failure and the solution. Evidence from Indonesia and the Philippines, for instance, shows that gaps between employers' expectations and actual skills are stronger for professionals than for other worker categories in East Asia (as is the time to fill vacancies at that level). This is particularly the case for skills such as creativity, problem solving, leadership, negotiation, and English, which, though higher in professionals, are lower in relation to the expectations that employers and employees alike have for these workers.[32] In fairness, tertiary education also prepares workers for nonprofessional careers, and thus gaps may be somewhat overestimated. But skilled production and nonproduction workers need some of the same skills as professionals, making gaps nonetheless relevant. And the fact that secondary TVET may prepare these workers better than college is alarming. Finally, as chapter 1 showed, it is also clear that higher education can potentially greatly improve most of these skills through the right pedagogy[33] and play a critical complementary role to other skill providers. Unfortunately, this is not happening.

Research and innovation

Beyond providing high-level skills, tertiary institutions, particularly universities, can support technological capability and innovation through basic and applied research and technology transfer in all three technology clusters. To assess how well they are progressing, this chapter reviews indicators of patenting, licensing, and university quality as ranked by various criteria. (Universities are only part of the innovation system, so their role cannot be fully isolated from that of other actors. They can, however, potentially support many innovation outcomes.)

FIGURE 2.15 Average monthly salaries of Thai employees reporting a particular skill as a top-three deficiency compared with employees not reporting skills as a top-three deficiency

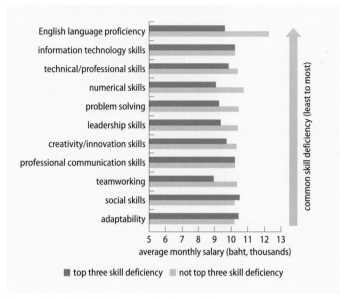

Source: World Bank Thailand IC Survey 2004 (employee module).

FIGURE 2.16 Average monthly salaries of Malaysian employees (in manufacturing) with very good versus very poor skills, according to employer

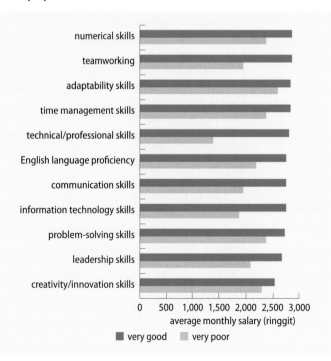

Source: World Bank Malaysia IC survey, 2007 (employee and employer modules).

FIGURE 2.17   Share of workers needing no training, by education level in the Philippines, 2008

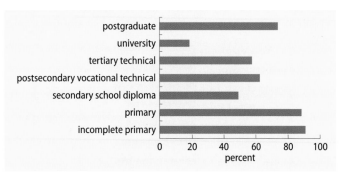

Source: di Gropello, Tan, and Tandon 2010.

TABLE 2.5   Number of patents granted by the USPTO, selected years

Economy	1992	2000	2008
Japan	23,151	32,922	36,679
Singapore	35	242	450
Taiwan, China	1,252	5,806	7,779
Korea, Rep.	586	3,472	8,731
Malaysia	11	47	168
Thailand	2	30	40
China	41	163	1,874
Indonesia	9	14	19
Philippines	7	12	22
Vietnam	0	0	0

Source: USPTO data.

Patenting

Patenting, while far from ideal as an indicator of the productivity of research and development (R&D), is generally the preferred metric,[34] and patents granted by the U.S. Patent and Trademark Office (USPTO) are preferred for several reasons.[35] First, because the criteria for submission, examination of patents, and decision to award patents differ across countries, the number of patents granted by any one country is not directly comparable with that of another, and the quality of the patents differs. Using data from a specific patent office eliminates this incompatibility. Because the United States has been the major market for East Asian economies, using data from the USPTO is appropriate. Second, applying to a foreign patenting office is more expensive. Therefore, only high-quality patents are submitted for approval by USPTO, reducing the noise in the data.

The number of patents granted to East Asian economies in 1992, 2000, and 2008 is shown in table 2.5. Japan led the field all three years by a wide margin, with more than 36,000 patents awarded in 2008.[36] In 2008 Korea was a distant second followed by Taiwan, China, though the number of patents accelerated after 1992.

China ranked fourth in 2008. As a mark of its acceleration, in 2008 it received four times as many as those granted to Singapore, from

roughly the same in 1992, moving ahead of the Southeast Asian countries. Vietnam—together with Mongolia, Cambodia, and Lao PDR, not listed in the table—did not receive any patents during this period.

A somewhat different impression is conveyed by table 2.6. As of 2007, Japan filed the largest number of patents with the World Intellectual Property Organization, followed by China, with Korea in third place. If measured by country of origin, Japan still leads, but Korea and China switch places.

Licensing

Royalty and license fee payments are taken as a proxy for technology absorption and technology production. China and Singapore stand out partly because of the presence of multinational corporations. Korea also purchases technologies from abroad, though the pace of increase has leveled off since 2005. Other economies in East Asia are not active in the market for technology because high-tech industries in these countries are dominated by multinational corporations that generally do not need to license technologies (figure 2.18).[37]

Japan is the major technology provider to East Asia in the sense that it maintains a surplus in this area, though it became a net provider of technology only in the past few years.[38] Korea and Singapore are emerging technology providers. Other countries' receipts are insignificant (figure 2.19).

In sum, Korea could emerge as a net provider of technology in the near future. Singapore is actively engaged in the trade of technologies in both directions through foreign affiliates. China is currently the leading importer. Other East Asian economies are not importing technologies from abroad or generating much by themselves.

Quality of universities

The quality and research capacity of universities play a key role in determining technological capability and innovation, though many other factors are at work. The top technology cluster and major innovator in East Asia has the higher-quality universities. China has been making positive progress in both broader and more closely university-related innovation and technology indicators, while all other low- and middle-income countries are making much slower progress in all indicators.

One measure of whether a university is "world class" is how it ranks on international indexes. Currently, two of the most respected are the Shanghai Jiao Tong University (SJTU) rankings and the Times Higher Education (THE) (formerly the *Times Higher Education Supplement*) rankings.[39] The SJTU ranking methodology focuses almost exclusively on research-related dimensions of university performance. Its criteria include the numbers of Nobel laureates among a university's faculty and alumni, the number of articles published in the journals *Nature* and *Science*, performance on the academic citation index, and university size. Because it contains broader elements in its ranking criteria, the THE ranking includes measures of the quality of teaching and skill provision in universities, such as surveys of employers to determine their perception of the quality of universities' graduates and graduate employment rates and salaries. The criteria also include an indicator on the number of international faculty on a university's payroll, which can be interpreted

TABLE 2.6 **World Intellectual Property Organization patent filings by origin and office, 2007**

Economy	Patent filings by office			Patent filings by origin
	Total	Resident	Nonresident	Total
Japan	396,291	333,498	62,793	501,270
Singapore	9,951	696	9,255	3,538
Korea, Rep.	172,469	128,701	43,768	174,896
Malaysia	2,372	670	1,702	1,144
Thailand	1,388	877	511	1,049
China	245,161	153,060	92,101	160,523
Indonesia	4,606	282	4,324	308
Philippines	3,265	231	3,034	310
Vietnam	0	0	0	13

Source: WIPO 2009.
Note: Data for Indonesia and the Philippines are for 2006.

FIGURE 2.18 **Royalty and license fee payments, 1995–2009**

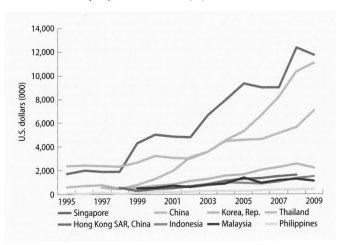

Source: World Development Indicators (WDI) database.

as a measure of the attractiveness of that university as a home to world-class instructors and researchers.

The relatively low quality of universities in East Asia is reflected in the 2009 THE ranking, which lists just nine East Asian universities in the top 50 (table 2.7). The nine are in Japan; Singapore; Hong Kong SAR, China; Korea; and China, which is the only middle-income economy among them. Thailand's leading university is ranked 138, Malaysia's 180, the Philippines' 262, and Indonesia's 351.

FIGURE 2.19 Royalty and license fee receipts, 1995–2009

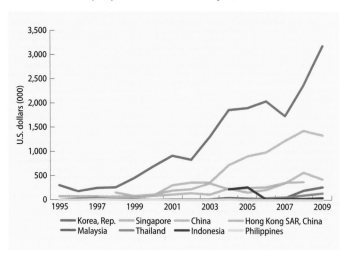

Source: WDI database.

SJTU ranking changes in the top 500 institutions and THE ranking changes in the top 2100 in the 2004–09 period confirm steep improvements for Chinese universities (table 2.8). The data show that China has been improving systematically since 2004, the year of the first SJTU ranking, doubling its top 500 institutions from 16 to 30 in a five-year period.

Published scientific output provides additional evidence that most East Asian economies lag behind OECD countries. Unsurprisingly, members of the leading technology cluster score the highest in terms of articles. They benefit from a solid base of primary and secondary education and have high-quality tertiary education. They invest heavily in R&D (and,

TABLE 2.7 Ranking of universities, East Asia, 2007, 2008, and 2009

School	Economy	Regional rank 2009	International rank		
			2007	2008	2009
University of Tokyo	Japan	1	17	19	22
University of Hong Kong	Hong Kong SAR, China	2	18	26	24
Kyoto University	Japan	3	25	25	25
National University of Singapore	Singapore	4	33	30	30
Hong Kong University of Science and Technology	Hong Kong SAR, China	5	53	39	35
Osaka University	Japan	6	46	44	43
Chinese University of Hong Kong	Hong Kong SAR, China	7	38	42	46
Seoul National University	Korea, Rep.	8	51	50	47
Tsinghua University	China	9	40	56	49
Peking University	China	10	36	50	52
Chulalongkorn University	Thailand	19	223	166	138
Universiti Malaya	Malaysia	29	246	230	180
University of Indonesia	Indonesia	31	395	287	201
Mahidol University	Thailand	34	284	251	220
Universitas Gadjah Mada	Indonesia	37	360	316	250
University of the Philippines	Philippines	39	398	276	262
Universiti Kebangsaan Malaysia	Malaysia	40	309	250	291
Universiti Sains Malaysia	Malaysia	43	307	313	314
Universiti Teknologi Malaysia	Malaysia	44	401–500	356	320
Universiti Putra Malaysia	Malaysia	46	364	320	345
Bandung Institute of Technology	Indonesia	47	369	315	351

Source: THE World University Rankings.

TABLE 2.8   Rankings of universities over time, 2004–09

Ranking	2004	2005	2006	2007	2008	2009
SJTU top 500						
Japan	36	34	32	33	31	31
Singapore	2	2	2	2	2	2
China	16	18	19	25	30	30
THE top 200						
Japan	5	10	11	11	10	11
Singapore	2	2	2	2	2	2
China	9	10	10	10	10	11

Source: SJTU Academic Ranking of World Universities.

as noted, receive more patents than other regional economies). Each is a source of a respectable number of scientific and technical papers when data are scaled to the total populations. With the notable exception of Singapore, even the region's leaders, such as Japan and Korea, produced fewer articles per million inhabitants than the world's top performers—Finland, the United Kingdom, and the United States (figure 2.20).

China is trying hard to move up to the top cluster by giving the highest priority to technology development through investment in tertiary education and R&D, and over these past 15 years it is closing the gap, as measured by the sharp increase in patents granted and the number of papers published in international science and engineering journals. These rose from 9,000 in 1995 to 41,000 in 2004.[40] Or, over a longer time frame, from 2,694 in 1980–84 to 48,552 in 2000–05 (table 2.9). But there is still a way to go to catch up with upper-income economies when these figures are compared with population.

The other East Asian economies also assign priority to innovation in their policy statements but are struggling to demonstrate results. They are, in fact, much further behind, trailing also several other middle-income countries outside the region. From 2000 to 2005, Korea produced an annual average of more than 20,000 scholarly publications, over 10 times more than the number of publications produced in Thailand and Malaysia.

FIGURE 2.20   Scientific and technical articles per million inhabitants, East Asia and the rest of the world, 2007

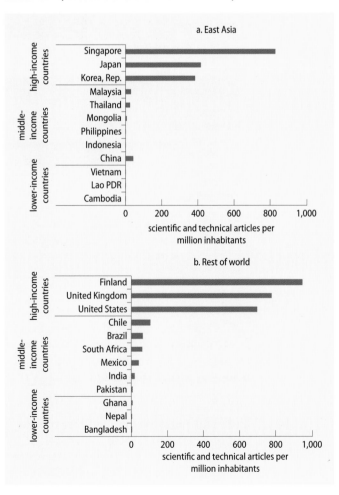

Source: WDI database.

TABLE 2.9   Yearly average number of publications, 1980–2005

Economy	1980–84	1985–89	1990–94	1995–99	2000–05
Singapore	253	597	1,142	2,501	5,177
Taiwan, China	642	1,644	4,326	8,608	13,307
Korea, Rep.	341	1,043	2,756	9,813	21,471
Malaysia	259	298	421	745	1,221
Thailand	394	446	557	926	2,059
China[a]	2,694	6,244	10,365	21,205	48,552
Indonesia	104	141	198	366	524
Philippines	237	207	246	329	474

Source: Yusuf and Nabeshima 2010.
a. Includes Hong Kong SAR, China.

FIGURE 2.21   Leading ways of acquiring technological innovation in firms, Malaysia, Mongolia, and Thailand

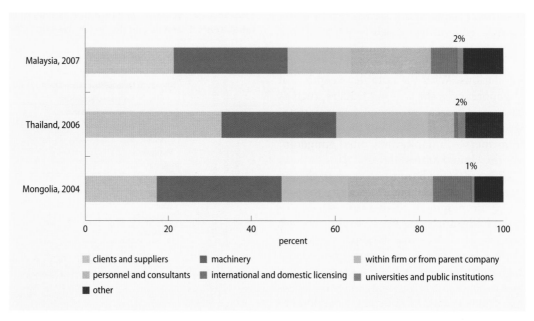

Source: World Bank ICSs (various years).

Most important, universities and other tertiary entities are not supporting technology assimilation and upgrading as they should. In the top technology cluster, only a few research universities are sources of ideas and engage in applied research with commercial applications. In all other countries, with the possible exception of China,[41] there is very limited engagement of universities in applied research and technology development, or even only

technology upgrading,[42] indicative of a disconnect between firms and universities, which is further explored in the next chapter.

In Malaysia, Mongolia, and Thailand, universities (and other public research institutions) are mentioned as a leading way of acquiring technological innovation (defined in a broad sense) by only 1 or 2 percent of firms (figure 2.21). In Vietnam only a marginal percentage of firms declared using research centers or universities as sources of product innovation (figure 2.22). A related firm survey in the Philippines also noted that innovations in new product lines for almost all the companies surveyed were based on their own R&D staff work, not university research. Strong engagement of universities in technology upgrading remains a challenge also in upper-income economies in East Asia and elsewhere, and it is evident that firms remain the main actors in R&D, but university contribution is higher. As an example, universities are cited as the source of technological innovation in the United Kingdom by about 27 percent of firms (with 11 percent mentioning universities as a high and medium source)[43] and in Singapore by more than 10 percent.[44] This suggests that universities in lower- and middle-income East Asia could do more to support technological capability (compatibly with the broader constraints of their technology cluster).

Conclusion

Looking ahead, it is clear that lower- and middle-income East Asian countries will need to do a much better job at providing the skills required by the labor market and to support innovation, while also starting to build higher research potential of their universities. The precise challenges and priorities vary by income group and country. Challenges are deeper and more widespread in lower-income countries and decrease at higher income levels. China's better performance from the perspective of R&D for innovation is aligned with its leadership position in the middle technology cluster, but skill-related gaps are persistent. Gaps relative to upper-income groups are evident in all dimensions. The immediate urgency for lower- and middle-income East Asia is to better understand why its higher education is not performing as it should, which is discussed in chapter 3 through the perspective of disconnects.

FIGURE 2.22   **Sources of product innovation at firm level in Vietnam**

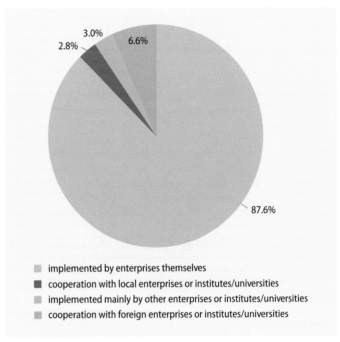

- ▨ implemented by enterprises themselves
- ■ cooperation with local enterprises or institutes/universities
- ▨ implemented mainly by other enterprises or institutes/universities
- ▨ cooperation with foreign enterprises or institutes/universities

Source: Vietnam Chamber of Commerce and Industry 2009.

Notes

1. These findings are somewhat conditioned by the ICS samples, which mainly cover manufacturing firms and a generally significant proportion of large and foreign-owned firms. The bias, however, can cut both ways. For instance, when including services in the Philippine firm sample—as done in the Employer Skill Survey (di Gropello, Tan, and Tandon 2010)—skills become much more of an obstacle, revealing possibly higher skill gaps in this sector. In the Indonesia Skill Survey (di Gropello, Kruse, and Tandon 2011), however, which incorporates a greater number of small and domestic firms, skills become less of an obstacle.

2. See Almeida (2009a) for details on the data sample and methodology. The surveys were conducted in 2002–05, and the samples were designed to be representative of the population of firms according to their industry and location within each country. The final sample consists of 10,215 firms in a wide range of sectors (manufacturing 78 percent,

services 20 percent, construction 1.3 percent, agro-industry 0.85 percent, and other 0.11 percent). Manufacturing covers several industries—auto and auto components, beverages, chemicals, electronics, food, garments, leather, metals and machinery, nonmetallic and plastic materials, paper, textiles, and wood and furniture.

3. Interestingly, while technological innovation or adoption loses significance after research and development is included (likely because of the high correlation between these two variables), technological innovation and Internet and computer use reinforce themselves in the explanation of skill gaps, indicating a cumulative effect on skill gaps of indicators of technological innovation, adoption, and application.

4. This relation is on the increase in Lao PDR and Cambodia, according to the last ICS.

5. A positive relation between time to fill skilled vacancies and openness in China and Indonesia, which does not translate into a positive relation with skills as an obstacle, initially looks like a puzzle. But, at least for China, where the export-oriented sector remains quite low skilled, it may simply suggest the presence of some other not strictly skill-related labor market–related factor, which has an impact on time to fill vacancies but is less likely to be picked up in the skill as an obstacle variable.

6. Although having many possible causes, some sectoral trends are troubling. In Indonesia metals and metal products, chemicals and chemical products, textiles, garments, and electrical machinery and equipment have all lost significant export shares since 2006 (International Monetary Fund 2010 Article IV Consultation: Indonesia). In the Philippines the heavy metals industry (including chemicals and machinery) has lost ground, as measured by share of manufacturing value added, falling from 44 percent in 2003 to 36 percent in 2007 (Tan 2010). In Thailand the electronic and electrical subsector's share of exports fell from 30.5 percent in 2000 to just more than 25 percent in 2007 (Doner, Intarakumnerd, and Ritchie 2010).

7. Judging from the continuous, steeply decreasing ratio of tertiary-educated workers in that sector (appendix C of this book).

8. di Gropello, Kruse, and Tandon 2011.

9. di Gropello and Sakellariou 2009.

10. OECD 2007a.

11. In Latin America, rates of return for tertiary education fluctuate at 14–28 percent (di Gropello 2006).

12. One cannot rule out that relatively lower returns in relation to the stock of tertiary graduates also indicate lower graduate quality.

13. UNESCO's ISCED 5A refers to the first stage of tertiary education not leading directly to an advanced research qualification (equivalent to a bachelor's degree). ISCED 6 programs are designed to prepare graduates for faculty and research posts and are the second stage of tertiary education (equivalent to a doctoral degree).

14. These findings hold when comparing tertiary-educated workers with journal articles.

15. The situation is much worse in the Philippines according to the number of students receiving advanced degrees in STEM fields. In 2004 only 315 received a master's degree in engineering, 203 in math and computer science, and 153 in natural sciences. Extremely few received doctoral degrees: 13 in natural sciences, 6 in engineering, and 6 in math and computer science (Tan 2010).

16. UNESCO Institute for Statistics Data Centre, 2009 data.

17. Sakellariou 2010a on the basis of labor force and household surveys.

18. All results are predicted results from a regression analysis with controls to isolate the effects of each single variable.

19. The response varies, according to how the surveys pose the question.

20. This conclusion does not rule out quality issues also in other countries, where the presence of quantity gaps may simply decrease the incidence of unemployment even if quality is low (likely to be the case in Cambodia and Vietnam), or limited potential for domestic absorption may explain while unemployment is more of an issue than vacancies (Indonesia) without discarding quality issues.

21. In Malaysia, Mongolia, and Thailand, gaps relate to both professionals and skilled production and nonproduction workers.

22. For Vietnam, results are directly comparing skills possessed by graduates with different education levels.

23. See also Abelmann, Chang, and Ayudhaya 2000.

24. This is also shown for Indonesia in di Gropello, Kruse, and Tandon (2011).

25. For Indonesia this is confirmed by the disaggregation of the most important behavioral skills included in di Gropello, Kruse, and Tandon (2011).
26. Cambodia is an exception for IT; such skills may still not fully be on the radar screen.
27. Farrell and Grant 2005.
28. AmCham-China 2010.
29. Lane and Pollner 2008.
30. Beyond the gaps underlined by employers, as visible in figure 2.16, technical and professional skills are among the largest skill gaps reported by employees in Malaysia.
31. See di Gropello, Kruse, and Tandon 2011; di Gropello, Tan, and Tandon 2010; and World Bank 2008 for further information.
32. This is visible from comparing appendix F of this book and appendix K of this book.
33. A study of higher education and information and communication technology skills, for instance, found that employers in the United Kingdom have increasing confidence in the information and communication technology skills that workers have developed through higher education: employers are pursuing the greater use of nontechnical graduates in roles such as technical support through the "substitution" of university-educated employees into roles that would previously have been filled by workplace trainees (Round 2003).
34. Scotchmer 2004.
35. Other indicators include enrollment in postgraduate programs, number of PhDs awarded, number of graduate schools and research institutes, number of scientific publications, and number of multinational corporation R&D centers.
36. In fact, among foreign countries, Japan receives the most patents (60 percent), followed by Germany. In any year, about half the USPTO-granted patents are to foreigners.
37. Even though multinational corporations have tended to locate their labor-intensive downstream operations in Southeast Asia, they generally hire more educated and skilled workers because, on average, the skill coefficients of their activities are higher than those of domestic industries.
38. Mok 2010.
39. Salmi and Saroyan (2007) discuss these rankings' limitations.
40. Chapman 2010.
41. In China university engagement in technology upgrading has been growing (Mok 2010), but specific data on sources of technological innovation at firm level are not available.
42. Mok 2010.
43. Laursen and Salter 2004.
44. Mok 2010.

Disconnects in Higher Education | 3

The analysis of skill demand and skill gaps in earlier chapters indicated clear shortcomings in the quality and relevance of higher education in low- and middle-income East Asia. Although higher education has the potential to be a leading contributor to regional competitiveness, it is not realizing its potential. It suffers from significant weaknesses in delivering relevant skills and contributing to technological capability and innovation—and ultimately growth—through higher productivity. As analyzed in this chapter, this failure reflects five main disconnects among skill and research providers and users (see figure 3.1): between higher education institutions (HEIs) and skill users; between universities and firms (now seen as research users) in the technology arena; between teaching and research (or HEIs and research providers); among HEIs themselves and HEIs and tertiary-level nonformal or enterprise-based skill provision; and between higher education and prior education levels. These two last categories represent disconnects between skill providers.

At the core of the higher education system are the HEIs and other critical institutional actors that supply and use skills and research, and the interrelation among all these actors. Higher education is not delivering as it

should because these different actors are not adequately connected. In other words, higher education in lower- and middle-income East Asia is not being managed as a system but instead as individual disconnected institutions. And because many education policy makers regard these disconnects as outside the immediate purview of the tertiary education system, they have not used them in formulating policies to improve higher education, thus keeping reforms inconsistent, piecemeal, and incomplete—in a word, ineffective.

The first disconnect: Between higher education and employers (skill users)

This first section reviews disconnects between HEIs and their main characteristics in terms of pedagogy, curriculum, and degrees—and employers, who constitute the skill users.

Curricula and pedagogy

Many low- and middle-income East Asian countries' curricular and pedagogical approaches do not meet the needs of services and manufacturing, nor do they allow students to acquire the needed generic skills,

FIGURE 3.1   Five disconnects in higher education

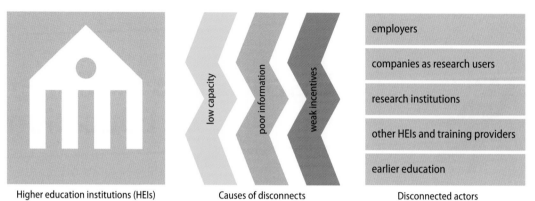

Higher education institutions (HEIs)   Causes of disconnects   Disconnected actors

---

BOX 3.1   Poor diversification in Cambodian higher education

Nearly 60 percent of all tertiary students study business, social sciences, or law, but fewer than 25 percent are in agriculture, education, engineering, health, or the hard sciences, even though many of these latter sectors provide—and will continue to provide—the most jobs. For example, fewer than 4 percent of students enroll in agriculture, even though the sector accounts for 29 percent of the country's gross domestic product (GDP) and supports the livelihood of 59 percent of the population. What accounts for this extreme polarization?

Recent evidence suggests that most students select their subject based on the advice and wishes—and, to a lesser extent, interests—of their family rather than on their own future labor market prospects, opportunities, and outcomes. A 2008 survey on youth employment reported that only one in five graduating secondary students based their decision on what to study on the job market; 7 of 10 followed their parents' advice. In the same survey, only one of three university and vocational training students chose their field of study because of market need. (Among university and vocational student respondents, 59 percent chose their field because of an interest in the subject.[a])

Lack of information seems to be one reason for these decisions, and students know little about demand for higher-level skills. No labor market information systems survey labor market demand, and

estimates of current or future demand for university graduates are lacking. In addition, there is no reliable tracking of the employment outcomes of recent university graduates.

The mismatch between graduate supply and demand has serious economic and social implications for Cambodia, such as high structural unemployment, with a pool of university graduates seeking jobs but without the skills demanded by employers. The mismatch can also constrain productivity and economic growth because employers fill positions with poorly qualified (and less productive) workers or scale back their growth ambitions. It can also stifle a country's attempts to diversify its sources of growth.

Cambodia can take some immediate steps in filling the information gaps. The government and universities could undertake tracer studies of university graduates and follow their employment experience. The results would provide information on the demand for skills for all jobs and those requiring higher skills and then signal overall graduate unemployment levels and supply-demand mismatches in particular fields. Additionally, universities could review their course curricula and teaching practices to better equip students with the types of skills employers demand.

Source: HRINC 2010.
a. BDLINK Cambodia Co. 2008.

---

often because teaching methods and practices are outdated. In Cambodia one survey found that teachers usually adopt a "teacher-centered" approach to instruction. Teachers

speak for the majority of classroom sessions, with little student interaction, teamwork, or time for problem solving.[1] Similar frontal, discipline-based practices also abound in China, Indonesia, Japan, Malaysia, and Vietnam.[2] This approach is usually ineffective in higher education, especially compared with a "student-centered" approach that encourages student interaction.

Data on fields of study indicate that most tertiary systems in the region's low- and middle-income countries have an uneven distribution of students across disciplines. Cambodia (box 3.1), the Lao People's Democratic Republic, and Indonesia notably have an extremely large share of tertiary students pursuing degrees in (a) social sciences, business, and law or (b) humanities, in general— at around 70 percent, 60 percent, and 50 percent, respectively (figure 3.2). Far fewer students are in other fields.

High-income economies such as Japan, the Republic of Korea, and Singapore

appear to have a much more even distribution of students across disciplines. Engineering and manufacturing, on the one hand, and social sciences, business, and law, on the other, are the two most popular groups of disciplines in these economies, but neither accounts for more than 40 percent of tertiary students. Moreover, the difference in shares of students enrolled in these fields and other disciplines is not nearly as large as in the low- and middle-income countries (figure 3.2).

This lack of diversification has implications for the responsiveness of their education system to new labor market demands. Low enrollment in science, technology, engineering, and math (STEM) fields is already a serious constraint for manufacturing in Cambodia and Mongolia, as illustrated by

FIGURE 3.2   Proportion of tertiary student enrollments by field of study, 2008

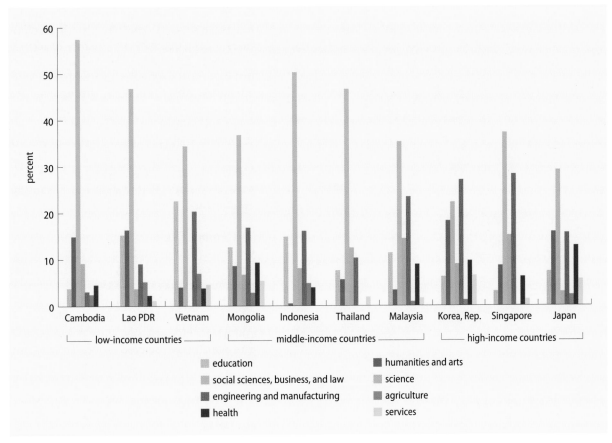

Source: UIS (UNESCO Institute for Statistics) Data Centre.

the current quantity gaps. While wage skill premiums continue to rise in these countries in manufacturing, no apparent increase in STEM fields is visible (figure 3.3), illustrating systemic rigidities. And in these and other countries this disconnect underestimates the true needs for STEM skills in the economy for innovation purposes.

In a country with limited course offerings, such as Cambodia, many students cannot obtain jobs because of a lack of opportunity to study certain fields and thus gain

FIGURE 3.3   Science and engineering enrollment shares and wage education premiums in manufacturing, Cambodia and Mongolia

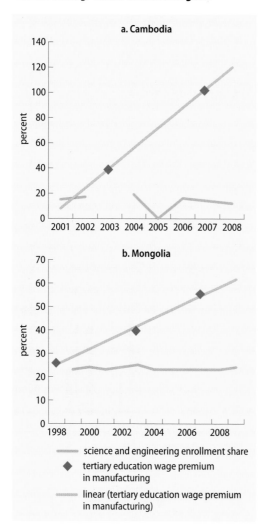

Sources: di Gropello and Sakellariou 2010; UIS Data Centre.

sufficient skills. Even countries with an economic structure more focused on services show gaps between education supply and labor market demand. Policy makers in the Philippines, for example, know that the courses of its higher education system have not kept track with changes in the financial services industry.[3]

Misalignment of institutional mix

Higher education systems are fairly varied in East Asia, with a mix of colleges, universities, and technical and vocational education and training (TVET) institutions providing professional certificates and diplomas through to bachelor's and postgraduate degrees. All countries have public and private institutions, and several have nontraditional delivery, such as distance higher education. (Appendix A illustrates the mix in each country.)

Evidence suggests that the institution-degree mix is misaligned with labor market needs in several countries, with implications for the quantity and quality of tertiary education graduates. TVET delivery is, for instance, still suboptimal or subpar in some countries. And Cambodia,[4] Mongolia,[5] and Vietnam,[6] for instance, have put very limited focus on college (as opposed to university) degrees (though college degrees may provide valuable intermediate skills relevant to manufacturing and services).[7] Most countries also have still relatively low shares of postgraduate students.

TVET/non-TVET

Often difficult employment prospects for graduates and relatively low tertiary completion rates have made the TVET subsector an attractive alternative to university education in many low- and middle-income countries. Historically, East Asian parents and youth have tended to prefer academic training, leading to unemployed university graduates alongside unfilled positions in basic trades.

Governments are shifting a greater proportion of those seeking tertiary education into

TVET, notably in middle-income countries. In China 40 percent of upper-secondary students and nearly 50 percent of tertiary students are enrolled in TVET (figure 3.4). In Malaysia nearly 60 percent of tertiary students are in TVET institutions. Nearly a third of Thailand's upper-secondary students pursue TVET qualifications, and almost 20 percent of tertiary students do. Indonesia has recently considered having 70 percent of its upper-secondary students in TVET programs.

Tertiary TVET has several advantages. It shapes the skill set of the next generation of workers, provides students with readily employable skills, and can help make up student undersupply in some fields. A recent World Bank study on the Philippines, for example, found that postsecondary TVET institutions have higher labor market relevance and adaptability (flexibility and responsiveness to changes) than universities. Similar results hold in Indonesia (figure 3.5).

It is thus unclear why countries such as Cambodia and Mongolia, which need more practical skills, have such low shares of TVET tertiary enrollment, especially because Mongolia, at least, is happy to accept TVET workers (as seen in the employment and remuneration analysis shown in chapter 1).

Still, skill-delivery gaps remain in TVET. Postsecondary TVET graduates in the Philippines, for example, lack relevant certifications in some technologically advanced fields, are of varying quality, and often need retraining.[8] Employers there, while acknowledging higher overall relevance to labor market needs, highlighted the limitations of postsecondary TVET education in several fields of study and the quality of teaching (see figure 3.5). In Indonesia employers felt the variety of fields of study to be less strong than in universities (see figure 3.5). Also in Indonesia those possessing a technical diploma lacked some generic skills.[9]

In Mongolia, as may be the case elsewhere, ineffective use of resources and outdated equipment undermine the quality of TVET. Public spending on TVET was roughly 6 percent of total public spending on education. Moreover, nearly half of that was

FIGURE 3.4   Share of upper-secondary and tertiary students enrolled in TVET

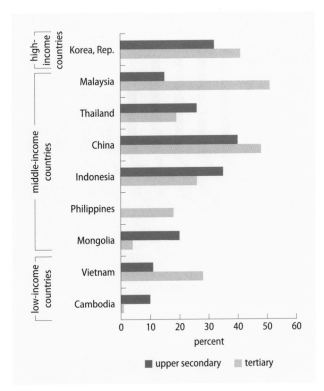

Source: Yilmaz 2009.
Note: The Philippines includes postsecondary students.

used for students' stipends, and less than 1 percent of that TVET budget was used for developing infrastructure and acquiring training equipment, both of which are severely inadequate.[10] These findings suggest an urgent need to improve the quality and relevance of current TVET education.

Given the strong social demand for higher education, coupled with skill shortages across a spectrum of sectors, countries could also do better at realigning their higher education institutions in relation to their core mission and the length of degrees provided with the needs of the skill users.

Colleges/universities

Second-tier universities or community colleges have different but equally important functions, which are to serve community and local development and develop a

FIGURE 3.5   **Employers' perceptions on general and TVET tertiary education, Indonesia and the Philippines, 2008**

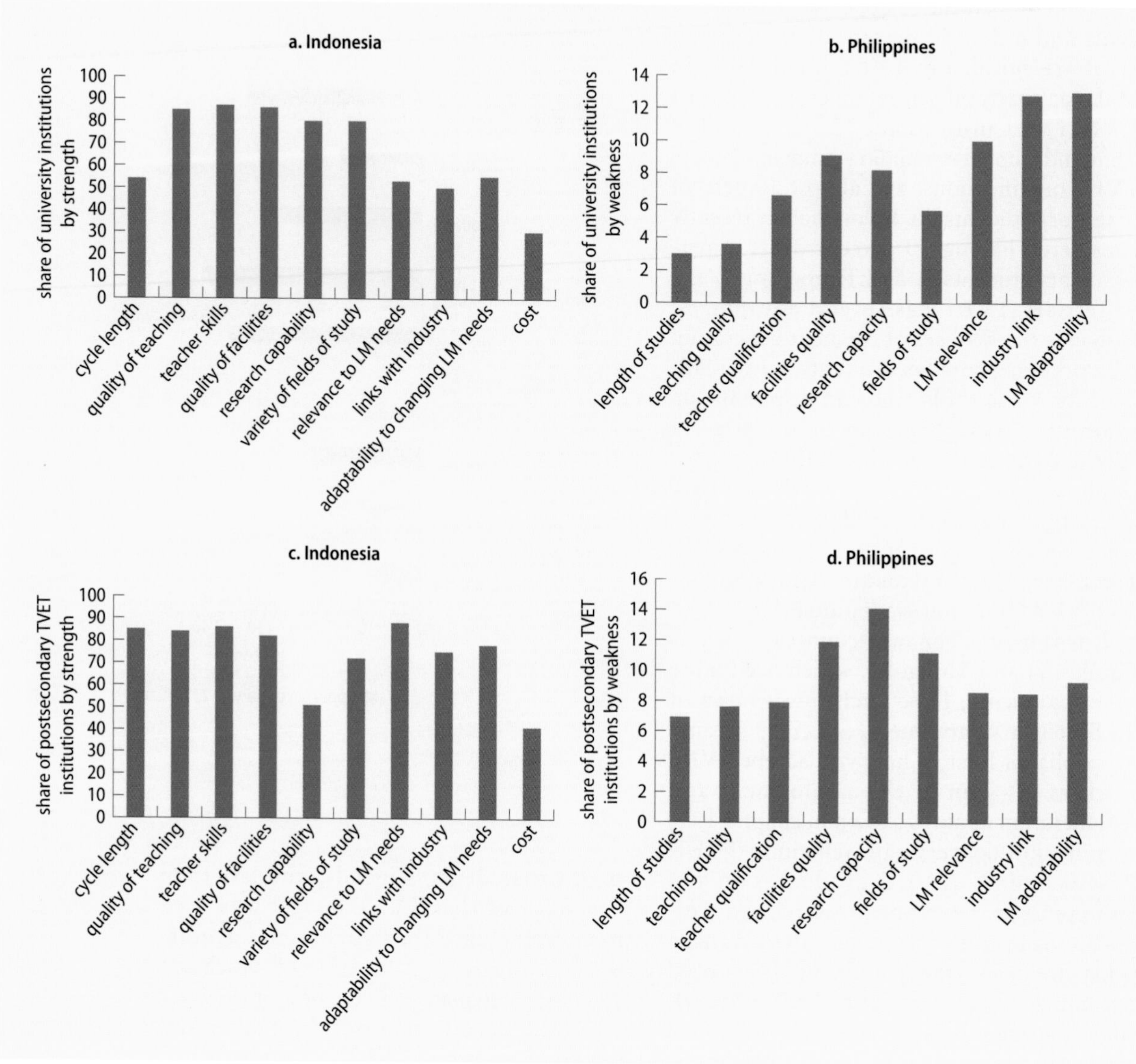

Sources: (a), (c) di Gropello, Kruse, and Tandon 2011; (b), (d) di Gropello, Tan, and Tandon 2010.

solid basis of some core generic skills and technical skills in some subjects. Mongolia, however, has only 11 schools offering preliminary and intermediate training for technical skills.[11] This number is probably insufficient to fulfill the needs of its labor market, given current gaps in English and even information technology that could be well provided in the context of shorter generic degrees.[12]

Postgraduate degrees

At the other end of the educational spectrum, the share of students enrolled in postgraduate studies may also not yet be sufficient in some East Asian countries. In 2000 Asia—principally East Asia—already had a large lead over other developing regions in the number of doctoral degrees awarded overall and probably in science and engineering disciplines (see appendix L).

TABLE 3.1 Earned science and engineering doctoral degrees, selected region or economy and selected field, 2006 or most recent year

Region or country	All fields	All science and engineering	Share of science and engineering (%)		
			Physical and biological sciences	Mathematics and computer sciences	Engineering
Asia	85,441	44,552	35	1	46
China	36,247	22,953	32	—	53
India (2005)	17,898	7,537	74	—	13
Japan	17,396	8,122	20	—	52
Philippines (2004)	1,748	56	0	23	13
Korea, Rep.	8,657	3,779	22	5	60
Taiwan, China	2,614	1,643	19	11	57
Middle East	5,759	2,902	45	8	20
Sub-Saharan Africa	2,064	679	37	0	21
Europe	97,840	53,119	44	8	26
United States	50,544	31,198	39	7	22

Source: National Science Board 2008.
— = not available.

Since 2000 the margin has widened considerably in East Asia's favor mainly because of a surge of degrees in China. The number of doctorates remains small, however, in relation to the stock in Europe (table 3.1 and appendix L), and almost all countries in the region have fewer than 2 percent of their tertiary students studying at the International Standard Classification of Education (ISCED) 6 level[13] (figure 3.6), in contrast to about 5 percent in western Europe and North America.[14]

Indeed, some countries' higher education systems may not be producing sufficient postgraduate students. There is no ideal ratio of postgraduate students: Korea, for example, has a fairly low ratio of students enrolled in advanced degrees and still manages to achieve enviable innovation outcomes. Many firms may not be interested in hiring workers with the profile of researchers, in particular in middle- and lower-income countries. Still, trends in education premiums suggest higher education systems may not be producing enough postgraduate students to meet the growing demand in some countries (figure 3.7). Beyond firms' needs, this growing demand is seen in the low share of highly qualified faculty in many countries (discussed further below).

FIGURE 3.6 Proportion of tertiary students enrolled in ISCED 6 programs

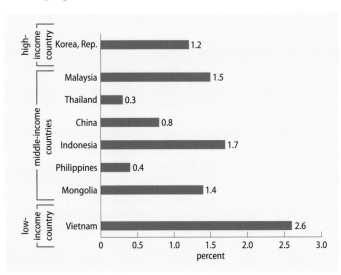

Source: Yilmaz 2009.

Reasons for the disconnect

A fairly widespread regional skill disconnect is apparent between what the current institutions deliver and what skill users need. Why? There seem to be three main groups of reasons, related to information, capacity, and incentives.

FIGURE 3.7   Wage education premiums, Indonesia, the Philippines, and Thailand

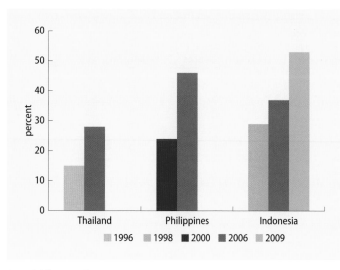

Source: Sakellariou 2010b.
Note: Postgraduate in relation to undergraduate; all results significant at 5 percent or 1 percent.

Poor information

HEIs may be unable to provide the skills that respond better to labor markets' needs because they lack information on demand. Instruments to provide institutions (and students) with labor market information are virtually absent, and mechanisms to channel inputs of firms in curriculum design and implementation are limited.

Low- and middle-income East Asian countries have weak links between industry and higher education in curriculum design. Many countries recognize the importance of strong links, but few have set up the necessary mechanisms. High-income economies in East Asia and elsewhere tend to have stronger university-industry links. (This is also visible from figure 3.10, which captures university-industry links in research and technology.)

These links are often the fruits of collaboration to ensure that pedagogy and curricula are aligned with what firms need. In New Zealand, for example, the Tertiary Education Commission requires HEIs to work closely with local businesses and industry training organizations to identify current and future skill needs. In Korea all polytechnics have to undertake regular visits to companies to keep their curricula updated, and companies

themselves are regularly invited to visit campus, to provide input.[15] Still, despite a greater emphasis on formalizing such links in recent years—not just for research but also for skill development and training as in the Philippines and Vietnam—they have remained mostly informal and piecemeal.

Overall, information on graduate employment, labor markets, and skills is still weak in the region (as seen for Cambodia earlier), contributing to lack of relevance of curricula and pedagogies. Institutions do not systematically attempt to gather recent graduates' feedback about the workplace relevance of their courses and training programs, which would allow those institutions to make changes in curricula and programs. In particular, only a few countries have effectively carried out and used graduate tracer studies.[16]

Nor do labor force and enterprise surveys fulfill their potential. While labor force surveys are conducted periodically in most countries and provide data on that area, including educational attainment, employment, and unemployment, they provide very limited information on the tertiary sector and its relevance to the labor market, because most do not include information on public or private education and type of training program.[17] Equally, enterprise (or census) surveys do not collect information on skill levels; nor do they ask employers about the types of programs and skills that are more relevant to their business needs or employees about the skills they most need or lack in their jobs.

Lack of university-industry links and other sources of information reflects country-specific conditions and legal frameworks, but it also more widely relates to lack of capacity and incentives, the principal cause for the broader disconnect between HEIs and skill users.

Low capacity

Pervasive lack of human capacity in higher education makes it hard to respond to labor market demand. The lack of qualified human resources has widespread implications for the relevance and quality of higher education, all the way from curriculum design to teaching and to research, also affecting the quality and quantity of university-industry links.

Academic faculty has a critical role in skill provision. First, they train future primary, secondary, and tertiary teachers who in turn shape the quality and relevance of the entire national education system. Second, they provide skills to future high-level research, technical, managerial, and administrative personnel who will lead government, business, and industry. Third, they are key incubators of the innovation and creativity that will enhance national productivity and competitiveness.[18] Lower- and middle-income East Asia are suffering from two main faculty-related constraints: higher and growing student-to-faculty ratios, and a low share of faculty with graduate degrees. The importance of these two challenges varies across countries.

As a result of the past decade's rapid expansion of East Asia's tertiary enrollments, which grew far faster than faculty numbers, student-to-faculty ratios are high in lower- and middle-income East Asia. Most low- and middle-income countries in East Asia have much higher student-to-faculty ratios than the Organisation for Economic Co-operation and Development (OECD) average of 15 to 1 (table 3.2),[19] having climbed or stayed relatively constant in most countries (except for the Philippines; figure 3.8). High student-to-faculty ratios affect teaching by leading to disproportionally high teaching loads and to less time for personal interaction with students and for professional development. They also affect the level of curriculum and degree diversification (particularly the possibility of offering college education and STEM fields, which require smaller classes). Indirectly they also affect research by decreasing the time left for research.

As student-to-faculty ratios have risen, many universities and institutions have hired lower shares of faculty with graduate degrees. This second constraint affects (a) the capacity of universities to offer postgraduate degrees; (b) teaching, to the extent that a master's degree is correlated with teaching;[20] and (c) research (more on this below). In Vietnam, for example, only 46 percent of academic staff in 2005 had graduate qualifications, and

TABLE 3.2   Student-to-faculty ratios in tertiary education, 2007

Economy	Student-to-faculty ratio
Cambodia	23:1
China	19:1
Indonesia	15:1
Korea, Rep.	16:1
Lao PDR	25:1
Malaysia	20:1
Mongolia	29:1
Philippines	23:1
Singapore	13:1
Thailand	37:1
Vietnam	30:1

Sources: Chapman 2010; UIS Data Centre.

FIGURE 3.8   Trends in student-to-faculty ratios, 2001–07

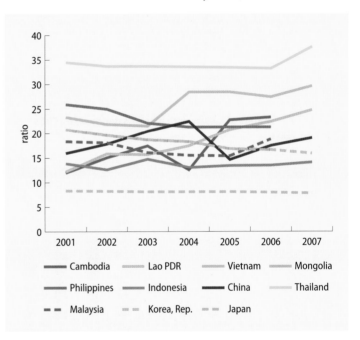

Sources: Chapman 2010; UIS Data Centre.

very few had doctorates (table 3.3 and figure 3.9). Worryingly, the share of faculty with doctorates has decreased since. About 53 percent of the faculty in Indonesia lacks master's degrees, as does 60 percent in the Philippines.[21] This proportion has been decreasing in the Philippines. This is in contrast with Korea; Mongolia; Taiwan, China; and Thailand, which have more than 70 percent of faculty with at least a master's degree.

TABLE 3.3   **Academic qualifications of faculty in a sample of East Asian economies**
percent

Economy	Total		Public HEIs		Private HEIs	
	Share with PhD	Share with master's degree	Share with PhD	Share with master's degree	Share with PhD	Share with master's degree
Low-income economies						
Cambodia (2008/09)	8	52	8	49	7	55
Vietnam (2005/06)	14	32	13	32	23	32
Vietnam (2008/09)	10	37	—	—	—	—
Middle-income economies						
Mongolia (2004/05)	20	65	—	—	—	—
Mongolia (2007/08)	20	66	23	65	15	68
Philippines (2009/10)	10	36	13	54	7	29
Indonesia (2007)	7	40	—	—	—	—
Thailand (2005)	—	—	26	59	16	66
High-income economies						
Korea, Rep. (1994)	59	24	—	—	—	—
Taiwan, China (1992)	46	26	—	—	—	—
Japan (2005)	41	17	—	—	—	—

Sources: Cambodia: HRINC 2010; Indonesia: World Bank Indonesia Higher Education Sector Assessment 2009; Japan: Newby and others 2009; Mongolia: National Statistical Office data; Philippines: Commission on Higher Education 2010 data; Taiwan, China, and Republic of Korea: China Higher Education Reform 1997/2009; Thailand: Commission on Higher Education 2008 data and World Bank 2009a; Vietnam: MOET 2005, 2010.
— = not available.

FIGURE 3.9   **Ratios of faculty with master's degrees and PhDs, various years**

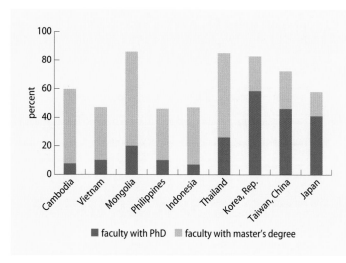

Source: Authors' extrapolation from table 3.3.

In Mongolia and Thailand, high proportions of faculty with a master's degree have, however, been achieved at the cost of a very high student-to-faculty ratio. One way or the other, middle-income countries face a faculty quantity-quality trade-off affecting their capacity to deliver high-quality teaching in a diversified institutional setting. Lower-income countries face a strong double quantity-quality challenge (particularly Vietnam).

Weak incentives
Even when sufficient capacity exists, lack of incentives for public institutions to produce graduates with the skills needed by firms may ultimately hamper all attempts to improve education relevance. In general, private institutions have more incentives to produce skills relevant to firm needs to attract and keep students, whereas public institutions have fewer, stemming from lack of clear accountability for results either to the government or to other stakeholders. Public institutions do not therefore focus on the outcomes of the education process. They are often "protected" by supportive financing policies that shield them from having to show results or compete against other institutions. And within public institutions, even highly qualified faculty may

not deliver on skills if not held adequately accountable to parents and students. Limited autonomy, too, in academic and administrative areas, generates another disincentive to tailor programs to the needs of the local community.

The second disconnect: Between higher education and companies (research users)

Engagement is weak. The limited contribution of universities to technology adaptation and upgrading in companies is suggestive of a disconnect between companies and universities in research and technology mostly applicable to lower- and middle-income countries but also to some upper-income ones. Figure 3.10 provides a snapshot of university-industry links in East Asia. The data include both skill-related and research-related links and, as such, cannot confer the full picture of university-industry links in research and technology. In particular, in the figure, were one to consider only research and technology, the links would be lower in Korea and Malaysia, where skill-related links are fairly developed. By contrast, were one to consider only research and technology, they would be higher in Japan.

Even so, the picture that emerges is one where high-income economies in East Asia and elsewhere, China, and to some extent Malaysia have stronger university-industry links than lower- and middle-income countries. Links in several middle-income countries of the region are also weaker than in their peers elsewhere, such as Brazil, Chile, and South Africa. The low intensity of links in Mongolia is aligned with its position in the lower technology cluster together with Cambodia and Vietnam.

In Thailand recent innovation surveys confirm that firms have very limited cooperation with universities in research and development (R&D) activities (figure 3.11).

However, some industries in Thailand show some interaction.[22] Firms in food, textiles, printing, synthetic rubber and plastics, telecommunications, and R&D regard

FIGURE 3.10 Intensity of university-industry links

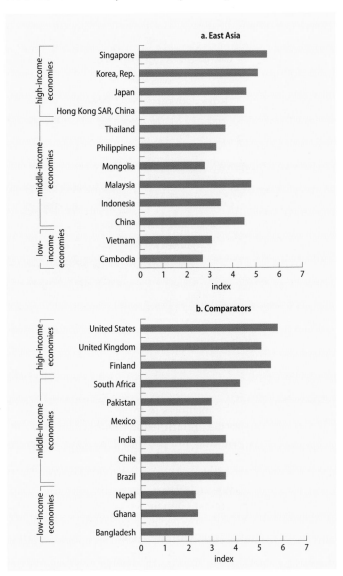

Source: KAM, 2009 data.

universities and research institutes as a "not unimportant" source of information.[23] Firms in petroleum, fabricated metal, telecommunications, and computer industries view universities as important partners in adapting or refining and troubleshooting technologies. This is understandable, given that many of these subsectors are technology intensive.

Low engagement is also confirmed in Indonesia and the Philippines.[24] At most,

FIGURE 3.11   **External collaboration for R&D activities, Thailand, 1999–2003**

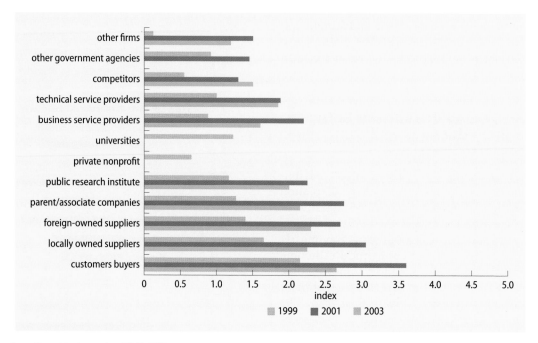

Source: Doner, Intarakumnerd, and Ritchie 2010.
Note: In 1999 and 2001, research institutes and universities are in the same category. They are separate from 2003. Scores: 0 = unknown, 1 = not at all, 5 = very intensely.

faculty members in these two countries have informal relationships with firms, mainly consulting and providing occasional technical assistance and training.

Collaboration is somewhat stronger in Malaysia (where, according to the 2007 Investment Climate Survey, about 13 percent of firms have declared to have looked for collaboration with universities on technological innovation) and China.

But even in China, demand from the enterprise sector is still low. According to a national survey of science and technology activities by the National Bureau of Statistics, only about a sixth of large and medium manufacturing enterprises had any form of collaboration with Chinese universities during 2000–02, and less than 3 percent of patents are jointly filed by firms and universities. Among private firms, only about half of surveyed firms collaborated with universities formally in 2007, though informal collaboration (sharing of equipment, laboratory space, and development of training programs) is more widespread, as it is in Japan, for instance.[25]

Finally, Korean universities, which have proven to be good trainers, are much less of a fertile source of ideas for established firms or for spin-offs.[26]

Some economies are, though, working more closely together. The authorities in Taiwan, China, for instance, have launched a program for promoting the excellence of universities and have made university-industry links one of the criteria for evaluating universities (and their faculty and students).[27] Small and medium enterprises in Taiwan, China, collaborate more with public universities than private ones and are gradually shifting the focus of collaboration from process innovation to product innovation, suggesting an increase in technological capabilities of these enterprises and the economy's technological maturity. University-industry links are also both stronger and on the rise in Japan and Singapore.[28]

Similarly, since 2001, and in line with its position as leader of the middle technology cluster, the Chinese government has encouraged closer university-industry collaboration, making the core missions of research universities teaching, research, and commercialization of technology.[29] Because of this push, patenting by universities has increased dramatically, and patents granted to universities now account for close to 30 percent of all patent grants in China.[30] Chinese universities are beginning to work with industry through contracts for technology services (particularly for technology transfer), patent licensing and sales, and university-affiliated enterprises. Revenues from these activities account for a quarter to a third of universities' research budgets. State-owned enterprises have been the most frequent users of universities' technology services, because these enterprises and universities are public entities, making such collaboration easier. Still, universities' technology links with private firms have increased significantly in recent years and now account for 40 percent of the total. (Foreign firms rarely collaborate with domestic universities because they generally rely on home- or advanced-country research.)

Thailand has separated university staff from the civil services to increase the flexibility of salaries and improve the relationship with firms through the Education Reform Act of 1999.[31] In the Higher Education Development Project, launched in 2001, the government identified seven areas of focus to improve research capabilities,[32] as more technology-intensive industries, such as engineering and the electronic and electrical sectors, capture larger shares of exports.

Reasons for the disconnect

Again, problems related to information, capacity, and incentives are reasons for the disconnect. Taking capacity first, a critical issue relates to the capacity of universities to undertake meaningful research and capacity of firms not only to identify but also to use the knowledge available at universities.[33]

Lack of capacity will hamper both collaboration itself and the results of this collaboration. Some of these capacity issues relate to the lack of skills of higher education graduates who stay in university (becoming faculty) or move to firms. In addition, faculty who lack business acumen and entrepreneurial talent may be reluctant to enter the business world, even if they have made promising findings and generated new ideas that can be commercialized. And lack of creativity and entrepreneurial skills on the firm side will be clearly unsupportive of innovative collaboration. Capacity constraints are likely to apply even more strongly to basic research.

A 2009 survey of a small sample of Indonesian firms identified poor technical quality of domestic graduates as a key constraint, along with lack of awareness of technological development abroad (most likely because of poor foreign-language skills). Firms also pointed to the lack of original, commercially relevant research originating in universities and the lack of a national or regional research hub within the country.[34]

Similarly, firms in Thailand's sugar industry were interested in cellulosic ethanol, given the current concern with energy conservation, but no Thai university possessed the expertise to help firms with R&D. These firms ended up collaborating with Japanese universities through the intermediation of a Japanese trading company.[35] Over time, a range of factors—weak academic capacity, mismatched supply and demand between universities and multinational corporations, and a political system marked by fragmented bureaucracies—have diminished the credibility of universities as a viable innovation partner for firms in Thailand.[36]

Elsewhere, an electronics firm in the Philippines identified the lack of qualified personnel for research and of facilities and tools for simulations and modeling in a particular field as the major impediments to innovation.[37]

Clearly, capacity to undertake research and support technological development in firms is constrained by low ratios of faculty with doctorates. Table 3.3 and figure 3.9

illustrate that the low ratio of faculty with doctorates in lower- and middle-income East Asia is in sharp contrast to the more than 40 percent of faculty with PhDs in Japan, Korea, and Taiwan, China. Countries with higher PhD ratios among their faculty also have higher researcher ratios (take Japan and Korea), translating into higher yearly scientific and technical publications (figure 3.12). While not the best proxy for technological support to firms, this indicator nonetheless captures some potential for it. Other elements, however, play an equally or even more important role in constraining university-industry links in research and technology.

Information failures are multiple and can be related to firms' lack of knowledge of existing technologies (inside or outside the country) generally and university offerings particularly. By contrast, universities may not be fully aware of industry's R&D and technology needs. More crucially, there is a lack of information among both firms and universities as well as governments on what types of university-industry links are most effective and in which economic settings, on the pros and cons of different approaches,

and on the kinds of industries and firms that can more successfully interact with universities.

As an illustration, among other factors, of information failures, according to a survey of manufacturing firms in Beijing, key barriers to collaboration some years ago included lack of efficient communication channels with universities, uncertainty of market perspective for research results, high cost to commercialize results of research, and immature technology from academic research.[38] Private enterprises in Shanghai have reported several major problems (ranked by proportion of responses): university R&D lagging behind market trends (22.5 percent), high costs associated with outsourcing to university (16.6 percent), lack of communication channels (13.8 percent), difficulty reaching mutually agreeable profit-sharing schemes (9 percent), and immature technology and lack of marketability of academic research (7.7 percent).[39] Because Beijing and Shanghai have the most active university-industry links, these results are likely representative of firms across the country.

Finally, without adequate incentives, universities and faculty may not be interested or even able to relate to enterprises.[40] On the firm side, lack of incentives to innovate will also lead to a lack of links. In fact, risk-averse firms with little exposure to new technologies and competition and a lack of technically skilled labor are often unwilling to bear the risks of or put up the financing to bring new technologies to market.[41]

As an illustration of weak incentives for university-industry links, research in Vietnam has found that the weak nature of the relationships between universities and firms could be attributed to four constraints: a credibility gap between industry and academia from both sides; bureaucratic regulations and attitudes not conducive to innovative partnerships and links; insufficient understanding of intellectual property rights and related matters, possibly constraining partnership efforts; and inadequate incentive structures and financial support programs.[42]

FIGURE 3.12 **Number of scientific and technical journal articles and number of researchers in R&D**

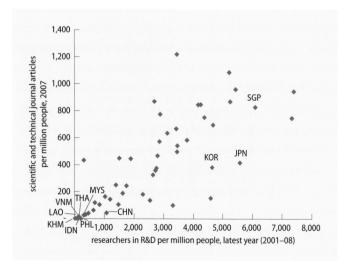

Source: WDI (World Development Indicators) database.

The third disconnect: Between higher education and research institutions (research providers)

Teaching and research have close complementarities. As chapter 1 illustrated, several authors have stated that there needs to be a link between tertiary education and research, while some have argued that the two elements are intrinsically intertwined, because active researchers can provide high-quality teaching, and interactions between researchers and students help improve research.

Whether students come into contact with research, the role that research plays in the academic program, or the extent to which the most recent developments in research are reflected in the curriculum, suggests economies of scope and, to some extent, scale between teaching and research at the tertiary level.

Most lower- and middle-income East Asian economies, however, show a wide disconnect between teaching and research.[43] Universities in many countries remain the domain of teaching, whereas research institutes, the government, and the private sector conduct practically all the research. Links between these two communities are weak, if they exist. In a given country, not all universities need to undertake research, of course, but teaching-research synergies should be exploited in at least a few institutions.

Country examples of the disconnect. Universities in Cambodia, for example, conduct very little research, and their connections with research institutes are weak. A recent study noted that research capacity is at a very early stage of development because of the inadequacy of research budgets, qualified researchers, and supporting infrastructure such as research facilities or laboratories.[44] Research and technical institutes conduct most of the country's research.

Teaching and research functions are often kept separate in the Philippines: universities and colleges have traditionally focused on teaching, and other institutions pursued research.[45] Recent efforts have been made

to bolster research output and capacity. For instance, the national congress created the Commission on Science, Technology, and Engineering in 2007 to study the state of the innovation system and recommend strategies for improving science and technology capabilities. The commission called for the creation of 20 councils, institutes, and administrative units outside the university system to pursue research in priority sectors. Yet the older trend continues. The Philippine Atmospheric, Geophysical, and Astronomical Services Administration, the country's climate forecasting agency; the National Academy of Science; and the Philippine Council for Industry and Energy Research and Development are all administered as governmental departments, rather than as university partners. And although awards and research grants to these institutions increased from ₱247.2 million in 2006 to ₱639.6 million in 2008,[46] none of the funds went to universities.

Universities in Malaysia and Thailand conduct more research than those in Cambodia and the Philippines, but research institutes still conduct most research. In Malaysia only 17 of the 254 R&D agencies are within universities,[47] spending US$94.8 million in 2005, compared with private sector entities' US$439 million.

In Thailand HEIs account for about 30 percent of total research expenditure, compared with 23 percent in government and 45 percent in the private sector. Most research conducted at HEIs is short-term applied research, as opposed to the research that is undertaken by the private sector and by research institutes, which provide 89 percent of the experimental research undertaken in the country.[48] Universities engage in research projects mainly as part of consulting services and technical or analytical services, because public funding levels are too low to fund capital investment. This keeps down the number of academics committed to long-term research: only 20 percent of Thai academics conduct research continuously.[49]

Even in China, where several universities have emerged as centers of excellence for both teaching and research in recent years, research institutes and government bodies still conduct most research, leaving teaching to HEIs. Such separation is rooted in the country's recent history. Between 1949 and 1979, the science and technology system followed a model under which research, including all innovation activities, was conducted by research institutes, manufactured by factories, and distributed by distributors. A multitude of central ministries coordinated these elements, creating a vertically rather than horizontally integrated system dependent on centralized, top-down allocations for necessary inputs.[50]

In recent years, however, links between HEIs and those conducting research have strengthened in China. National programs specifically designed to elevate the importance of research in higher education have been implemented since 2002. Project 985 aims to turn China's top universities into world-class research universities by introducing elements of competition for resources. Competition for "985" designation is fierce because selected institutions receive substantial central government funding, with matching funds from provincial governments.

But Chinese universities have yet to become key drivers of innovation, particularly relative to public research institutes, indicating that separation between teaching and research functions is still prominent. Universities have consistently spent less than public research institutes, accounting for less than 10 percent of total R&D expenditures from 1997 to 2006.[51] In addition, with expanding corporate R&D, higher education's share in both national R&D expenditure and personnel has in fact trended downward in recent years, accounting for 8.5 percent and 14.6 percent, respectively, in 2007. Moreover, interaction between public research institutes and universities largely focuses on recruiting university graduates.[52]

Non-Asian trends. East Asia's divide between teaching and research functions contrasts with trends elsewhere. The German and Swedish higher education systems, developed according to the Humboldtian vision of the unity of research and teaching, emphasize blending these two elements across all disciplines and require that teaching be informed by research.[53] The OECD has noted that even Eastern European countries, in which there was a clear separation between teaching and research characteristic of socialist regimes, have been restructured posttransition according to the Humboldtian vision.[54] Closer to Asia, New Zealand's parliament has passed a law that only those actively involved in research can teach at degree level.

Reasons for the disconnect

The overall approach to managing teaching and research is partly at fault. Most countries have been adopting a model of separation between teaching and research that has not been conducive to enhancing research in universities. This approach has further debilitated the already weak capacity of universities to undertake research, while there are few incentives for universities and research institutions to collaborate on, say, common projects, with the consequence that useful synergies between research at HEIs and research institutes are not exploited.[55] Beyond constraints in resources, the lack of incentives to pursue research in universities (alone or in collaboration with research institutes) is thus also to blame. And even more so is the lack of incentives to pursue meaningful and productive research (resources need to be well used).

The fourth disconnect: Among higher education institutions themselves and between these institutions and training providers (horizontal disconnect across skill providers)

HEIs themselves (and those institutions with other skill providers at about the same level or postemployment level) are not well connected to each other in much of lower- and middle-income East Asia, and this has led to weak skill transmission to graduates. Indeed, because the links and complementarities among institutions have generally not been well understood or built upon by institutions and governments, the development of higher-level skills and competencies has been inhibited. Although some encouraging steps have been taken, the connection between different HEIs and these institutions and, for example, firm training, on the one hand, and the development of different skill acquisition pathways, on the other, has not been well or coherently managed across the region. And it is one of the reasons that the skill supply system has been unable to ensure more flexible, efficient, and even equitable skill acquisition.

The situation in Mongolia is illustrative of fragmentation between TVET and non-TVET providers. Despite the demand from employers for vocational skills, public investment in TVET is limited, and links between universities and TVET skill providers are scarce. Facilities and machinery are often outdated and faulty, faculty rarely share their expertise with TVET institutions, the different skill providers' curricula are not aligned, transfers between university and TVET tracks are not easy, and private providers are not part of a regulatory and monitoring framework.[56]

Thailand is similar: students have little mobility across institutions because of a lack of formal links among different skill providers. Curricula between university and vocational tracks are, for instance, rarely aligned, making it difficult for students to pursue multiple paths to skill acquisition. And the story repeats itself across the region.[57]

Reasons for the disconnect

What has caused this fragmentation among skill providers? Part of the underlying problem appears to be the lack of a well-developed and unifying framework for different skill providers. Such a framework, commonly referred to as a *national qualifications framework*, can help provide substantial links among institutions. When well developed, it can provide more effective overall governance to address fragmentation and ensure that students and workers can move horizontally and vertically between education and training levels[58] and the formal/nonformal education and training system, through a strengthened skills certification.

National qualifications frameworks are at an incipient stage in lower- and middle-income East Asia[59] (and not fully developed also in some upper-income economies), and the underlying concept has yet to take hold: instead of a more modern focus on outputs and adherence to a market-oriented policy agenda, the skill provision systems in East Asia remain focused on inputs. Instead of stressing competencies acquired, East Asian education systems emphasize inputs and the institutions that teach the skills. Job mobility and thus labor market efficiency have suffered. Malaysia is one step ahead of other lower- and middle-income countries in this dimension.

Fragmentation among skill providers has also arisen from a lack of focus on concrete competencies. Indeed, most countries in the region have no competence-based training systems, which would shift the emphasis from what courses a trainee or student has taken and when to what the trainee or student can do. Such systems focus on the skills needed for performance in a job and put pressure on instructors and institutions to deliver these skills. They are usually modular and, in theory, facilitate flexible entry and exit and recognize different routes for skill acquisition. Lack of incentives to focus on the skills that matter, lack of links with industry in curriculum development, and lack of capacity to adopt a competency-based approach may have prevented the development of such an approach in East Asia. In turn, the absence of such an approach creates fewer incentives for institutions to relate with industry.

The fifth disconnect: Between higher education and earlier education (schools) (vertical disconnect across skill providers)

The quantity and quality of earlier education, particularly secondary education, have a strong influence on tertiary education, and transition points across education levels are critical. But low- and middle-income East Asian countries show a disconnect in this area, too. This is illustrated by the fact that the outcomes of earlier education levels and the transition between levels are constraining higher education outcomes one way or another in the different countries, suggesting a lack of comprehensive vision of the education sector.

FIGURE 3.13   **Secondary and tertiary gross enrollment ratios, 2007–08**

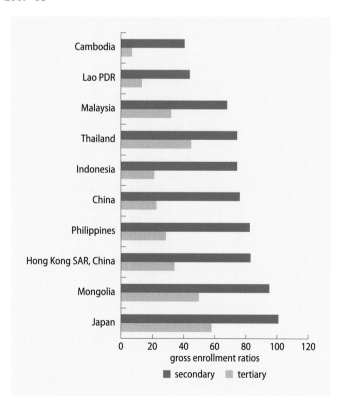

Source: UIS Data Centre.

Secondary and tertiary enrollments

Secondary and tertiary enrollments are necessarily related (figure 3.13). While the relationship is not necessarily linear, with Malaysia and Thailand performing better than expected,[60] countries with higher tertiary enrollment ratios tend to have higher secondary enrollment ratios. Similarly, the share of workers with tertiary education is highly conditioned by the share of workers with secondary education (figure 3.14). The difference between the share of workers with tertiary education and the share of workers with at least secondary education indicates that the share of workers with secondary education has had to grow even faster than the share of workers with tertiary education. While secondary enrollment is not yet a constraint across low- and middle-income East Asia, it may become one as countries seek to extend coverage. In some countries, such as Cambodia and Lao PDR, low secondary enrollment is already a constraint to getting a wider talent pool.

While low- and middle-income countries have either improved or maintained their secondary completion levels (figure 3.15), a comparison of tertiary enrollment rates with secondary completion rates[61] indicates that secondary completion may already be a binding constraint for expanding tertiary education in Cambodia, China, Indonesia, and Thailand. Thus, expansion may need to be related to efficiency improvements in secondary education and in the transition from secondary to tertiary education.

Tertiary and earlier academic performance

Academic performance at the tertiary level is closely related to earlier academic performance. Indeed, performance in secondary education has been shown to be a strong predictor of both access and outcomes in tertiary education. Research has shown, for instance, that students who have taken academically advanced courses in high school are more likely to perform better and

FIGURE 3.14   Trends in shares of workers with secondary and tertiary education, four East Asian economies, various years

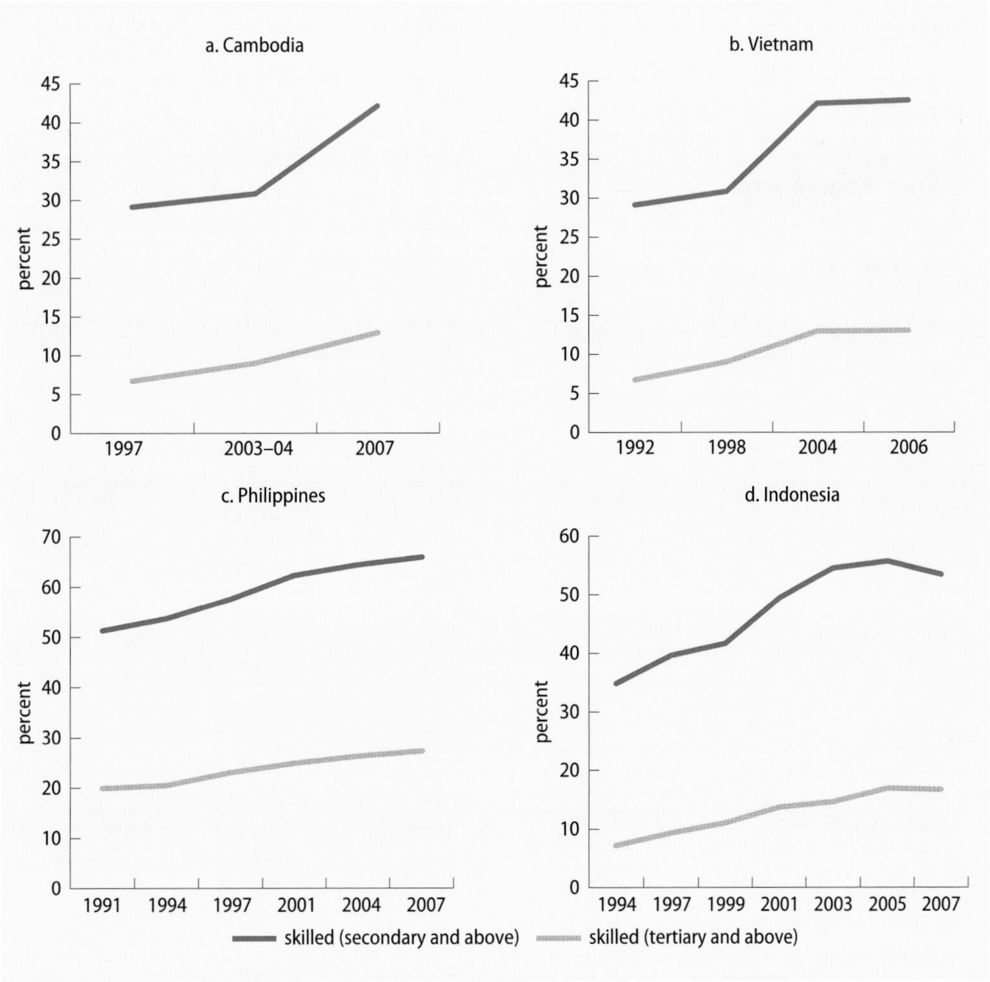

Source: Labor force surveys, various years.

complete college than those who have not.[62] This finding is consistent with prior research that found that advanced mathematics and algebra in the eighth grade are strong predictors of whether students enrolled in a four-year college and completed a bachelor's degree.[63]

According to one U.S. study, graduation rates for better prepared Latino students were on par with white students.[64] And researchers have found that the quality of high school education (measured by the quality of coursework and test scores) was a

stronger predictor of college completion than a student's socioeconomic status.[65] Finally, results of international assessments across 132 countries found a positive correlation between math and reading scores of 15-year-olds and the quality of higher education in their countries (based on university rankings, number of researchers, and number of patents). Indeed, after including GDP per capita in the regression model, the study found that math scores of 15-year-olds were a better predictor of higher education quality than GDP.[66]

FIGURE 3.15   **Secondary education completion**

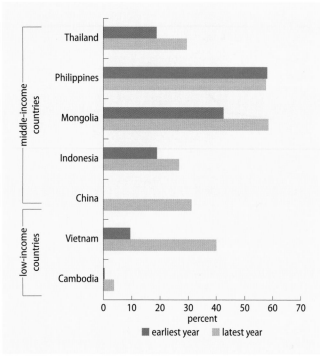

Source: Sakellariou 2010b.
Note: Data for China are for large cities only, so they are not directly comparable to the other surveys. Years are 2005 for China (earlier year missing); 1998/2006 for Indonesia, Mongolia, the Philippines, Thailand, and Vietnam; and 1999/2007 for Cambodia. Figures for China and Thailand are underestimated.

A couple of indicators show the same interrelation and how it can constrain in East Asia. First, in alignment with the low quality of tertiary graduates, lower- and middle-income East Asian economies show weaknesses in literacy and numeracy skills at the lower-secondary stage. The most recent Trends in International Mathematics and Science Study (TIMSS) data (tables 3.4 and 3.5) highlight gaps of middle-income Asian economies in numeracy and science relative to high-income Asian and non-Asian economies—and more broadly the international average—suggesting continuous gaps in numerical skills. While the international average and the performance of some high-income economies, such as the United States, Korea, and Taiwan, China, have been increasing, that of Malaysia—traditionally a

strong performer in math according to the TIMSS—has been gradually declining, and Thailand has not done much better. The Philippines is the weakest TIMSS performer among the tested Asian countries. In Indonesia the significant improvement in Programme for International Student Assessment (PISA) scores between 2003 and 2006 in reading and math subjects[67] was partly reversed between 2006 and 2009, underscoring its significant gaps in relation to the OECD average in 2009 (figure 3.16). The country also needs to reverse its stagnating TIMSS results.

Second, countries with a higher TIMSS score in math and science have higher STEM enrollment shares in tertiary education later (figure 3.17). The relation may be even clearer if one considers the quality of these STEM skills (as seen in the poor quality of engineers in several countries). A similar relation holds between TIMSS scores and journal publications (figure 3.18): higher TIMSS scores are associated with more publications.

While only illustrative, this evidence suggests that the low or relatively low (in relation to high-income East Asia) TIMSS scores of Indonesia, Malaysia, the Philippines, and Thailand are constraining these countries from achieving better STEM and innovation outcomes in tertiary education.

Tertiary inclusiveness and prior education

Tertiary inclusiveness is clearly related to inclusiveness at earlier education levels. The inequities in access to tertiary education, documented in chapter 2, at least partially originate in the lack of access to earlier education levels (figure 3.19). Beyond showing the cumulative effect of dropouts at different levels and grades on the completion of the secondary cycle, these plots also demonstrate variation in primary and secondary education access and survival rates by rural and urban populations, wealth, and gender: larger gaps between the two lines in each graph indicate greater levels of inequity, whereas perfectly overlapping lines indicate complete equity between groups.

Cambodia shows significant inequities in access to and survival in prior education levels across all dimensions. Indonesia seems to have a relation between high inequity across urban and rural areas in tertiary and secondary education (while inequities of access to tertiary education by income level seem to have an impact later). In Thailand, underscoring the relation between tertiary and prior education levels, the generally lower levels of inequity in access to tertiary education also seem to reflect lower levels of inequity at prior education levels (beyond other reasons). The gender inequities in favor of females in secondary education are replicated at the tertiary level, as clearly visible in Mongolia, the Philippines, and Vietnam (figure 3.20).

Gender

Gender inequities now cut both ways, given steady improvements for females in access to secondary and higher education in several countries, including Malaysia, Mongolia, the Philippines, Thailand, and Vietnam. There is much evidence on the benefits of promoting girls' education. Results of PISA 2006 show the benefits of investing in girls' education: girls outperformed boys in math and science in some countries but consistently outperformed boys in reading in all OECD countries and some developing countries. It is imperative for countries to ensure that their girls have access to education—including access to higher education.[68] However, although in some countries, such as Cambodia and probably China, females remain discriminated against, in others, such as Thailand, it is now males who may be falling behind at the entrance of lower- and upper-secondary education.

The inequities in completion disfavoring males in Mongolia, the Philippines, and Vietnam may in theory be related to having admitted a wider mixed-ability pool of males in the first place, requiring some caution in

TABLE 3.4   Eighth-grade TIMSS scores for mathematics, selected East Asian economies, 1999, 2003, and 2007

Economy	1999	2003	2007
Taiwan, China	585	585	598
Korea, Rep.	587	589	597
Singapore	604	605	593
Hong Kong SAR, China	582	586	572
Japan	579	570	570
United States	502	504	508
International average	487	466	500
Malaysia	519	508	474
Thailand	467	—	441
Indonesia	403	411	397
Philippines	345	378	—

Sources: Gonzales, Guzman, and others 2004; Gonzales, Williams, and others 2008; Mullis and others 2000.
Note: Economies are ranked by their score in 2007.
— = Not available.

TABLE 3.5   Eighth-grade TIMSS scores for science, selected East Asian economies, 1999, 2003, and 2007

Economy	1999	2003	2007
Singapore	568	578	567
Taiwan, China	569	571	561
Japan	550	552	554
Korea, Rep.	549	558	553
Hong Kong SAR, China	530	556	530
United States	515	527	520
International average	488	473	500
Malaysia	492	510	471
Thailand	482	—	471
Indonesia	435	420	427
Philippines	345	377	—

Sources: Gonzales, Guzman, and others 2004; Gonzales, Williams, and others 2008; Mullis and others 2000.
Note: Economies are ranked by their score in 2007.
— = Not available.

interpreting their results, but this possibility is quite unlikely, particularly in Mongolia and the Philippines, given the significant relative gap in completion. This gap suggests other issues related to retaining males in the secondary cycle. Indeed, opportunity costs are potentially high among the poor and higher for males than females in the secondary school age range, leading to dropout of otherwise talented students.[69]

FIGURE 3.16   PISA 2009 scores for East Asia, United States, and OECD

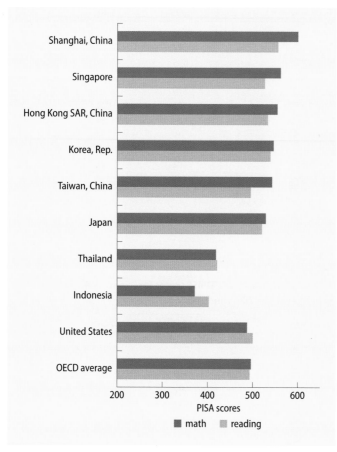

PISA scores

■ math ■ reading

Source: OECD 2010b.

Ethnicity

Inequities by ethnic group seem to be sharper than gender inequities. Although data on access to primary and secondary education by ethnic group are not always reliable in labor force or household surveys, evidence suggests discrimination in several countries.[70] Vietnam's minorities have attendance rates of 89 percent for primary education, 85 percent for lower-secondary education, and 52 percent for upper-secondary education (as of 2008), well below the national average.

In Vietnam inequities by ethnic group are visible in completion (figure 3.21). They are likely to reflect both differences in access and in quality of schools.[71] Several studies point to cultural and awareness issues, but the

absence of comprehensive policy measures for ethnic minority groups means they are not being tackled (primary and secondary equity interventions focus on fee exemptions).[72]

While they start early, inequities by ethnic group are most often further exacerbated in the transition between secondary and tertiary education, raising additional issues for addressing this disadvantage.[73] Even the few benefits and policies in favor of these groups initiated at the secondary level are generally not pursued further, creating new barriers to entry. This was still the case in Vietnam in 2008 and in Thailand in 2006 where ethnic groups had a much worse transition rate than the majority (figure 3.22).[74]

Urban or rural location

Inequities in other areas are worrisome. The significant losses of rural students at the entrance of lower and upper secondary in Indonesia and Thailand, going beyond poverty gaps, are particularly problematic. They suggest barriers to entry, such as lack of schools, which become an impediment for possibly bright students. Other data suggest that in Vietnam, Mongolia, and the Philippines inequities are already evident in secondary education and are reflected then in tertiary education (figure 3.23). Also in these three countries, as well as in Indonesia, inequities are further exacerbated in the transition between secondary and tertiary education (figure 3.24), suggesting insufficient action to retain rural students throughout the education cycle.[75]

Income

Income remains the biggest constraint in Cambodia for both access to and survival through the secondary cycle. Poor students are likely to drop out or not enroll because of high direct and opportunity costs. They can access only a few need-based scholarships (at all levels) and generally go to lower-quality schools.[76]

Tertiary entrance examinations

Ethnic minorities, rural students, and other groups are disadvantaged in their access to high-quality higher education. Entrance examinations used to determine places for students at universities are inherently linked to issues of access and equity because successful performance in these examinations is the result of prior academic experience. Evidence for this finding is seen notably in Vietnam and China. In Vietnam students from disadvantaged groups score lower marks on the National University Entrance Examination (without this being related to ability, as shown in chapter 2) and are less likely to enroll in high-quality tertiary education institutions.[77] While the Ministry of Education and Training sets the cutoff marks needed to enroll in tertiary institutions for mathematics, physics, and chemistry, higher-quality universities require better entrance examination scores.

In China aspiring tertiary students must take a national entrance examination in addition to the senior secondary diploma examination to enter tertiary education. Some recent research has noted significant disparities in access across provinces despite similar test scores: one study reported that applicants from Beijing needed a slightly lower score to enter tertiary education than those in Hunan.[78] Other research has shown that students from areas with higher concentrations of tertiary education opportunities need lower scores than students from other provinces. These findings may result from the quota system, which favors students from regions with stronger tertiary systems.[79]

Steps taken
Even when countries have started to address inequities, outcomes have not always turned out as expected because of weaknesses in policy design.[80] China is well known for having instituted policies to ease the plight of minority and disadvantaged groups, including interventions targeted beyond the education sector,[81] and has been generally active in supporting ethnic minorities through the education cycle itself.[82] Autonomous government officials have the right to determine the education plans, curricula, and language of

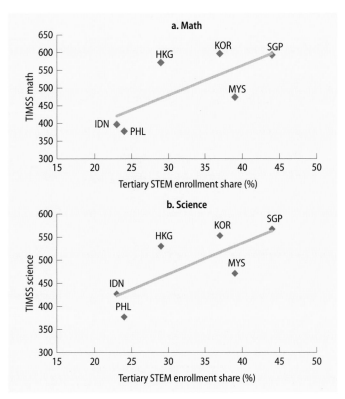

FIGURE 3.17   Relation between TIMSS scores and STEM enrollment shares

Sources: EdStats database; TIMSS 2007 database.

instruction at the primary and secondary levels following government principles and goals (such as the universalization of compulsory education). This has led to schools using minority languages for instruction in all subjects up to the end of senior secondary education. (Chinese is taught only as a second language.)[83]

Despite a policy to improve minority enrollment in mainstream institutions in place since 1951, most ethnic minority students are still concentrated in ethnic universities, which are weak in science and engineering and tend to direct minorities into languages and teacher studies—fields that traditionally do not allow much upward economic mobility. Moreover, when ethnic minorities are enrolled in mainstream institutions, they may have difficulty in performing well.[84] These results may be related to weaknesses in quality of teaching

FIGURE 3.18   Relation between TIMSS scores and journal articles

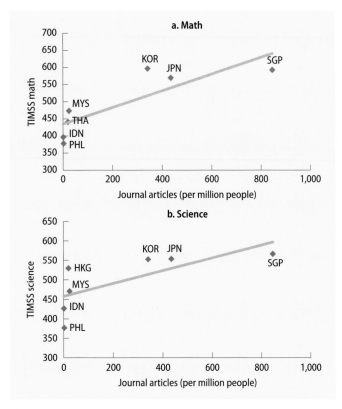

Sources: EdStats database; TIMSS 2007 database.

Curricula may not be sufficiently well aligned between the secondary and tertiary cycles, the case in Mongolia and Thailand.[86] This misalignment may be partly responsible for some of the dropouts between secondary and tertiary education. Yet countries such as Korea and Singapore have been successful at creating a solid higher education system by aligning their secondary and tertiary systems well.[87]

Inclusiveness of tertiary education clearly depends on inclusiveness early on, requiring a bold and comprehensive approach to tackle disadvantage. There is, for instance, still too little use of distance education at the secondary level, and scholarships to cover transport costs to urban centers, to address the urban-rural gap, are limited.[88] And comprehensive packages, including affirmative action policies, to address the multiple disadvantages faced by ethnic minority groups are extremely rare. Moreover, when they are implemented, they do not always have the desired effects.

Beyond the specific measures, implementing comprehensive approaches to tackle quality and inclusiveness is constrained by gaps in information, capacity, and incentives. Fortunately, information is now improving through the use of international standardized tests in primary and secondary education. Equity statistics are, however, still weak in some countries.[89] Policy makers need to be well informed with disaggregated data as to why certain groups are more vulnerable than others and why these groups tend to be poorer—and have a deeper understanding of what has determined the success of groups who have been able to improve their circumstances despite long-term disadvantage.

Equally, equipping students with information about the tertiary education application process is critical. In many countries (and not just in East Asia), the lack of information for students on college choices or procedures, as well as adult guidance, is a significant nonmonetary barrier to access, particularly for disadvantaged groups whose parents are much less knowledgeable about higher education.

of the Chinese language in the secondary education provided to ethnic minorities, highlighting the need for standards and alignment between cycles.

Reasons for the disconnect. The evidence suggests that policy makers in low- and middle-income East Asia may not be putting enough emphasis on the connections between education levels, or fully understanding these interrelationships— and so the need to address them early and consistently. A comprehensive vision of the education sector is missing. Math results in secondary education, for example, clearly influence outcomes later, requiring at minimum a coordinated effort to improve secondary education quality.[85] Low- and middle-income East Asia may not be making enough effort at that level.

FIGURE 3.19   **Estimated survival rates for children ages 13–19, Cambodia, Indonesia, and Thailand**

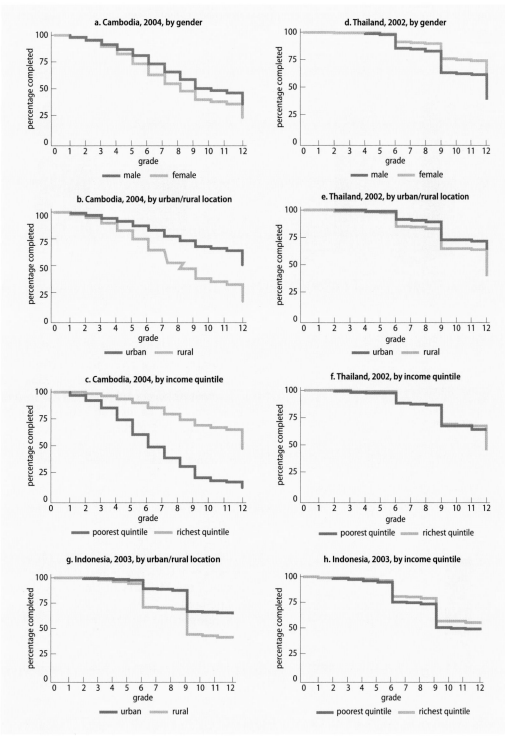

FIGURE 3.20   Secondary and tertiary education completion rate by gender, Vietnam, Mongolia, and the Philippines

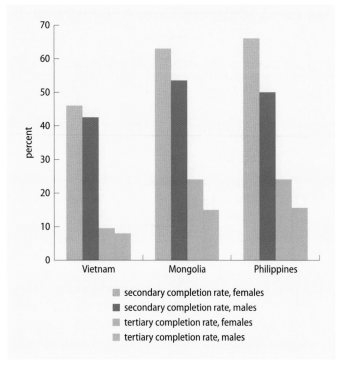

Sources: Household and labor force surveys, most recent years.
Note: Tertiary education is proxied by university education in Mongolia and the Philippines; secondary education goes up to only grade 10 in the Philippines. Secondary completion rates are calculated in relation to the 17–21 age range; tertiary completion rates are calculated in relation to the 22–28 age range.

FIGURE 3.21   Secondary and tertiary education completion rate, by ethnic group, Vietnam, 2008

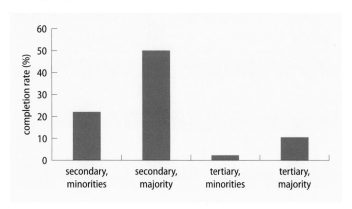

Source: VHLSS 2008.
Note: Secondary completion rates are calculated in relation to the 17–21 age range; tertiary completion rates are calculated in relation to the 22–28 age range.

FIGURE 3.22   Tertiary enrollment in proportion of secondary completion by ethnic group, Vietnam, 2008, and Thailand, 2006

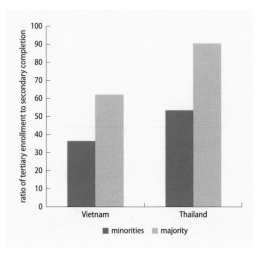

Sources: VHLSS 2008; Thailand 2006 Labor Force Survey.
Note: Secondary completion rates are calculated in relation to the 17–21 age range; tertiary enrollment rates are calculated in relation to the 18–22 age range.

Understanding the interrelationships between educational levels and planning and implementing successful packages is also constrained by lack of institutional and human capacity, as well as the right financing and nonfinancing policies at all levels. Finally, governance overall, including accountability mechanisms and the management arrangements of the government in relation to the education sector, also influences the way interrelationships are understood and built upon. For instance, in the Philippines and Thailand the separation of higher education management from the ministries of education (through the Ministry of University Affairs in Thailand and the Commission of Higher Education in the Philippines) has not been conducive to an overall vision of the education sector. In Thailand this separation has by now been addressed.[90] But also in other countries where policy and operational responsibilities are confused, an integrated approach has been difficult. These considerations lead to the next and last section of this chapter.

Conclusion and moving forward

This chapter has argued that failure to deliver on skills and research reflects five main disconnects among skill and research providers and users at the core of higher education systems. With limited systematic quantitative or qualitative information, it is difficult to make generalizations on comparative intensity of disconnects across countries, but the evidence presented in the chapter points to these disconnects being present all around lower- and middle-income East Asia (table 3.6). Cambodia, Indonesia, Mongolia, the Philippines, and Vietnam have been repeatedly used to illustrate some of these disconnects. China, Malaysia, and to a lesser extent Thailand tend to perform better along most dimensions than other countries. In particular, China, in line with its position of leading the middle technology cluster, is being more successful in building links with firms in the technology arena than other lower- and middle-income countries, while Malaysia has an edge in linking skill providers. Upper-income countries, reflecting their better skill and innovation outcomes, appear to have many less or less-intense disconnects, though links between HEIs and firms in research and technology remain more of a challenge for them as well. This fact indicates that some disconnects are likely to be more difficult than others to address.

This chapter has also argued that many of the disconnects in higher education in low- and middle-income East Asia have their origin in information, capacity, and incentive gaps, which point to market and policy failures. Public policy can address these disconnects. Not all the policies are strictly related to higher education,[91] and not all actors and interactions at the core of higher education systems will respond the same way to higher education policies, but they clearly have a tremendous role. Figure 3.25 shows a simplified picture of the potential impact of three main pillars of higher education policy—financing, management, and stewardship—on the five

FIGURE 3.23 **Secondary and tertiary education completion, by urban or rural area, Vietnam, Mongolia, and the Philippines**

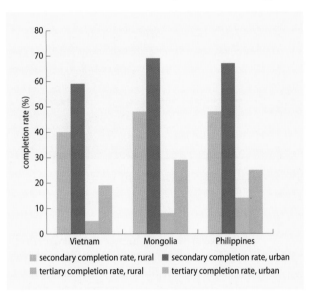

Sources: Household and labor force surveys (most recent years).
Note: Tertiary education is proxied by university education in Mongolia and the Philippines; secondary education goes up to only grade 10 in the Philippines. Secondary completion rates are calculated in relation to the 17–21 age range; tertiary completion rates are calculated in relation to the 22–28 age range.

FIGURE 3.24 **Tertiary enrollment in proportion to secondary completion by urban or rural area, selected economies**

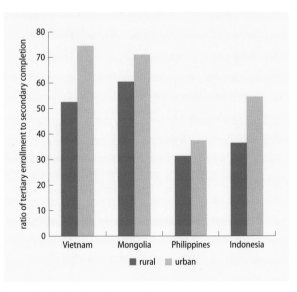

Sources: Household and labor force surveys (most recent year).
Note: Tertiary education is proxied by university education in Mongolia and the Philippines; secondary education goes up to only grade 10 in the Philippines. Secondary completion rates are calculated in relation to the 17–21 age range; tertiary enrollments are calculated in relation to the 18–22 age range.

TABLE 3.6   Intensity of disconnects by income and technology cluster group

Disconnect	Lower income LTC	Middle income LTC	LMTC	MTC	UMTC	Upper income TTC
Disconnect 1: HEIs and employers						
Disconnect 2: HEIs and companies in research and technology						More advanced in Japan; Taiwan, China; Singapore
Disconnect 3: HEIs and research institutions						Less advanced in Korea, Rep.
Disconnect 4: HEIs among themselves and with training providers						
Disconnect 5: HEIs and earlier education institutions (schools)					Incomplete evidence	

Source: Authors' elaboration.
Note: The darker the area, the larger is the disconnect. LTC = lower technology cluster; LMTC = lower-middle technology cluster; MTC = middle technology cluster; UMTC = upper-middle technology cluster; TTC = top technology cluster.

disconnects through higher capacity, stronger incentives, and better or more information. To every policy pillar are associated critical policy levers that are the object of the next chapters. The figures are simplified because only the most obvious relationships between policy pillars and disconnects are shown—in fact, the policy pillars have the potential to influence all disconnects with the right policy levers. Figure 3.25 illustrates how some of the policy pillars work.

Many of the disconnects are related to financing. For instance, disconnects in research and from secondary to tertiary education suggest that too few financial resources may be available for research and scholarships. Low enrollment in STEM fields in several countries, a disconnect with skill users, also suggests underspending in these fields. Developing or attracting faculty with PhDs may require financial decisions, such as offering scholarships to brilliant students to study in prestigious universities abroad. It may also require offering internationally competitive faculty salaries as is done at the top universities in Singapore; Hong Kong SAR, China; Korea; and Japan. Japan pays its top-level academics over three times more than China does.[92] Adequate financing can thus improve higher education's capacity to conduct research, hire high-quality faculty, develop technical and engineering courses, and install laboratories. Financing decisions can also provide HEIs with incentives to improve performance. For example, firms and governments can improve skill outcomes by allocating funds to universities according to graduation and employment indicators. Finally, funding for scholarships can help increase the pool of talented students getting access to university.

So public financing can address the disconnects. Greater and more efficient public spending, combined with additional private resource mobilization, can tackle the disconnect with earlier education by supporting student transitions from secondary to tertiary education through scholarships and loans (addressing capacity constraints). Greater and more efficient public spending can also tackle the disconnects between universities and firms in skills and research and between teaching and research provision by supporting higher funding for research and STEM skills in universities combined with performance-based funding (addressing capacity and incentive constraints). These policy levers are explored in depth in the next chapter.

Several information, capacity, and incentive constraints and the related disconnects are related to management. For instance, limited information on skill and institutional outcomes—or the research and technology needs of firms—suggests a market failure not yet corrected. Even if institutions receive sufficient funds for highly qualified faculty, insufficient autonomy to select staff and decide on their academic programs makes it difficult for them to deliver what firms need. A lack of accountability of university management to representative university boards may also not be conducive to universities fulfilling the needs of skill or research users, as would be the lack of competition among institutions.

Management of the public sector can help tackle the disconnect between HEIs and skill and research users through the right mix of institutional autonomy and accountability. The right accountability structures will also help address other disconnects. Qualification frameworks have, for instance, a direct impact on improving the incentives and information for coordination among HEIs. Chapter 5 reviews policies related to the management of the public sector.

Beyond managing the public sector, governments also need to coordinate and handle actors and connections not under the direct administrative authority of the departments of higher education but whose performance is critical to the sector. In other words, governments need to exercise appropriate stewardship of the overall system. The lack of interaction between HEIs and firms to some extent reflects a lack of information on what works and legal and financial incentives to connect. Disconnects between skill providers and users are also related to a private sector not fulfilling its potential because of overregulation. Stewardship will require expanding the capacity to coordinate higher education departments with other departments, actors, and ministries; private HEIs; the links between HEIs and firms in skills and research; and increasingly the links between the domestic and international higher education markets. Adequate stewardship of the higher education system can help solve the disconnects between skill users and providers through effective promotion and regulation of the private sector (addressing incentive, information, and even capacity constraints). It can also address the disconnects between firms and providers in skills and research by sharing best practices on what works and by putting in place the right legal and financial incentives (addressing incentive and information constraints). Stewardship-related policies are reviewed in chapter 6.

BOX 3.2 **The rationale for public intervention in higher education**

The overall policy direction, oversight, regulation, and quality control of the system. The government has the primary responsibility for establishing the main strategic directions, providing the core regulations, and setting up the accountability and quality assurance framework needed to address opportunistic behavior and asymmetric information. Capacity building can also be provided.

Accurate and timely information about the supply, demand, and value of particular skills and other education outcomes and outputs. This function can entail supporting learning outcome assessments; education management information systems; and firm, labor force, and household surveys.

Funding "public goods," such as R&D and science, technology, engineering, and math, and addressing scale economies needed to finance centers of excellence. The government may need to dedicate an increasing share of its resources to create the framework for innovation and excellence that the market alone may fail to create because of benefits difficult to internalize or prohibitive initial investment.

Funding the access of key vulnerable groups that are left out but deserve an opportunity to participate. There continues to be a strong scope for public intervention on equity grounds.

Funding minimum teaching needs to provide basic coverage that the market may fail to provide for positive spillovers, while giving institutions an incentive to perform without necessarily stifling them with rules. This calls for funds to be provided according to transparent and performance-based criteria.

FIGURE 3.25   Relationships between disconnects and policies

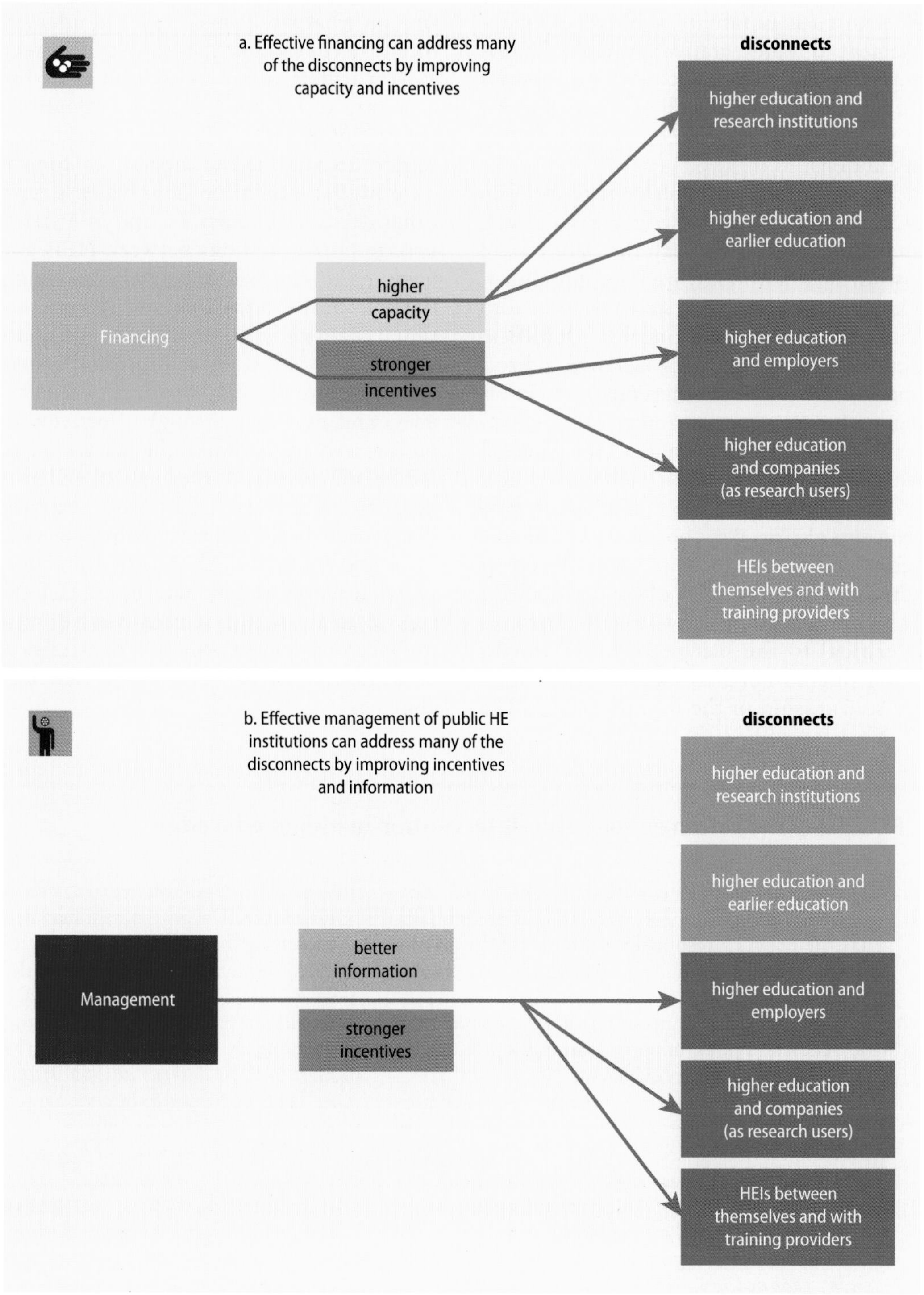

a. Effective financing can address many of the disconnects by improving capacity and incentives

disconnects

higher education and research institutions

higher education and earlier education

Financing

higher capacity

stronger incentives

higher education and employers

higher education and companies (as research users)

HEIs between themselves and with training providers

b. Effective management of public HE institutions can address many of the disconnects by improving incentives and information

disconnects

higher education and research institutions

higher education and earlier education

Management

better information

stronger incentives

higher education and employers

higher education and companies (as research users)

HEIs between themselves and with training providers

(continued next page)

FIGURE 3.25   continued

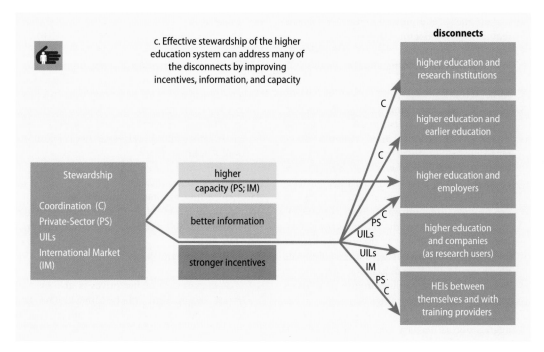

Source: Authors' elaboration.
Note: Only stronger relations shown; the intensity of shade indicates intensity of impact.

In light of these considerations and the above diagnostic, it is clear that public policy can have a profound role in improving higher education outcomes by tackling the disconnects. Box 3.2 reviews the case for public intervention in higher education.

The next three chapters delve into the three most critical public policy areas: financing, management of public institutions, and stewardship of the higher education system.

Notes

1. HRINC 2010.
2. Kennedy and Lee 2008; World Bank 2008.
3. Government of the Philippines 2007.
4. HRINC 2010.
5. World Bank 2010d.
6. World Bank 2008.
7. Smeaton and Hughes (2003) define *interme-diate skills* as those located above routine skills and below professional skills that are required to operate effectively in jobs with a

relatively high level of skills and fair degree of responsibility. Examples of intermediate skills include effective communication (in local and foreign languages); personal skills (interest, motivation, interpersonal skills, leadership); computer skills; and technical knowledge of some disciplines (such as economics, law, and business).

8. di Gropello, Tan, and Tandon 2010.
9. di Gropello, Kruse, and Tandon 2011.
10. World Bank 2010d.
11. World Bank 2010d.
12. Appendix A shows that other countries in the region, such as Cambodia and Vietnam, may also not have achieved a healthy balance among universities, colleges, and non-degree-granting skill providers, judging from the types of HEIs and workers' gaps in information technology, English, or even work attitude skills, indicating that this poor mix may be contributing to the skill shortages prevalent in the region (though China, with its large number of "tier III" institutions, appears better positioned to deliver these types of skills).

13. The ISCED 6 programs are designed to prepare graduates for faculty and research posts and are the second stage of tertiary education (equivalent to a doctoral degree).
14. According to United Nations Educational, Scientific and Cultural Organization (UNESCO) Institute data.
15. Mok 2010.
16. These studies are commonly used to elicit information from recent graduates—about three to six months after convocation—regarding field of study, employment, and job-search methods and, if working, information about the employer, starting pay, and relevance of training received to the job. These studies can provide useful information to institutions and policy makers on the relevance of different academic programs to the job market, as well as on skills most needed in the workplace, which would allow them to make adjustments to curriculum and training programs to make graduates more employable.
17. Only Thailand and Vietnam provide a disaggregation of tertiary education by field of study in their household surveys.
18. Chapman 2010.
19. Underneath these aggregate data is much variation across institutions, academic disciplines, and types of schools, as well as within countries.
20. Chapman (2010) provides support for a positive correlation between teaching and a graduate degree.
21. In the Philippines, the relative lack of qualifications among tertiary faculty results from a combination of several factors, including the fact that lower-level schools were upgraded to HEIs and had the faculty only to instruct at the secondary level; moreover, low compensation to faculty does not make teaching at the tertiary level attractive.
22. Doner, Intarakumnerd, and Ritchie 2010.
23. The survey scale metric was as follows: 0 = unknown, 1 = not important, and 5 = very important.
24. Hill and Tandon 2010; Tan 2010.
25. Wu 2010.
26. Mok 2010; Sohn and Kenney 2007. The Korean government has also encouraged university input into creating and developing regional science parks, though only in recent years (Mok 2010).
27. Mok 2010.
28. Mok 2010; Motohashi 2005.
29. Approximately 150 research universities have been so designated.
30. Only about 10 percent of these patents are directly marketable, however (Wu 2010).
31. Doner, Intarakumnerd, and Ritchie 2010.
32. These were agricultural biotechnology; environmental hazardous waste management; environmental science, technology, and management; energy and environment; chemistry; postharvest technology; and petroleum and petroleum technology (Doner, Intarakumnerd, and Ritchie 2010).
33. Kodama and Suzuki 2007.
34. Hill and Tandon 2010.
35. Doner, Intarakumnerd, and Ritchie 2010.
36. See Brimble and Doner (2007) and Schiller and Brimble (2009) for more on these arguments.
37. Tan 2010.
38. Guan, Yam, and Mok 2005.
39. Wu 2010.
40. The importance of incentives is also evident from Wright and others (2008), who find that faculty in second-tier European universities have limited time and few incentives to conduct applied research and engage in patenting, even if this activity is subsidized. For purposes of recognition and promotion, publication in scientific journals takes precedence.
41. Carney and Zheng (2009) contend that Singapore firms' risk aversion has generated conflicting innovation incentives and ultimately undermined innovative activity. A 2009 study of the Malaysia Innovation Climate Survey by the firm Alpha Catalyst found that Malaysian firms, particularly in manufacturing, were unwilling to invest in new product processes without guaranteed success.
42. Ca 2006.
43. Although an exceptional case, an upper-income country like Korea, where most applied research is still carried out by public or private research institutes or by *chaebol*, which have historically received the state's strong financial support to set up their own in-house research units, also shows this type of disconnect (Mok 2010).
44. HRINC 2010.
45. Tan 2010.
46. Tan 2010.
47. Yilmaz 2009.
48. Yilmaz 2009.
49. Yilmaz 2009.
50. Wu 2010.

51. Wu 2010.
52. Wu 2010.
53. OECD 2008a.
54. OECD 2008a.
55. As a matter of fact, there is even often a separation between teaching and research within universities themselves.
56. World Bank 2010d.
57. World Bank 2009a.
58. These include different types of institutions and courses (such as short and long courses).
59. Indonesia is still at the pilot stage of developing a framework based on the Australian model. The Philippines is relatively more advanced in the design and implementation of a model more focused on addressing the needs of vocational and technical education. Although only in its initial stages of implementation, Thailand's Commission on Higher Education is aiming to institute a national qualification framework over eight subject groups over the next five years.
60. This performance is owing to a large share of TVET tertiary education in Malaysia and distance tertiary education in Thailand.
61. Because these rates involve different cohorts, caution is needed.
62. Hoachlander, Sikora, and Horn 2003.
63. Ingles and others 2002.
64. Fry 2004.
65. Fry 2004.
66. Michaelowa 2007.
67. di Gropello, Kruse, and Tandon 2011.
68. OECD 2007b.
69. di Gropello 2006.
70. In China, participation and survival rates at the primary and secondary levels for ethnic minorities are far lower than for Han Chinese (Ma 2010). In Mongolia, Kazakh children enjoy relatively high rates of access at the primary level but exhibit lower transition rates to the secondary level than the majority population by almost 10 percentage points (World Bank 2010d).
71. According to a recent study, the ethnic minority students demonstrating greater access to higher education most often live in urban areas and in households that are smaller, have a smaller proportion of children, have larger shares of parental education, and have higher levels of income (Linh, Thuy, and Long 2010).
72. World Bank 2010g.
73. In Mongolia, for example, Kazakh students demonstrate lower transition rates to tertiary education, partly because the language of instruction (Mongolian) is introduced in classrooms in Kazakh provinces only at the beginning of the secondary level (World Bank 2010d).
74. Strictly speaking, these are not transition rates, because the tertiary gross enrollment ratio is an average of the different grades, so using the gross enrollment ratio underestimates transition. The trends across groups are likely to be the same, however. Caution is also needed because these indicators are comparing different student cohorts.
75. In Vietnam, for instance, the evidence on determinants of access for rural students is clear. Among regions, young people in South Central Coast are more likely to enroll in tertiary education than those in Red River Delta. By contrast, young people in North East are less likely to go to colleges than those in Red River Delta, and young people living in urban areas are more likely to attend college than those in rural areas. Among the determinants of tertiary education access, both head of household and head of household's spouse's education levels have strong effects: if they have only primary education or no formal schooling, children living in such households are less likely to go to college. Also, those living in households whose heads have high school degrees or tertiary degrees are more likely to go to college and university (Linh, Thuy, and Long 2010).
76. Evidence in Cambodia indicates that those with higher levels of head of household education, in the top three income quintiles, and living in urban areas have far higher educational attainment (Sakellariou 2010a).
77. Linh, Thuy, and Long 2010.
78. Luan 2007.
79. Loyalka 2009.
80. Malaysia is a successful example of affirmative policies in middle-income East Asia, for its Bumiputera ethnic group (Mukherjee 2010).
81. It has eased access to political office for these populations, loosened fertility restrictions, and implemented several affirmative policies.
82. Scholarships and boarding for primary and secondary education have been offered to most students in pastureland and mountainous regions in China since 1995. This policy was in place long before the national scheme of Two Exemptions and One Subsidy, which exempted

minorities from tuition fees and provided a subsidy to minority families whose children are enrolled in primary and secondary education.

83. Information Office of the State Council of the People's Republic of China 2005.

84. Wu 2010.

85. In Korea serious attention to math and science at the secondary level started in 1973 with the so-called movement to scientificize the whole people, performed in conjunction with the government's strong industrial push during the same period. Sorensen (1994) shows that a similar emphasis on math and science soon followed at the tertiary level.

86. Several reports (World Bank 2009b, 2010d) note the lack of links between secondary and tertiary curricula in these two countries. They encourage more direct intervention by tertiary academics in designing secondary curricula and instituting more standardized upper-secondary leaving examinations.

87. OECD 2008b.

88. di Gropello (2006) has shown that educational attainment and rural-urban disparities in East Asia remain hampered by variables such as distance to school, availability of basic services, school fees, cash and noncash transfers, lack of learning materials, and lack of alternative cost-effective delivery methods, such as distance learning.

89. They are weak for ethnic groups particularly.

90. It was done through the creation of a Commission of Higher Education within the Ministry of Education (Fielden 2008).

91. Some policies involve actions to support firms and research centers, for instance, which derive from broader economic and political decisions. This is the case of fiscal, financial, and liberalization policies to encourage innovation in firms. Some others involve actions at other education levels. While not directly under the authority of higher education, these policies need to be carefully considered because they affect actors that are part of the higher education system and therefore the outcomes of higher education reforms. The combination of all these policies ultimately decides the success of higher education reform.

92. Rumbley, Pacheco, and Altbach 2008.

Financing Higher Education 4

Solid financing is the backbone of a well-functioning higher education system, but the systems in East Asia's low- and middle-income countries are not delivering the skill and research outcomes they need, as seen in the disconnects—often funding related—discussed earlier. In part this is because public financing goes to institutions regardless of whether they are addressing public goods such as research, externalities, or equity concerns. Public funding can then address the disconnects. For instance, it can help tackle the disconnect with early education by supporting student transitions from secondary to tertiary education through scholarships and loans. Or it can tackle the disconnects between universities and firms in research and technology by supporting higher funding for research in universities. The region thus needs to identify priority areas for support and strategies to fund them. Public funding will have a critical role to support research, science, technology, education, and mathematics (STEM) fields, and equity measures in lower- and middle-income East Asia. But because public resources are scarce, countries will also need to use them more efficiently and effectively and be innovative in mobilizing additional resources. This chapter has three parts.

It starts with a broad review of financing needs, continues with a review of funding strategies with emphasis on the role and efficiency of public financing and strategies to mobilize additional resources, and concludes with a brief summary of policy options.

Financing needs

Many of the outcome gaps and related disconnects and constraints are related to funding. This section investigates how costly it would be to achieve better outcomes in a sample of lower- and middle-income East Asian countries and, in light of the high costs, suggests priority areas for funding. Before proceeding, a brief caveat is in order: the aim of this section is to provide a broad order-of-magnitude estimate of financing needs if countries were to ramp up investments in quality and quantity, without regard to current budget constraints. The estimates are not public investments but should be thought of as overall financing needs that could be covered by myriad sources (public, private, philanthropic). This section highlights the trade-offs between quality and quantity that countries will face when financing their systems. Pursuing both quality and quantity in equal measure would be very costly without greater efficiency of expenditures, a strong sense of priorities, and private finance leveraging.

Simulation analysis

A demographic-based model, in which coverage targets and quality-improvement policies are independent variables, can estimate education expenditures in light of achieving these targets. In performing these simulations, this chapter has adapted the United Nations Educational, Scientific and Cultural Organization's Education Policy and Strategy Simulation Model to estimate financing needs for four regional countries. (Details of the architecture of the model are in appendix M.)

This chapter presents the model's results for two scenarios: (a) expanding coverage and improving quality (illustrative for countries with lower tertiary gross enrollment ratios, or GERs, using Indonesia and Vietnam) and (b) maintaining coverage and improving quality (illustrative for countries with higher tertiary GERs, using the Philippines and Mongolia).

All scenarios have ambitious targets and interventions to provide an upper financing bound, though student-teacher ratios and student-classroom ratios were maintained, saving on costs.

Expanding coverage and improving quality: Indonesia and Vietnam
Financing simulations for Indonesia show that a steep ramp-up of tertiary investment will be required to expand coverage and improve quality. Interventions to increase faculty qualifications, salary and administrative costs, and faculty training costs—as well as costs for central administration, curriculum development, and monitoring and evaluation—all imply larger financing gaps over current public expenditure.

Recurrent expenditures make up more than 95 percent of the projected quality improvement interventions. They rise over time from nearly US$2,000 per student per year to nearly US$8,000 over the decade. While the majority of these recurrent costs

finance salaries, improving faculty qualifications through fellowships also constitutes a robust share of recurrent expenditure at nearly 10 percent.

The financing gaps that these projections imply for Indonesia over current expenditures are large. Indeed, Indonesia will need to increase expenditure per student dramatically over the near term, since in 2008 it was spending only about 13 percent of gross domestic product (GDP) per capita per student (in public money). If public expenditures are maintained, to institute these interventions the financing gap will grow from about 150 percent of GDP per capita to more than 500 percent by 2019 (table 4.1).

To widen access and raise quality, Vietnam also will have to mobilize significant additional resources, mainly on increased recurrent expenditures (about four-fifths on salaries, followed by training, upgrading faculty qualifications, and administration). Per student expenditure will need to increase from US$1,500 to about US$4,000 over the next decade.

If 2007 public expenditure levels are maintained, these projections imply a large financing gap. Tertiary expenditure per student, measured as a percentage of GDP per capita, will likely need to increase by three to four times its current levels by 2015, and by several orders of magnitude thereafter (table 4.2).

Maintaining coverage and improving quality: The Philippines and Mongolia
The financing simulation for the Philippines similarly projects large and increasing recurrent expenditures. The model projects that expenditures need to grow from nearly US$6,000 per student per year to about US$10,000. More than 95 percent of these expenditures are recurrent, and of those recurrent expenditures, salaries constitute by far the largest share (over 88 percent of recurrent expenditure), followed by administrative costs and costs for faculty qualification upgrading (both estimated at about 5 percent of recurrent expenditure). As with Indonesia and Vietnam, these figures represent expenditures several orders of

magnitude above what the Philippines currently spends. If 2007 per student expenditure levels are maintained as a share of GDP per capita, the financing gap between needs and budgetary outlays is projected to reach about 300 percent of GDP per capita over the coming decade (table 4.3).

Mongolia's smaller volume of tertiary enrollments and higher student-teacher ratios place recurrent expenditure projections slightly lower than those for the Philippines. In later years, the simulation projects recurrent expenditures per student to rise to more than US$7,000 per year, while capital expenditures remain low. Recurrent expenditures rise abruptly as more faculty complete fellowships and training. Overall, these figures imply a financing gap of 335 percent of GDP per capita by 2018 (table 4.4).

Summary

While these estimates are several orders of magnitude above what Indonesia, Mongolia, the Philippines, Vietnam, and most other countries in the region are now spending on tertiary education, they should be put in context. The estimates are broadly in line with what neighboring countries and other middle-income countries are spending on higher education. Per student tertiary spending is more than US$12,000 in Japan, nearly US$10,000 in Brazil, and nearly US$7,000 in Chile.[1] The United States spends US$24,370 per tertiary student per year, and the Organisation for Economic Co-operation and Development (OECD) average is US$11,512.[2]

Funding priorities

Attaining these spending targets appears very challenging in the short to medium term for all countries and should not be the cost norm for higher education in lower- and middle-income East Asia. This suggests the need for greater selectivity in the targets and in the activities to finance.

In line with the analysis of chapter 2, it is clear that not all countries need broad

TABLE 4.1   Gap between projected per-student expenditure needed and current levels, Indonesia
percentage of GDP per capita

Year	2008 tertiary expenditure	Projected tertiary expenditure needed	Gap between projected levels needed and 2009 levels
2011	13.3	156.9	143.6
2013	13.3	222.1	208.9
2015	13.3	325.9	314.6
2017	13.3	778.3	765.0
2019	13.3	579.8	518.1

Source: Authors' calculations based on model presented in appendix M.

TABLE 4.2   Gap between projected per-student expenditure needed and current levels, Vietnam
percentage of GDP per capita

Year	2007 tertiary expenditure	Projected tertiary expenditure needed	Gap between projected levels needed and 2009 levels
2011	61.7	151.8	90.1
2013	61.7	186.9	125.2
2015	61.7	236.3	174.6
2017	61.7	321.2	259.5
2019	61.7	579.8	518.1

Source: Authors' calculations based on model presented in appendix M.

TABLE 4.3   Gap between projected per-student expenditure needed and current levels, the Philippines
percentage of GDP per capita

Year	2007 tertiary expenditure	Projected tertiary expenditure needed	Gap between projected levels needed and 2009 levels
2011	11.6	303.1	291.5
2013	11.6	359.6	125.2
2015	11.6	430.7	174.6
2017	11.6	536.4	259.5
2018	11.6	633.6	341.1

Source: Authors' calculations based on model presented in appendix M.

coverage increases in the short to medium term, notably Indonesia and the Philippines. Increasing coverage is costly, raising quantity-quality trade-offs. It may also be difficult to reduce student-faculty ratios across the board, implying that the higher differentiation of the

TABLE 4.4 Gap between projected per-student expenditure needed and current levels, Mongolia
percentage of GDP per capita

Year	2007 tertiary expenditure	Projected tertiary expenditure needed	Gap between projected levels needed and 2009 levels
2011	17.1	117.5	100.4
2013	17.1	151.0	133.9
2015	17.1	199.3	182.2
2017	17.1	280.2	263.1
2018	17.1	352.6	335.5

Source: Authors' calculations based on model presented in appendix M.

higher education system in colleges and other short-term institutions required by the labor market of some countries may be achievable only gradually. And increasing faculty qualifications may be possible only selectively, so only a few universities will probably ever develop credible research capacity (given the high requirements for faculty qualifications). Realistic targets will also vary by income-technology cluster.

In line with being more selective in the targets is setting priorities for what higher education activities countries should spend on. Chapter 3 suggested that activities with high externalities or market failures are probably underfunded in the region and thus need to be prioritized. This is further supported in this chapter through an analysis of funding for research, cost constraints, and equity-enhancing interventions in the region. No separate analysis is made for investment in STEM fields, but the low enrollment shares in several countries of the lower and middle technology clusters suggest that this is also an area with high positive externalities (for its links with innovation) that is being underfunded. While the focus here is on underfunded activities, spending also needs to continue or even be boosted on gradually increasing coverage in some countries, maintaining support to social science fields, and allowing for greater curriculum and degree diversification when needed.

Funding for research
The tight relationship between journals and tertiary research spending shows the benefits

of research in higher education (acknowledging that journals are not the best metric to capture the desirable effects of research) and that obtaining results has a cost (figure 4.1). Chapter 1 showed that there is at least potential and need for better supporting small and medium enterprises in technological development in lower-income countries, thus justifying higher focus on research. Without investment in tertiary research, disconnects between research and teaching in higher education will continue.

Lower- and middle-income East Asia spend much less than upper-income East Asia in university research (figure 4.2). Overall, the low research spending of most lower- and middle-income East Asian countries points to a lack of priorities for research in higher education spending, low overall spending on research and development (science and technology), and low allocations of this spending for higher education. They also spend less than other lower- and middle-income countries outside the region.

Cost constraints for poor and disadvantaged groups and country responses
With large education needs and little leeway in public funding, most countries in the region are starting to rely more on student fees to finance their institutions.[3] Although positive from the perspective of state budgeting, using this source brings inclusiveness challenges.

This section documents the fee structures and related cost constraints that students in the region face—as well as the country financing policies to address these constraints. The aim is to show that countries are still underspending on inclusiveness-enhancing measures and to set the context for further discussion of what approaches could tackle inclusiveness.

Rich and poor countries operate with limited fiscal means and less than optimal institutional capacity, using a familiar mix of funding sources to finance higher education: tuition fees, government subsidies, and income from other sources. Tuition fees are equivalent to about a third or half of public university revenue in four of the five countries, but only around a tenth in the Philippines (table 4.5).

The costs of tertiary education (tuition fees and associated living costs) affect how much a cash constraint can discourage otherwise talented students from enrolling and completing higher education. But financial aid can reduce that constraint.

The variables influencing the decision to pursue a tertiary education can be classified as monetary and nonmonetary, with three types of monetary barriers (box 4.1). While these barriers will be affected by many variables, financial aid—in the form of assistance programs, scholarships, or loans—could address at least some of these constraints. It is the "net" costs (the costs less the financial aid) that really matter.

Several East Asian countries have financial aid policies to help students overcome the cost constraint. It is important to assess the full extent of the constraint. But the data do not allow a calculation of "net costs" because few household surveys include information on, say, scholarships. Secondary quantitative information can help in assessing the likely true costs.

Mongolia and Vietnam have used a fairly effective combination of instruments to increase access among the poor, and Thailand has been a pioneer in the use of student loans. But all lower- and middle-income countries in the region could implement more and better financial aid policies. Beginning with a review of countries that have a combination of instruments to tackle inclusiveness (Vietnam, Mongolia, China), this section then reviews countries that have more specific instruments (Indonesia, Cambodia, Thailand, Malaysia).

Vietnam. In 2009, tertiary education costs (tuition fees, extra-class fees, living and accommodation costs) based on fees were estimated at 70 percent of household income for the poorest quintile, and 30 percent for the richest quintile (table 4.6).[4]

FIGURE 4.1   Research and development spending in tertiary education as a share of GDP and journals, latest available year

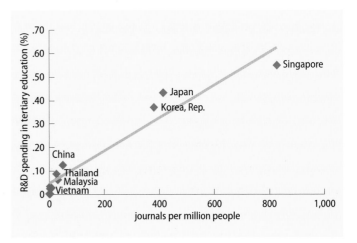

Sources: EdStats database; UIS (UNESCO Institute for Statistics) Data Centre.

FIGURE 4.2   Research and development spending in tertiary education as a share of GDP, latest available year

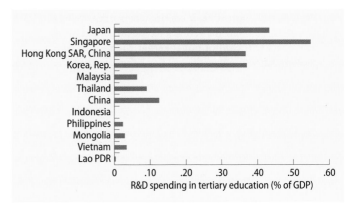

Source: UIS Data Centre.

TABLE 4.5   Snapshot of public university revenue breakdown by proportion of funding source, selected economies
percent

Economy	Government subsidies	Tuition fees	Other income
China (2004)	47	30	23
Indonesia (2009)	56	38	6
Mongolia (2008)[a]	35	54	11
Philippines (2006)	73	11	16
Vietnam	50	45	5

Sources: China: OECD 2009a; Indonesia: World Bank 2010c (average of 82 universities); Mongolia: World Bank 2010d; Philippines: Orbeta 2008; Vietnam: World Bank 2010f.
a. The government subsidy for Mongolia comprises funds from the state budget and the State Training Fund.

BOX 4.1   Determinants of higher education access

Both the academic literature and available data (mainly household surveys) show that the decision to attend tertiary education has monetary and non-monetary variables.

Monetary variables

Family income determines whether the student can afford the costs of the college. There are three monetary barriers to entry into tertiary education: the cost-benefit barrier, the cash-constraint barrier, and the debt-aversion barrier.

Cost-benefit barrier: A certain segment of the population (usually, lower-income or minority groups), when deciding on whether to attend university or not, performs a cost-benefit analysis of the costs of and expected returns to higher education. The barrier arises when the group decides that the cost of attending university is greater than its expected return to the education investment.

Cash-constraint barrier: Also known as the "liquidity" constraint, it occurs when students who have decided that the returns to education outweigh the costs still cannot put together the resources to obtain entry to universities. They believe in the value of higher education but simply cannot afford to attend university even after pooling internal (family funds, savings, and wages) and external (grants and loans) funds. Financial aid, particularly the amount of aid, will increase liquidity.

Debt-aversion barrier: Described by the economist Richard Thaler as an "internalized liquidity constraint," debt aversion arises when an individual does not want to borrow even if he or she believes that the benefits of higher education outweigh the costs. Debt aversion occurs when this individual refuses to use the funds at his or her disposal because part of the funds might be loans, which at some point will have to be repaid.

Nonmonetary variables

Parental education, race and ethnicity, gender, and geographical location—all play a role in the college decision-making process. So does prior academic achievement, measured by the rigor of secondary courses and the quality of that education.

Sources: Johnstone 2004; Usher 2005.

TABLE 4.6   **Vietnam: Tertiary education costs per month, 2009**

Income quintile	Average monthly costs (US$)	Average monthly income (US$)	Higher education costs (% of income)
Poorest	67	95	70.1
Near poorest	83	152	54.2
Middle	95	212	44.8
Near richest	108	264	41.1
Richest	126	461	29.6

Source: Linh, Thuy, and Long 2010.

To address these constraints, Vietnam has a comprehensive package of strategies and instruments, including the expansion of the student loan scheme and the application of several other aid mechanisms.[5] It has encouraged fee deductions and exemptions for the poor, revamped its aid scheme, and fine-tuned its loan program. Cost-recovery mechanisms rapidly increased the share of tuition fees in the total revenue of higher education institutions. While this strategy has helped Vietnam expand the subsector rapidly without creating a heavy burden on the state budget, it has also jeopardized the capacity of some students and their families to pay. This risk has been mitigated to an extent: access to higher education by income quintile has become more equitable over time, as the gap between the number enrolled from the poorest quintile and the number enrolled from the top income quintile has significantly declined, particularly in comparison to its middle-income neighbors (figure 4.3). This is not the result only of policies for higher education. Vietnam has also been active in supporting more equitable access to higher-quality primary and secondary education, providing a larger potential pool for tertiary education.[6] But tertiary education policies have complemented these efforts by supporting the higher transition of secondary graduates to tertiary education.

Since 1998 Vietnam has instituted policies to encourage fee deductions and exemptions, benefiting poor and ethnic minority students. In 2006 about 22 percent of disadvantaged university students were benefiting from significant fee deductions of up to 50 percent of tuition.[7]

Vietnam has also had student aid schemes since the mid-1990s. Since 2006 students from ethnic minorities have received lump-sum assistance of about D470,000 (US$25) a month—about a third of their overall monthly higher education costs. Recent evidence from household surveys confirms that the program is well targeted, with benefits accruing largely to poor and ethnic minority groups.[8] Since 2007 scholarships for poor students were also revised to cover the full tuition fees.

In addition to scholarships, Vietnam reformed its student loan scheme in 2006, increasing the amount of the loan by more than 250 percent (from D300,000 per month to D800,000 per month, or US$15 to US$41 per month) and lengthening the repayment period. The scheme now supports 29 percent of students enrolled in 103 universities.

Despite these positive steps, challenges remain, mainly to support greater equity in the access and completion of ethnic minority groups. Persistent inequity in completion rates indicates that the mechanisms are better at supporting initial enrollment than retention, which may require an examination of the way these mechanisms support students while enrolled. Tying some of these

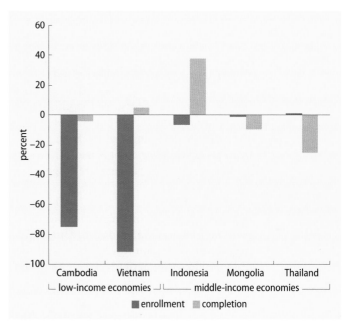

FIGURE 4.3   Change in ratio of tertiary enrollments and completions for the poorest and richest quintiles, selected East Asian economies

Source: Sakellariou 2010a.
Note: Cambodia data are from 2009 and 1999; Indonesia data are from 2009 and 1998; Vietnam data are from 2008 and 1998; Mongolia data are from 2007 and 1998; Thailand data are from 2006 and 1996. Vietnam data include junior colleges and Indonesia data include tertiary diplomas.

aid instruments to performance (or at least completion) could also be worth exploring, as would focusing more on pretertiary education and increasing the scholarship amount.

Mongolia. Mongolian bachelor's degree students pay an average of US$270 per academic year, roughly 16 percent of gross national income per capita, higher than in most OECD countries, on par with the Republic of Korea, and lower than in Chile. The fees in private tertiary institutions are similar. When living expenses are included, an average student has to spend nearly US$400 a year.[9]

Like Vietnam, Mongolia has also relied on a fairly effective mix of loans and scholarships to improve access to higher education. The State Training Fund provides about 28 percent of funding to tertiary education through grants and loans, with a need-based component.[10] On average, a recipient student would receive 80 percent of tuition. These instruments help offset the cost of education for about 40 percent of students in the subsector, which may explain the higher coverage and relatively lower inequity in Mongolia. While a significant fraction of the grants are need-based, they could be better targeted because of legislation that expanded eligibility to the children of civil servants. Today, about 40 percent of recipients are the children of civil servants (table 4.7), though this proportion has been declining slightly. If loan recipients are employed for eight consecutive years, five in a rural area, the loans are forgiven.

China. Tuition fees in 2004 were prominent sources of financing and in the absence of financial aid could present a large cash-constraint barrier to enrollment and completion, particularly for the poorest students. In Beijing average university tuition fees per year range from US$615 to US$806.[11] Tuition fees are set differently for different courses and programs. The tuition for science and engineering ranges from US$674 to US$806 in these universities, and for languages and medicine,

between US$732 and US$879. In addition to these fees, associated living costs are also high in China.

A combination of monetary instruments eases the barriers for the disadvantaged, but the outcomes have been mixed.[12] The government has instituted both need-based and merit-based scholarship programs to cover tuition and living expenses. A national school-based loan program offers loans through commercial banks, to be repaid within six years of graduation. And loans by the National Development Bank must be repaid within 10 years after graduation.

Universities have the autonomy to administer financial aid—based on need or merit. But researchers have noted shortcomings. Need-based aid, administered by the state and by universities, is granted only to students majoring in the sciences or attending a first- or second-tier university. And the average scholarship amount, only about 15 percent of the average tuition fee, is too small to really make a difference (table 4.8). The student loan program, not income contingent, covers only a small proportion of students. A short repayment period is also taxing for

TABLE 4.7   Mongolia: State Training Fund recipients, by program area

Grants	2003		2004		2005	
	Number	Percentage	Number	Percentage	Number	Percentage
Need-based grants	8,119	23.3	13,294	33.5	13,831	33.5
Disadvantaged group grants	2,216	6.4	2,454	6.2	2,149	5.2
Merit-based grants	153	0.4	149	0.3	126	0.3
Public employee family grants	15,915	45.7	16,335	41.2	16,428	39.8
Loans	8,409	24.2	7,390	18.6	8,696	21
Total	34,812	100	39,622	100	41,230	100

Source: World Bank 2010d.

TABLE 4.8   China: Net payment in regular universities, 2008

Average tuition (US$)	Living cost (US$)	Scholarship (US$)	Loan (US$)	Work study (US$)	Net payment (US$)	Net payment (% of gross family income)
895	141	138	62	37	799	30

Source: Min et al. 2009 in Ma 2010.

many recipients. Overall, even after scholarships and loans, students still need to spend on average about 30 percent of their gross family income on higher education (fees and living costs), a ratio that is certainly higher for lower-income families.

Other lower- and middle-income countries in the region have had a more piecemeal approach to tackling inclusiveness issues. Indonesia and Cambodia have relied mostly on scholarships, and Thailand and Malaysia mostly on loans, with mixed effects.[13]

Indonesia. Private spending, primarily for tuition fees and levies, constitutes the bulk of financing for higher education.[14] In 2009 the average spending per student per year was about US$2,200 in public institutions (tuition fees, student fees, and living expenses) and about US$1,200 in private institutions. Supporting one tertiary education student can cost up to a third of yearly income (figure 4.4), a share likely to be much higher for the poorest quintile, and even higher if the student is in a public institution.

To spur demand among the poor, the government introduced a full and partial scholarship scheme, but the scheme is targeted to students already enrolled in tertiary education, ignoring high school leavers who do not have the economic means to enroll. This may explain why enrollments in tertiary education remain very inequitably distributed in the country. Moreover, financial aid awarded to students enrolled in tertiary education covers only 3 percent of the cost,[15] even though, according to national law, students are required to cover only up to 33 percent of tertiary educational costs. This may explain why Indonesia is the only country where completion gaps between the poorest and wealthiest population quintiles have been increasing (figure 4.4). While 20 percent of students from the poorest quintile are eligible for scholarships, these groups rarely receive scholarships because of narrow eligibility criteria (scholarships are also merit based). Overall, scholarships cover only 5.6 percent of the student population.[16]

FIGURE 4.4   Indonesia: Tertiary education expenditure as a percentage of annual household income

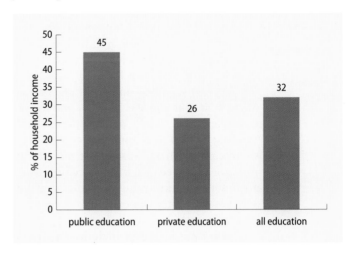

Source: World Bank 2010c.

Cambodia. Scholarships are the primary means of helping students overcome cost constraints. In 2000 a circular from the prime minister was issued to regulate the proportion of fee-paying students in public higher education institutions and stated that a third of students enrolled in public higher education institutions could be fee paying, with the remaining two-thirds on scholarship.[17] Scholarship students do not pay tuition fees, but the share of scholarships is modest and declining: 15.3 percent of students held scholarships in 2004–05 and 12.3 percent in 2007–08.

Over the past few years, Cambodia's Department of Higher Education has developed the selection processes to use the scholarship scheme to promote equitable access to higher education, improving the equity of access for the poorest (see figure 4.3). But much more remains to be done. Of the scholarships awarded, 60 percent are based on merit and 40 percent go to priority candidates. Of the priority scholarships, females receive 15 percent, the poor 15 percent, and those from rural areas 10 percent. So the proportion of need-based scholarships remains low. Moreover, the financial support has been significantly less than the cost of study and living (in effect, this is merely a tuition-free mechanism).

Thailand. The poorest household spends on average US$112 per month in higher education, about one-eighth of the spending of the richest household.[18] But for the poorest families, private spending on education is about 60 percent of their total income, and for the wealthiest, less than 1 percent (figure 4.5). Sending a child to school thus represents a significant financial burden for poor families, not only because of high costs associated with attending higher education but also because of the opportunity costs of forgone earnings.

These figures do not include loans, and Thailand has increased access to higher education through student loan programs.[19] Thailand has also instituted a grant and scholarship scheme to increase tertiary access among the poor, such as the One District Scholarship and scholarships for low-income students, but coverage has remained very limited. It is Thailand's student loan program for needy students that

has increased participation. To help lower-income students, government loans have to be repaid over 15 years at a 1 percent interest rate. To faciliate administration, the loans can be provided directly by universities (box 4.2).

Results have been encouraging: there is evidence of significant effects on the participation of the poorest to higher education. These results could be improved with better targeting. There is also evidence suggesting that universities have extended loans to underqualified applicants to boost enrollment.[20] The government is now attempting again to introduce an income-contingent loan system.

Malaysia. Tuition fees tend to be lower than in other countries, but total living costs are higher. Loans are the primary form of financial aid for higher education, but the mechanism does not work equally well across fields and could be better targeted. A study to assess the effects of socioeconomic status on university education and social and economic mobility at the University of

FIGURE 4.5   Thailand: Private expenditure in higher education, by income quintile

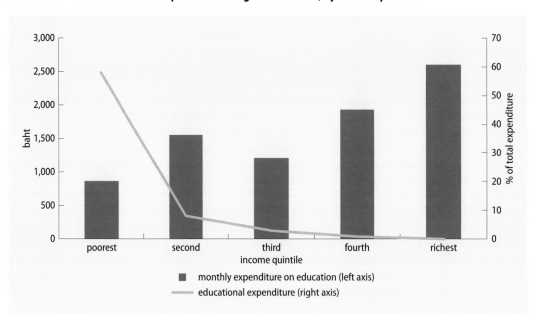

Source: Socio-Economic Survey 2006, as cited in World Bank 2009a.

BOX 4.2   Evaluating the Student Loan Fund in Thailand

The Student Loan Fund, instituted by the Thai government in 1996, was to increase access for low-income upper-secondary, vocational, and undergraduate students. The loans cover tuition fees, education-related costs, and living expenses. Only students from households earning less than US$4,300 a year are eligible for the need-based fund. Over the first decade of implementation, US$5.7 billion was disbursed to more than 2.6 million students.

A recent evaluation examined the fund's targeting and whether it increased access for low-income students. Upper-secondary students were better targeted than undergraduate students. Only 7 percent of student loan recipients in upper secondary were nonpoor, compared with 19 percent of undergraduate student loan recipients. The success in targeting upper-secondary students can be attributed partly to the closer relationships schools have with students and their families.

There were significant effects on the decision to participate in higher education for those students whose family income was close to the poverty line,[a] but few effects on students with somewhat higher income, implying that the income limit for the loan was set too high.

Source: Tangkitvanich and Manasboonphempool 2010.
a. The poverty line is approximately US$888 (B28,650) per year.

Malaya concluded that lower-income students were bound for certain disciplines, whereas upper-income students dominated fields with traditionally higher returns.[21]

While benefiting both public and private sector institutions, a positive feature rather unusual for the region, Malaysia's student loan program could also be better targeted. The National Higher Education Fund Act 1997 provides for student loans to faciliate access to public and private higher education: full loans to students with family incomes below US$900, partial loans to cover tuition fees and part of living expenses to students with family incomes between US$1,001 and US$1,380, and partial loans to cover tuition fees for students with family income greater than US$1,381.[22] Together with affirmative action policies pursued since 1971, these loans were instrumental in increasing Bumiputera enrollment in universities (reaching 60 percent of overall enrollment in 2006). But while the coverage of the scheme and the volume of loans dispensed have increased, it is not means tested, implying that there could be significant leakages to the nonpoor. Very few loan recipients are not Bumiputera.[23]

Summary. First, countries should move to need-based scholarships, because merit-based ones do not promote inclusiveness. Second, comprehensive packages—including fee deductions for disadvantaged groups, need-based scholarships, and student loans—have been more effective in addressing inclusiveness than more piecemeal approaches. Third, the effectiveness of specific instruments (separate or in a wider package) has varied significantly across countries depending on design and implementation. Scholarships and loans have been more effective when covering a significant proportion of tuition costs and at least some living costs. Broad-based application across universities and fields has worked better than more selective application, when carefully targeted to disadvantaged groups.

How to fund priority activities

How should underfunded activities be financed? There is a clear case for public financing to support research and STEM capacity—and to address inclusiveness. Research and STEM are two areas with high positive externalities. While the initial costs can be high, the social benefits are even higher, particularly in relation to their link with innovation. Private financing tends to underfund these activities. For inclusiveness the case is based on the failures in capital markets: cost constraints are binding. So far, most scholarships have indeed been financed with public money in the region.

Countries thus need to assess their ability to allocate more public spending to higher education and, even more important, to finance key activities. This will help higher education institutions address skill and research disconnects—providing students with better skills and increasing the talent pool entering tertiary education, and building the capacity of institutions for research.

The scarcity of public resources requires better targeted resources and performance-based allocations. More efficient financing will also improve the match between skill provision and needs (first disconnect) and research provision and firm needs (second disconnect) by tying funds to relevant skills and research.

To maximize the leverage of public funds, it will be important to attract more private funds and correct market failures by providing student loans. Within a coherent financing framework, private funding would not only complement public funding in financing some of the above activities but also focus on system expansion and diversification (targeting some other country priorities, such as increasing enrollment or service-related disciplines) through public and private delivery.

Increasing and prioritizing public spending

Public spending ratios vary substantially in East Asia and are not necessarily lower than in high-income East Asia (figure 4.6). Tertiary spending in relation to GDP is lowest in the Lao People's Democratic Republic, Cambodia, and the Philippines. Ratios are higher in Vietnam, Indonesia, and particularly Malaysia. Spending ratios also differ substantially across high-income East Asia, with Hong Kong SAR, China, and Singapore

spending significantly more than Japan and Korea.

These trends are the result of how countries deal with funding trade-offs and tight budgets for the allocation of public funding across levels of education. In a few high-income economies in the region, Japan and Korea, for example, the long-standing policy has been to prioritize public funds for earlier levels of education, a policy stance that has had important implications for the strategies to expand and improve higher education over the years. Japan and Korea have relied heavily on private funding (both through public and private delivery). Middle- and lower-income countries in the region have not mobilized similar absolute levels of private sector finance for their systems. While they should strive to do more, public funding will remain critical.

Comparing public expenditure per tertiary pupil as a share of GDP per capita with countries outside East Asia, spending is generally on the low side in East Asia's middle-income countries even compared with other middle-income countries in other regions: Brazil, India, and Mexico all outspend them, apart from Malaysia (figure 4.7).

In a troubling trend, expenditure measured this way has also tended to decrease across the region, especially in Cambodia and Lao PDR, where absolute per pupil tertiary expenditure was already low (figure 4.8). Middle-income countries have also reduced such spending but, except for Malaysia, by much smaller margins.

These data suggest that several countries may have scope for further public spending in tertiary education, but do they have the potential? A look at the ratios of tertiary spending to total education spending and of total education spending to GDP casts light on this issue. According to these two indicators, Mongolia and Thailand are the countries with most potential.

Hong Kong SAR, China; Singapore; and Malaysia spend the most on tertiary education as a share of total education, at around 30 percent (figure 4.9). Japan and Korea allocate less than 20 percent of their public education spending to tertiary education, as do the Philippines, Thailand, Mongolia, Lao PDR, and Cambodia. A comparison with lower- and middle-income countries outside the region can suggest some room for reallocation within education budgets.

But the real room for intrasectoral reallocation in favor of tertiary education is probably not very large, given the many competing needs in other parts of the education system[24] and the fairly low overall education spending as a share of GDP in several countries (figure 4.10). This is particularly so for Lao PDR, Cambodia, and the Philippines. Thailand and Mongolia may have more leeway. (Tertiary education shares have also been growing in most countries since the beginning of the decade, thus providing less scope for reallocation.)

To increase spending in tertiary education, Lao PDR, Cambodia, and the Philippines should consider increasing their education spending in relation to GDP. High tax shares to GDP would suggest more potential for public spending increases.

Given the many competing needs, prioritizing public spending and improving efficiency in the allocation and use of public funding will be critical. In cases such as Vietnam, Indonesia, and Malaysia, which already spend above the average in tertiary education, a first imperative will be to ensure higher public spending shares for research, STEM, and scholarships. Further evidence comes from comparing overall public tertiary spending in relation to GDP with tertiary research spending in relation to GDP (figure 4.11) across East Asian economies. While these two indicators are not strictly comparable (research and development funds include both public and private funds), they offer insights into the different priority given to research within public budgets for higher education. It is definitely much lower in lower- and middle-income economies than in upper-income ones. In the middle technology cluster, China leads.

Lower- and middle-income East Asia need to increase public spending for research in tertiary education. There is no ideal benchmark,

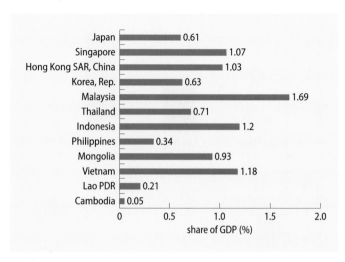

FIGURE 4.6   Public tertiary expenditure as a share of GDP, latest available year

Country	share of GDP (%)
Japan	0.61
Singapore	1.07
Hong Kong SAR, China	1.03
Korea, Rep.	0.63
Malaysia	1.69
Thailand	0.71
Indonesia	1.2
Philippines	0.34
Mongolia	0.93
Vietnam	1.18
Lao PDR	0.21
Cambodia	0.05

Source: UIS Data Centre.

and lower-income and lower technology cluster countries clearly do not have the same room or even scope for increases in research as other countries. But further effort is needed. And in a broader sense, funding for research can also support the development of future researchers for both universities and the private sector. Scholarships for talented students in Thailand illustrate this option well (box 4.3).

Increasing efficiency of public spending

Prioritizing public spending will be neither successful nor sufficient without efficiency improvements.

Efficiency gaps
Most countries could be more efficient in the way they use and allocate public resources—as is also evident from the large spending gaps. For example, a very simple comparison of higher education outcomes— the STEM share and the number of journal articles—and spending indicators[25] suggests that Cambodia, Malaysia, the Philippines, and Vietnam are less efficient than Korea in supplying STEM, and that Malaysia and Thailand are less efficient in translating

FIGURE 4.7   **Public expenditure per tertiary pupil as a share of GDP per capita, 2006–07**

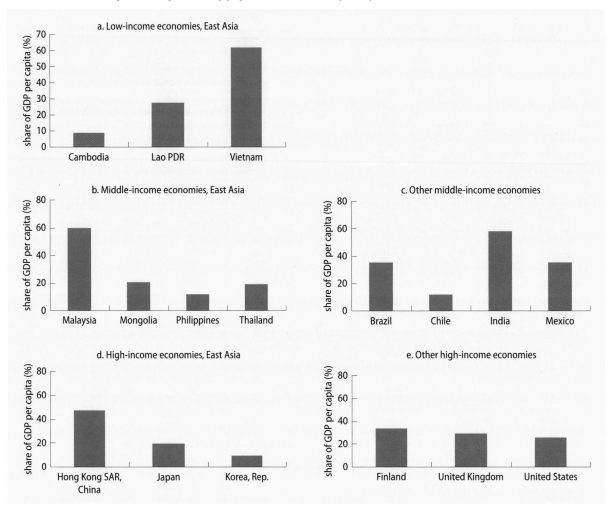

Source: UIS Data Centre.
Note: Although some countries have 2008 data, the 2006–07 range was maintained for comparability across countries.

funds into journal articles than Japan and Korea (figures 4.12 and 4.13).

Some of these differences may simply be caused by different levels of private resources invested into the system, either through fees in public institutions or private delivery. And they suggest different uses of funds as much as inefficient use and allocation of these funds (for instance, a limited priority on STEM spending). But there is no obvious relation between private fees in public institutions and results, and private delivery tends to be more focused on teaching than research and

within teaching on non-STEM fields. Malaysia's high spending indicators in relation to the outcomes suggest some inefficiency.

Beyond the poor targeting of their scholarships, most countries spread their public resources for teaching and research too thinly among institutions, and few have competitive (or other performance-driven) funding to trigger systemic change.

Governments across the world are turning to allocating resources to develop premier research (and teaching) universities. This move toward directing substantial resources to a few premier institutions is partly a response to the large resources universities need to undertake high-level research (and teaching), which makes selectivity important. Harvard University had an endowment of US$37 billion, and annual spending of US$3.2 billion, and per student spending of US$105,041 before the crisis. Other top universities have expenditures in similar orders of magnitude.

Dedicating substantial resources to a few premier institutions that attain international standards, in teaching or research, can be one way to reverse a trend of low-cost and low-quality education. Pursuing this path, governments need to identify programs or departments (not necessarily an entire institution) that have good potential.

Most high-income (and a few middle-income) East Asian economies have started moving this way. Through the World Premier International Research Center Initiative, Japan intends to make Tokyo, Tohoku, Kyoto, and Osaka universities, as well as the National Institute for Material Sciences, a public research institute, its core research bodies.[26] Korea is raising the caliber of its universities through the Brain Korea 21 Project.[27] The government in Hong Kong SAR, China, has set up five research centers under the Hong Kong SAR, China, Research and Development Centers Program to lead and focus research on 13 priority sectors.[28] In Taiwan, China, the authorities have allocated a budget of NT$65 billion for the Developing Top Grade Universities and Research Centers to be spent between 2008 and 2015.

Some middle-income countries also have started to move in this direction. Malaysia identified four universities as its main research universities. China identified 100 research universities for increased support (about 6 percent of its universities). With these exceptions, however, most countries in the lower and middle technology cluster are still thinking of roughly equal allocation of resources across institutions. Illustrating a new mindset, the Philippine government will spend US$70 million in 10 years to set up the Engineering Research and Development for

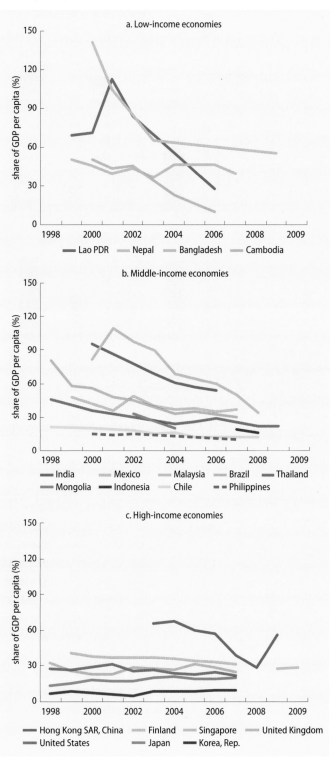

FIGURE 4.8   Public expenditure per tertiary pupil as a share of GDP per capita, 1998–2009

Source: EdStats database.

FIGURE 4.9   **Public tertiary education expenditure as a share of total public education expenditure, 2006–07**

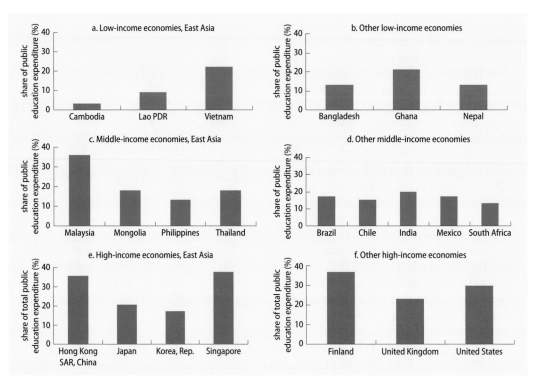

Source: UIS Data Centre.
Note: Although some countries have 2008 data, the 2006–07 range was maintained for comparability across countries.

FIGURE 4.10   **Overall public education expenditure as a share of GDP, latest year**

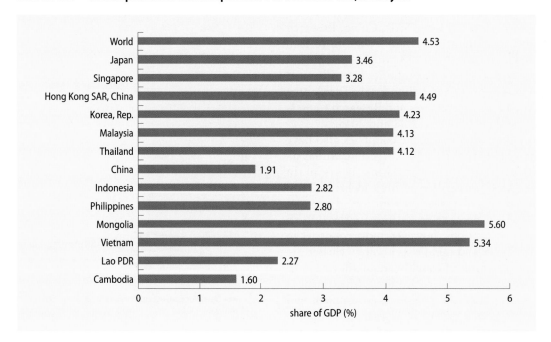

Source: WDI database.

Technology Program, a consortium of eight top engineering universities.[29]

Some gradualism for investing in centers of excellence is warranted. It is important to create an environment that allows excellence to emerge, and once identified, to build on the comparative strengths of various institutions and their academic offerings. This requires setting up a more autonomous and competitive governance framework for all universities (discussed in the next chapters). Also useful is a competitive (or other performance-driven) process to target the resources at the best research institutions. In Japan research funding is allocated through competitive bidding rather than being distributed in predetermined amounts. More generally, performance-based allocations can trigger systemic changes in quality—improving the effectiveness of both teaching and research (even in fields that have less scope to be financed with public funds).

Lower- and middle-income East Asia still have a long way to go to improve allocation mechanisms of public funds to improve skills and research. Most countries, usually in a centralized system, still use historically negotiated budgets (table 4.9), leading to

FIGURE 4.11   Research and development spending and total public spending in tertiary education, latest available year

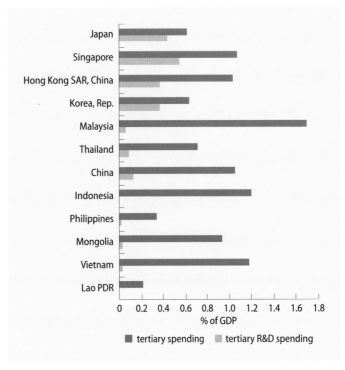

Source: UIS Data Centre.
Note: Data on tertiary spending as a share of GDP for China are estimates.

BOX 4.3   Overseas scholarships for outstanding students from Thailand

The Thai government has various scholarship and loan programs. Some are explicitly targeted at the poor to increase access among disadvantaged groups. Others are merit based and aim to develop the technical skills of the next generation of Thai leaders, both in academia and government. Among the two most prestigious of these types of scholarships are the King Scholarships and the Anandamahidol Scholarships.

King Scholarships. The King Scholarships were established in 1897 by King Rama V and are awarded to outstanding students every year. The scholarship presentation was stopped in 1932 because of political instability but was restored in 1964 by the current king, Rama IX. Several scholarships are given

to secondary school graduates each year to continue undergraduate study in foreign countries. The candidates are selected by academic performance, writing tests, and interviews.

Anandamahidol Scholarships. The Anandamahidol Foundation was established by King Rama IX to provide graduate-level study scholarships for students willing to continue postgraduate studies in high-income countries. The scholarships' main goal is to support students pursuing degrees in one of the eight fields identified as crucial for national development, including science and technology.

Source: World Bank 2009a.

FIGURE 4.12 **Tertiary spending per student as a share of GDP per capita and STEM enrollment share, latest available year**

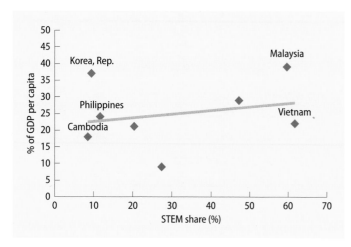

Sources: EdStats database; UIS Data Centre.

FIGURE 4.13 **Tertiary spending per student and journals per million people, latest available year**

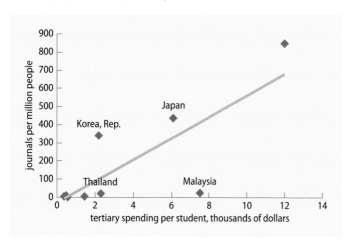

Source: EdStats database; UIS Data Centre.

institutions, countries can foster higher quality and address critical research and skill disconnects.

Competitive funds, by promoting excellence in research and teaching, can support more selective resource allocation. Higher education institutions submit their funding proposals along with their development plans, with key performance indicators.[30] The funds are then used to fund equipment, facility improvement, and staff upgrading and professional development. Part of the appeal of competitive funds is that they can reduce the incentives to use enrollment expansion to sustain financial viability—and they encourage faculty to devote time to teaching and research, improving quality across the system (box 4.4). Student fees can then be used by institutions for supplemental investments. To improve relevance and research capacity, funding could be awarded to the disciplines and courses related to labor market needs.

One of the most effective means to hold institutions accountable is the government's power of the purse. In theory a government could simply remove or reduce funding to institutions that fail to comply with approaches or fall behind on goals. But reducing funding for public universities, particularly original budget allocations, is extremely difficult. One way around this is to have diverse financing mechanisms beyond the base fund, to incentivize institutions' performance. At a minimum a formula funding allocating funds in proportion to the number of students is already a move in the right direction for negotiated budgets. Several mechanisms can enhance performance,[31] beyond the competitive funds reviewed above:

Performance contracts. Governments sign regulatory agreements with institutions to set mutual performance-based objectives.

Performance set-asides. A portion of public funding for universities is set aside to pay, on the basis of various performance measures.

Payment for results. Output or outcome measures are used to determine all or a portion of the funding formula. For example, universities are paid for the number of students that graduate, sometimes at higher

inefficiencies. Only China, Malaysia, and Thailand have moved to formula funding. Indonesia has also been experimenting with competitive funds and performance-based grants. Mongolia and Vietnam started introducing some competitive funding for research.

Moving forward

By being more selective and performance based in resource allocations across

TABLE 4.9 **Block grants in East Asia**

Economy	Historically negotiated budget	Formula funding	Voucher-based allocation	Performance-based contracts
High income				
Japan	○	○	○	●
Singapore	○	●	○	●
Hong Kong SAR, China	○	●	○	○
Korea, Rep.	○	●	○	●
Middle income				
Malaysia	●	●	○	○
Thailand	●	●	○	○
China	●	●	○	○
Indonesia	●	◕a	○	○
Philippines	●	○	○	○
Low income				
Vietnam	●	○	○	○
Lao PDR (National University of Laos)	●	○	○	○
Cambodia	●	○	○	○

Sources: Raza 2010 on the basis of Expert Survey 2010, except Singapore, which was taken from Ministry of Education, Singapore 2005.

Note: ○ = none/not applicable; ◕ = partial.

a. Formula funding incorporating performance indicators piloted in five autonomous universities (and some nonautonomous universities) in Indonesia.

BOX 4.4   Competitive funds as an innovative financing tool

A few countries—including, to a degree, Indonesia, Mongolia, and Vietnam in East Asia—have competitive funding schemes to allocate resources to higher education institutions. Output oriented and targeting a range of sector issues, they can increase cost-effectiveness and enhance educational quality and relevance.

Under most competitive funds, institutions compete for investment on the basis of their own planning and choices. An independent body selects the best projects based on potential, performance, and track record, encouraging a culture of fair competition. Its choices are based on transparency in objectives, eligibility, and other criteria—and usually peer evaluation.

Competitive funds offer several advantages. They provide incentives for institutions to perform. They encourage institutions to clarify their mission and strategy and plan for the medium term. And they can handle complex indicators of impact and success tailored to institutional characteristics and needs.

Competitive funds over the past few years have supported activities ranging from traditional investments to systemic reform. In Bangladesh and Indonesia they have lifted quality by providing grants for equipment, libraries, laboratories, buildings, and university programs.

A critical component of a successful competitive fund is capacity: the government needs to set the rules of eligibility, selection, and implementation, and institutions to supervise projects.

On the downside, these funds offer less predictability than formula funding, but they can stimulate systemic change.

Source: World Bank staff reports.

---

prices for graduates in certain fields of study or with specific skills.

Many countries use payment for results and performance contracts to improve institutional accountability for quality, efficiency, and equity, though they may also use them to penalize the institution for underperforming.

The Indonesian government is using performance-based grants in the form of block grants for autonomous universities (and some nonautonomous universities). This allows flexibility and some accountability. Performance-based grants provide budgetary support, conditional on the universities' meeting certain performance targets at the department and unit level.[32]

In Singapore, to accompany the corporatization of the National University of Singapore and the National Technological University in 2006, the government adopted new ways of holding them accountable. Besides requiring an external quality assurance process, the government mandates policy agreements and performance contracts. Policy agreements allow the Ministry of Education to provide strategic direction to the higher education sector with clear goals for universities to guide them in formulating policy and ensure that they are following the necessary conditions to receive government funding. Performance contracts are established with each university for five years. These set out the goals for teaching, research, service, and organizational development. Linked to each goal are clear targets and performance indicators. The ministry also sets workforce targets linked to public financing.[33]

Korea has also focused more on accountability for public financing. In 1995 all major funding programs were restructured along the lines of performance contracts. The government evaluates the institutions' achievements against preset criteria. Under the Brain Korea 21 project and the New Universities for Regional Innovation project, contracts are established between participating institutions and the government. If the institutions breach the contract, they face government-imposed penalties, usually financial.

These mechanisms may, however, have led to excessive regulation in Korea, highlighting the difficulty of achieving the right balance between accountability and autonomy (see chapter 5).[34] More generally, there may be some tension between performance contracts and higher accountability to university boards if the contracts limit the capacity of the boards to freely fix at least some institutional objectives.

Performance-based funding requires caution in its design, particularly performance set-asides, if there are no clear precedents. The value of performance set-asides depends on the amount and the indicators to assess institutional success. The set-aside can vary from 5 percent to 100 percent, and indicators can also vary from 1 to 12 or more. But South Carolina provides a cautionary tale in the United States. South Carolina allocated 100 percent of its recurrent budget on numerous performance indicators. The program failed simply because institutions could not comprehend a clear vision of success because of the many indicators and standards built into the system.[35]

Countries can also improve the targeting of scholarships and loans to the poorest and disadvantaged groups. Targeting is a particularly serious issue in Cambodia, Indonesia, and Mongolia. To improve targeting, governments need the capacity to identify disadvantaged students, inform them of aid opportunities, and monitor their performance once enrolled.

Finally, efficiency gains can be made at the level of individual public institutions. Scholars have noted two main ways for governments to promote internal efficiency and sustainability: by moderating costs to conserve resources and by maintaining or increasing the rate at which students complete their programs and receive degrees.[36]

Mobilizing private funding and developing student loans

Recent research points to two interrelated elements of successful pro-equity financing for higher education: variable fees for students and income-contingent loans. Where these instruments have been implemented well, higher education systems have increased access for the poor and disadvantaged while recovering costs.

Variable fees
Countries across the globe charge varying tuition fees, depending on their higher education structure. Japan, Korea, and the

United States, all countries with steep private sector participation in higher education, charge fairly high tuition fees as measured by percentage of GDP per capita. Canada and the United Kingdom, by contrast, have larger public sector financing and lower tuition fees.

Variable (or liberalized) fees—set by universities—offer several benefits over a flat fee. They can increase the resources entering the higher education system by being open ended, and they can increase competition among universities, increasing quality and relevance, as well as the efficiency of resource use.[37] And by being akin to income transfers to targeted income groups, they have the potential to be more equitable than other approaches to revenue generation, especially when they are set at higher rates for those who can afford them and are combined with redistributive policies to help poorer students pay those fees.[38]

In most variable fee schemes, the government usually places a ceiling on the maximum[39] and has most students make at least some contribution toward their education, though exempting qualified poor students from fees based on need and equity helps ensure that they are not excluded or sent to low-cost and possibly low-quality institutions. Otherwise, requiring students to pay at least some of the cost generally improves their motivation and performance. Of course, governments will differ in what the variable fee structures and ceilings should be to ensure access, equity, and cost-recovery.[40]

East Asia has more scope for using variable fee schemes, by applying more systematically differentiated fee structures, determined either by the government or by the universities. Vietnam has a partly differentiated fee structure (through partial fee deductions, and liberty to fix higher fees for students enrolled outside the regular student quota), a strategy applied with some success. Combined with redistributive policies to promote access, variable fees can be progressive. Despite lack of formal evaluations, Mongolia and Vietnam argue for need-based scholarships. Supporting stronger university-industry links and nontuition private resources are other ways to leverage private funds (box 4.5).

Income-contingent loans
A second pillar of an effective financing scheme for higher education is income-contingent loans. Traditionally, student loan programs have been either a conventional mortgage-type loan (the loan of choice in many countries, which usually requires repayment after graduation with varying repayment periods) or an income-contingent loan. Capital for a mortgage-type loan[41] may come from the government or a lending institution. If the government is not the lender underwriting the loan, it can provide interest subsidies and default assurance, while allowing the lender to administer the loan. These types of loans can be means tested, and target students below a certain income threshold, or they can be academic merit loans, which target students who score high on entrance or exit exams. To ensure equity, loan designers also need to take into account the choice of higher education institution (public or private, accredited or not), location (in state, out of state, foreign), and status of study (full time or part time)—all factors that may affect loan access.

More governments recognize that income-contingent loans are better for access (box 4.6). Repayment is contingent on the future income of the borrower: people with low earnings make low repayments, and people with low lifetime earnings do not repay the loan principal in full. Such a loan protects a student from excessive risk and can

TABLE 4.10   Average tertiary tuition fees
percentage of GDP per capita

Economy	Tuition fees
Australia	34.8
Canada	20.6
Japan	60.3
Korea, Rep.	56.7
New Zealand	38.5
United Kingdom	18.5
United States	36.7

Source: OECD 2008b.

BOX 4.5   Matching funds in Hong Kong SAR, China, and Singapore

One of the key reasons Hong Kong SAR, China, and Singapore have mobilized public and private funding for university research is that they both have effective government matching-fund programs and favorable tax incentives. By using public-private partnerships, they have strengthened the capacity for raising the independent income of colleges and universities and contributed to a philanthropic culture supporting higher education.

Starting in 2002, Hong Kong SAR, China, provided nearly HK$7 million of seed money to 12 institutions to improve fund-raising capacity. To encourage private donations to higher education, the government also raised the ceiling for tax-exempt donations from 10 percent of income or profits to 25 percent. And to support research in universities, it created a national fund of HK$1 billion for matching grants on a ratio of 1 to 1. Under the scheme, the government set a floor—a guaranteed minimum that each institution could access by raising donations to that amount. This structure gave smaller institutions a fair chance to raise funds while encouraging competition among institutions and raising the profile of private philanthropy.

Singapore has also mobilized large funds for university research through its matching-fund program. Although the government has traditionally invested a relatively larger share of public resources in university research, it has augmented this investment by encouraging private participation. Starting in 1991, it began encouraging philanthropic support to research universities with a matching ratio of 3 to 1. Private donations were also eligible for double tax deductions.

The success of both schemes points to strong institutional capabilities, as well as conducive legislative climates and applicable tax laws.

Source: Sutton Trust 2004.

BOX 4.6   Advantages of income-contingent loans

Income-contingent loans have three main advantages over conventional mortgage-type loans.

Credit reputation. A bank- or government-guaranteed mortgage-type student loan protects the bank or the government in case of default but offers no protection to the borrowers. If a student is unable to find employment that enables him or her to repay the loan, he or she may have to declare bankruptcy, impairing access to credit later in life.

Access to loans. Conventional mortgage-type bank loans usually are available only to students of threshold economic means, whereas government income-contingent loans are available to most students.

Repayment. Conventional mortgage-type loans are generally characterized by a repayment period where the borrower makes set payments over a specified period. Without the income-contingent part of the loan, a borrower may have difficulty in repaying the borrowed amount plus interest.

Source: Johnstone 2004.

---

promote efficiency (by the protection from risk) and access (fees financed by the loans free resources for access).

How large should loan entitlement be? Experts argue that it should be enough to cover tuition fees and living expenses.[42] And it should carry an interest rate similar to the government's cost of borrowing. For students (only while they are students), this means that their tertiary education is effectively free, financed through taxation and an income-related government contribution. While they are students, they pay nothing at the time, a fact compatible with government efforts to improve access. Ministries of finance, of course, bear the burden of upfront costs and receive repayments only later. Income-contingent loans have been applied with varying success across the world, starting with Australia (box 4.7). Most other countries with income-contingent loan programs are in Europe.

But student loan schemes are not without financial risk. They may differ in the underlying objectives and in organizational structure, sources of initial funding, student coverage, loan allocation procedures, and collection methods. However, they almost always share a common trait: they are highly subsidized by governments. Unlike commercial loans, a sizable proportion of the total student loan outlay usually is not paid back. Experts note that this gap between total loan disbursements and overall loan recovery is the result of two elements: (a) built-in interest rate subsidies, incorporated in the design of the loan scheme, and (b) inefficiencies in running the scheme, in substantial repayment default and high administration costs. Lending conditions for almost all government-sponsored loans are "softer" than those for regular commercial loans. This is a student

subsidy in the sense that the borrower is not required to pay back the full value of the loan received, thanks to below-market interest rates on the loan, periods when no interest is levied on outstanding debt (both during study and in grace periods after study), and repayments not linked to inflation.

Some general steps can improve the financial viability and cost recovery of loan schemes. Governments can reduce the built-in subsidies (hidden grants). They can improve the efficiency of loan schemes through containing administration costs. Or they can reduce repayment leaks caused by default.

Some countries have taken steps in these directions. The Canada Student Loan Program, for example, charges a zero nominal interest rate, subsidized by the government, during the period of study, whereas the post-study repayment rate of interest is high (prime plus 2.5 percent), resulting in an overall loan system repayment ratio that nears 100 percent.[43] In the Czech Republic the interest rate charged throughout the period of the loan is fairly high (above 12 percent), resulting in an overall system repayment ratio of more than 108 percent. Japan's loan programs have

---

BOX 4.7   The higher education contribution scheme in Australia

Australia became the first country to adopt a national income-contingent loan policy to finance higher education, in 1989. Under the Higher Education Contribution Scheme, all Australian undergraduates pay a uniform tuition fee (in 1989, the fee was $A 2,250 a year), to be repaid in proportion to future income. The fee could be either an upfront fee, in which case students received a discount, or a deferred fee, in which case repayment was delayed until after graduation. The minimum income threshold for repaying the loan was set at $A 27,700 in 1989, with graduates paying 2 percent of their taxable income; the rate was progressive, rising to 4 percent for those at higher incomes. In 1997, average charges for courses increased by 40 percent, and more important, a differential fee

structure was introduced. And the income threshold at which repayment was mandatory was decreased to $A 23,000.

Apart from revenue generation, the main aim of the scheme was to improve access, particularly among disadvantaged youth. It partly succeeded because—though overall higher education participation increased when it was introduced, and though students from higher income levels were more likely to attend university—the participation rate for students from lower-income backgrounds did not decrease. And the differential fee structure initiated in 1997 increased higher education enrollment for students from all backgrounds.

Source: Johnstone 2004.

charged higher interest rates and achieved an overall recovery ratio of 68.3 percent (implying a 30 percent government subsidy).

Clearly, these options may not be the most attractive for countries confronting the tension between cost recovery and equitable inclusion. The key issue is cost-effectiveness. At what level should the built-in loan subsidy be set for student groups, particularly the poor and disadvantaged, to ensure adequate revenue, appropriate opportunity, and desired outcomes?

Hong Kong SAR, China, and Korea offer useful lessons for how to reconcile fiscal sustainability with equity through tiered student loans. Korea enacts no fewer than six different types of student loan schemes—targeted to different segments of the population—to increase access and promote cost recovery.[44] The separate loan schemes administered by Korea's Ministry of Education, the Human Resources Development Fund, and the Korea Research Foundation aim to increase access of poor students to higher education. These loans target poor students, particularly from farming and fishing villages; offer interest rates of less than 1 percent; are administered through private commercial banks; and are guaranteed by the government. Schemes administered by the Government Employees' Pension Corporation, the Korea Teachers' Pension, and the Korea Labor Welfare Corporation target the children of government employees, teachers and their children, and industrial accident victims, respectively. While still highly subsidized by the government, they are offered at higher interest rates and strongly enforce repayment after graduation. With their emphasis on cost recovery, they cross-subsidize the equity-focused loan schemes, helping ensure sustainability.

Hong Kong SAR, China, is also well known for its multitiered student loan system. In the early 1990s, when Hong Kong SAR, China, decided to recover more higher education costs through tuition fees, the Local Student Finance Scheme was separated into two tracks.[45] An Extended Loan Scheme (not income contingent), charging a higher interest rate of 4–5 percent a year, targeted

applicants who failed the means test by a slim margin; applicants less able to pay for their university education received more assistance. A separate non-means-tested loan was developed for other students in public universities who passed the means test. The interest rate for these loans is the government's no-gain-no-loss rate, 1.5 percentage points below the average best lending rate of note-issuing banks. This rate covers the government's risk in disbursing unsecured loans. An administrative fee is charged annually to cover the full cost of processing and administering the loans, further enhancing cost recovery.

If the region expanded such programs more widely, governments would have to upgrade the financial management and fiduciary capacity of the agencies charged with administering and monitoring. These programs would require governments to have systems for identifying qualified individuals and calculating their repayment amounts—and ensuring collection. This could require coordination with the social security or tax authority (together with interventions targeted to earlier education levels).

For most countries in East Asia, the combination of fees, scholarships, and loans[46] can increase equity and access to tertiary education. While fees are a necessary form of cost recovery, they should ensure the equality of opportunity for poorer and more vulnerable groups. There is clear potential for scholarships when living costs are high and returns are lower for some disadvantaged groups. But fairly high higher education returns and cost-saving considerations make loans particularly attractive.

Summary of policy priorities

East Asia's low- and middle-income countries are not delivering the skills and research outcomes they need. Many of the disconnects are related to funding. The precise challenges and related priorities differ for individual countries, but all countries face some common imperatives.

First, they need to be selective in deciding their targets and priorities. In line with the analysis of chapter 2, it is clear that enrollment increases are not urgent or even advisable in all countries. Only a few universities will ever be able to develop credible research capacity (given the high requirements for faculty qualifications). By contrast, most research, STEM fields, and scholarships are underfunded, making them a priority area.

Second, countries need strategies to fund priority activities. There is a clear case for public financing to finance research, STEM fields, and inclusiveness. (Private funding would complement public funding in financing some activities and focus on increasing coverage and diversification.) Countries could consider continuing to mobilize public resources, while prioritizing them better. And because public funds are scarce, countries should find ways to allocate them more efficiently, attract more private funds, and correct the source of market failures by offering student loans.

Mobilizing and prioritizing public funding. Countries should assess the scope for increasing public spending. The ratios of tertiary spending to total education spending, of total education spending to GDP, and of taxes to GDP show the potential for increasing public spending. On the first two indicators, Mongolia and Thailand have more potential than the others. All countries should increase their shares of public spending for research, STEM fields, and scholarships.

Increasing the efficiency of public funding. Because few countries have much flexibility to ramp up their tertiary expenditures quickly, more efficient use and allocation of public funds applies particularly in the short and medium terms. Greater efficiency requires being more selective and performance based in the way public funds for teaching and research are allocated across institutions and better targeting of equity-enhancing measures.

Leveraging private funds and correcting the source of market failures. One way to increase private funds is to design more efficient and equitable fee structures. Combined with loan schemes, these policies can increase access for the poor and disadvantaged while helping to recover costs.

Lower- and middle-income countries face the challenge of improving and prioritizing their financing policy for their higher education systems. Meeting this critical challenge will bear fruit only within a more flexible and competitive higher education system—the topic of the next two chapters.

Notes

1. OECD 2008b.
2. OECD 2008b.
3. As visible from the snapshot presented in table 4.5 and further evidence from Salmi (2009).
4. Linh, Thuy, and Long 2010.
5. Linh, Thuy, and Long 2010.
6. For instance, fee exemptions introduced at secondary education have been shown to have increased enrollment and completion of secondary school in Vietnam according to rigorous econometric analysis (World Bank 2010g).
7. Sakellariou 2010b.
8. World Bank 2008.
9. World Bank 2010d.
10. World Bank 2010d.
11. Ma 2010. The figures have been converted from renminbi (RMB) to U.S. dollars at a rate of US$1 = 6.83 RMB as of May 2010.
12. Loyalka 2009 as cited in Ma 2010; Ziderman 2004.
13. The Philippines has done very little overall in terms of equity (Orbeta 2008).
14. World Bank 2010c.
15. Directorate General for Higher Education, Ministry of National Education [Indonesia] 2009.
16. Moeliodihardjo 2010.
17. World Bank 2010e.
18. These figures are not directly comparable with the amounts in figure 4.5, which are calculated in Thai baht.
19. World Bank 2009a.
20. Ziderman 2004.
21. Singh 1973 cited in Mukherjee 2010.
22. World Bank 2007a.
23. Mukherjee 2010.
24. For a richer discussion of the trade-offs involved in funding various levels of education, see Mingat, Ledoux, and Rakotomalala (2010). The authors provide financing simulations for Sub-Saharan Africa under five

varying scenarios for progress toward universal primary education under the Education for All Fast-Track Initiative Framework, as well as tertiary education expansion. The authors draw attention to the implications of such scenarios, such as raising the share of education in the national budget, reforming the service delivery arrangements to manage costs, diversifying the flow of students beyond lower-secondary education, and enlarging the role of private finance in postsecondary education.

25. Tertiary spending per student as a share of GDP per capita is used for the STEM share, given that the cost of providing these courses is likely to be quite dependent on local conditions; simple tertiary spending per student is used for the journal indicator, given the closer correlation with international salary costs.
26. Mok 2010.
27. Mok 2010.
28. Mok 2010.
29. Tan 2010.
30. These indicators include faculty strengths in course offerings, academic qualification, research and publications, student graduation rates, employment rates, and student evaluation results.
31. World Bank 2007.
32. Raza 2010.
33. Ministry of Education, Singapore 2005.
34. Byun 2008.

35. Salmi and Hauptman 2006.
36. Salmi 2006.
37. Barr 2008.
38. Barr 2008.
39. This is true at least for public institutions. Private institutions are generally—and should be—exempt from fee caps.
40. The use of fees can be maximized by charging variable fees at the institutional and course level; higher-quality institutions and in-demand or higher-paying disciplines can charge greater fees.
41. This section draws heavily on a review on student loan design by Johnstone (2004).
42. Johnstone 2004.
43. Ziderman 2006.
44. Ziderman 2003.
45. Ping Chung 2007.
46. Programs to increase access to high-quality secondary schools and courses, particularly targeted at vulnerable groups, could have a particularly high payoff, as shown by the example of the Urban Systemic Initiative in the United States. This initiative, which was designed to provide opportunities for disadvantaged youth to participate in high-level math and science courses, showed positive effects on access to advanced math and science courses, as well as reductions in disparities between (a) African Americans and whites and (b) Latinos and whites in science and mathematics course enrollment (Martinez and Klopott 2005).

Managing Public Higher Education | 5

Financial capacity forms an essential pillar of effective higher education. What helps tie it together is effective management of public institutions and stewardship of the higher education system. This chapter deals with the management of public institutions; chapter 6 addresses the stewardship of the system, with emphasis on private institutions and the interactions between higher education institutions and skill and research users (the firms). Public tertiary institutions are critical in East Asia because, notwithstanding significant differences across countries, 70 percent of all students are enrolled in the public sector. Several information, capacity, and incentive constraints and the related disconnects are related to management. For instance, even if institutions receive sufficient funds for highly qualified faculty, insufficient autonomy to select staff and decide on academic programs makes it difficult for them to deliver what firms need. At the same time, lack of accountability of university management to representative university boards may not be conducive to universities' fulfilling the needs of skill or research users. Examples abound that poor management of public institutions has caused many of East Asia's disconnects. In this context, good management of the

public sector can help tackle the disconnect between higher education institutions and skill and research users.

This chapter focuses on managing public institutions through the optics of autonomy and accountability. Higher education worldwide in the past two decades has moved to market approaches, attempting to achieve efficiency gains. But markets, even for education, need regulators to oversee a correct balance between autonomy and accountability—a balance that many of East Asia's low- and middle-income countries have yet to find. These countries should aim at comprehensive autonomy, in both academic and procedural aspects. Their most important accountability move will be to strengthen the mechanisms to nongovernment stakeholders (communities, households, students, and academic and other staff) to ensure that autonomy translates into more socially efficient outcomes. But governments remain crucial in the process. And they need to separate long-term vision and policy direction, which they should direct, and quality assurance, where they have a critical role, from operational management, which they should grant to higher education institutions and intermediate "buffer" bodies. They must also generate program ownership, which early, demonstrable success at a few top institutions can generate.

How decision making is shared across actors and how accountability is structured to translate autonomy into results are the two critical decisions that regional policy makers face in managing the public sector. The following discussion reviews the case for providing higher education institutions with greater decision-making autonomy while supporting strong accountability, then moves to the main characteristics and issues related to autonomy and accountability in the region. It concludes with a summary of the main policy implications.

Global moves to autonomy

Encouraged by governments, higher education sectors worldwide in the past two decades have increasingly adopted market-like behavior in the hope of achieving efficiency gains—often in the form of greater institutional autonomy (box 5.1)—as they moved from state-controlled to state-steered systems. A crucial theme in this transition was structuring an alternative system of accountability, for higher education is not like other goods and is plagued with market failures that have traditionally justified a larger role for government. These include externalities, information asymmetry (at different levels of the sector), and the potential for monopolies. The government thus has a clear role to play, but too strong a grip on higher education institutions or "protective" behavior (such as guaranteed financing) undermines incentives to reform. A key challenge is thus how to balance autonomy with accountability—and within accountability, how to build on the different potential mechanisms available in a decentralized setting.

Institutional autonomy increases the number of lines of accountability. But even as institutions become more autonomous, governments typically continue to play an important role in setting priorities and expecting results (system oversight), thus defining the first of three accountability relationships—a "compact" relationship (figure 5.1).[1] In an institutional autonomy setting, front-line service providers become, at least potentially, more transparently accountable to their "clients" (local community, students, and parents) through the second accountability relationship—the "client power" relationship.[2] A third, the "internal management" relationship, refers to the internal control and quality measures that need to be in place to ensure the accountability of the institution management or of the faculty to the institution (box 5.2).

Research in the past few years[3] has highlighted the importance of autonomy for developing world-class universities and innovation.

BOX 5.1   Institutional autonomy defined

Institutional autonomy is the "degree of freedom of the university to steer itself"[a] or the "condition where academia determines how its work is carried out."[b] Allowing for increased institutional autonomy means that governments increasingly exit from the day-to-day management of the tertiary sector, allowing universities and other higher education institutions to determine their own path. Underlying the notion of autonomy are efforts to encourage institutions to have the freedom to make choices about their internal management and governance, given ideally existing market-driven incentives.

a. Askling, Bauer, and Marton 1999, 177, and Marton 2000, 23f, both as quoted in Bladh 2007.
b. Neave and van Vught 1994, 295, as quoted in Bladh 2007.

The key message is that autonomy combined with competition is conducive to innovation, especially for institutions closer to the technological frontier.

Enhanced autonomy can also support a better match between output from tertiary institutions and labor market needs.[4] It also allows higher education systems to work with the community to develop programs for developing skills needed by the local labor market (box 5.3).

One study[5] examined how different policies and institutions affect the number of new tertiary graduates[6] as a proxy for investment in tertiary education in 19 countries of the Organisation for Economic Co-operation and Development (OECD). The authors found that, on the supply side, the greater responsiveness of supply of tertiary education (as measured by input flexibility, output flexibility, and accountability) had a positive effect on the number of graduates produced. On the demand side, they found that higher internal rates of return also had a positive effect on graduate numbers, but that financing systems (the ratio of education costs to available financing—an index for liquidity constraints) had a negative effect.

Autonomy for low- and middle-income East Asia

Less affluent East Asian countries face the huge challenge of having to manage large and increasing public higher education systems—scaling up many times to thousands of institutions and to hundreds of millions of students—while making sure that these systems address the skill and innovation needs of their economies. Most do this using centralized management structures and limited institutional autonomy, but many are failing—as seen in earlier chapters.

Institutional autonomy, with accountability, could have huge benefits for skill development and innovation in low- and middle-income East Asia. This is largely because greater incentives, arising from more flexible governance structures, and greater use of local information allow better matching

FIGURE 5.1 Accountability relationships in an institutional autonomy setting

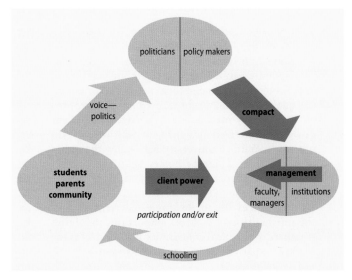

Source: Authors' elaboration based on World Bank 2003.

of skills and research between higher education institutions and the labor market (first and second disconnects) for differentiated local needs and for quality-enhancing choices. Greater incentives are also positive for resource mobilization, which is a basis for wider coverage and higher quality.

Autonomy on its own, however, is unlikely to achieve its potential without well-functioning accountability mechanisms. For example, universities may have the autonomy to align their curriculum to what firms need but may only really do so if a combination of government, students, and parents holds them accountable for graduates' future employment performance.[7] Universities may also have the autonomy to hire the human resources to support an innovative research program for firms but may do so only if the government or the firms hold them accountable for research commercialization.[8] Adequate accountability structures have other benefits. Qualification frameworks have a direct effect on improving the incentives and information for coordination among higher education institutions (fourth disconnect), and governance arrangements for the management of higher education (separating policy from operational

---

BOX 5.2   Translating autonomy into more socially efficient outcomes

The main argument for higher institutions' autonomy lies in the potential gains that flexibility in substantive and procedural issues provides in responding to changes in the labor market, in addressing differentiated local needs and in allowing quality-enhancing choices. None of these benefits will really materialize, however, if the client power and internal management relationships do not work. While a university may know the needs of its local community better than the central government, those needs are most likely better addressed if the community can directly express its preferences by, for example, participating in the university board. More important, involving members of the local community may be necessary to ensure that the university uses its knowledge to satisfy local needs.

Similar reasoning holds for student involvement. And as important are possibilities for students to express preferences by voting with their feet (the "exit" option).

Beyond client power, internal control and quality measures (illustrating the internal management relationship) are also essential to support quality-enhancing choices in higher education institutions. Such measures typically include self-administered quality assurance (including self-evaluations), tenure systems, and other performance incentives for faculty, as well as university boards that can hold university management accountable for its decisions. Institutional autonomy without a culture of internal quality—including holding staff and management accountable for performance—runs the risk of simply not producing the desired outcomes.

BOX 5.3   Addressing local labor market needs in the United States and Mexico

Clemson University[a] in South Carolina, United States, by partnering with the carmaker BMW, transformed itself from a predominantly agriculture and mechanical engineering school into a significant contributor to automotive and motor sports research. The school made the switch because South Carolina has in recent years become a U.S. hub for the automotive industry.

In Mexico, curriculum reform has enhanced the prospects of the University of Monterrey. The university requires students to take part in local

development projects as well as obtain professional skills.[b] It has wide representation of external members on its board (external stakeholders control the direction of the institution) and grants a leading role in decisions to faculty and students. The university has been particularly successful at setting up a wide network of business incubators, business accelerators, and technology parks.

a. Przirembel 2005, as cited in Salmi 2007.
b. Salmi 2007.

---

management) could even have positive consequences for the interrelation between education levels (fifth disconnect).

The evidence on the effects of autonomy in East Asia is less widespread than for OECD countries, as real autonomy is still rare or, in some countries, very new.[9] Still, the partial evidence now presented points to some early successes of autonomy and, when this

information is available, backs up the point that autonomy needs to be accompanied by accountability.

Effects of autonomy at institutional level

There are a few positive examples of what autonomy can achieve in East Asian institutions. In Thailand, a few universities that have moved out of the government bureaucratic structure have begun to successfully position themselves as value-adding partners for several growth industries. Prince of Songkla University, for instance, has created new master's and PhD programs in chemical engineering focused on bio-based chemicals and fuels that include expertise in biomass agronomy, chemical engineering for biomass processing, saccharification, and fermentation. An emphasis on biochemicals and polymers makes the programs very useful to firms operating in the rubber industry.[10]

The Hong Kong University of Technology became an internationally ranked university within a decade of its founding in 1991, aided by two factors. First, its first-tier faculty recruitment policies were successful, tapping into the potential of the Chinese diaspora, thanks to its level of academic and administrative freedom (including freedom to fix salaries). Second, the university related well with local and regional firms through a significant presence of external members from businesses in the University Council, and it had substantial freedom to partner with firms both in and beyond Hong Kong SAR, China, and to launch regional initiatives.[11]

Finally, Pohang University of Science and Technology (POSTECH) in the Republic of Korea, which specializes in science and technology, is a private university that has achieved world-class status over the past decade. The university has always had high levels of management autonomy and used performance indicators. It also has expanded its collaboration with many companies in the electronics and mechanics sector.[12]

Effects of autonomy at country level

Some early country-level evidence shows the positive effects of autonomy alongside accountability. For instance, while it is not possible to flesh out the precise relationship between recent Chinese trends in institutional ranking, patents, and journals (see chapter 2) and the autonomy of its institutions, there is a positive relationship because autonomy increased at the same time. Indeed, many reforms have been under way in Chinese higher education, including priority of resource allocation to its flagship universities and very strict output monitoring, but the contemporaneous increase in autonomy (box 5.4), extended to both teaching and research institutions, as well as further support of private higher education providing some enhanced competition, has played a role. The Chinese case appears to illustrate the positive effects of a combination of additional resources and governance reforms aimed at increasing both accountability and autonomy.

Another example, though more incipient, is Singapore. The evidence suggests that following the move toward higher autonomy for its universities (see box 5.4), the National University of Singapore has seen its performance pick up along several dimensions. In the mid-2000s, while active in publishing journals and in patenting, the National University of Singapore in a context of increased competition fell from 18th in 2004 to 33rd in 2007 (based on 2006 results) of the *Times Higher Education Supplement* (*THES*) ranking.

Such difficulties motivated the government's 2006 decision to corporatize the university. As a result of greater flexibility in structuring recruitment offers, including the provision of generous start-up research grants and reduced teaching loads in initial years for top researchers—and management flexibility to support market adjustment allowances for faculty in fields with high market demand (such as medicine and finance)—the number of research collaboration agreements, invention disclosures, and patents granted to the National University of Singapore increased significantly. In addition, the university developed relatively quickly a wide range of new interdisciplinary educational programs such as nanotechnology and interactive digital media.[13] While it is still early to appreciate the full effects of the reform, since 2006 the National University of Singapore has

---

BOX 5.4   East Asian autonomy

The countries that began reform in the mid- to late 1990s have generally followed a gradualist approach. The Korea Education Reform Plan of 1995 greatly liberalized the private higher education institutions in Korea, which had previously had very little autonomy.[a] Korea's public higher education institutions, however, remain highly centralized with limited autonomy.

Malaysia extended limited autonomy to all its 17 public universities. But despite a strong blueprint for reform, implementation was poor.[b] Indonesia and Thailand selected a few universities for autonomy. (In Indonesia, after some early reforms, momentum slowed, then accelerated, then slowed again.) China pushed a more ambitious reform toward the end of the 1990s, decentralizing responsibilities to provincial authorities and achieving fairly high levels of autonomy for universities, though under strict regulations.

In the mid-2000s, Japan and Singapore launched reforms geared toward more extensive autonomy. Japan, through the National University Corporation

Act of 2004, extended autonomy to all its national universities, 87 of its total of 157 public universities.[c] In 2006 Singapore pushed through extensive autonomy for its two premier public universities, the National University of Singapore and Nanyang Technological University, after accepting the recommendations of the Steering Committee to Review Autonomy, Governance and Funding, set up in 2004. These two universities were incorporated as not-for-profit companies in separate acts, joining Singapore Management University, which already had this status.

Elsewhere, recent attempts at reform in Cambodia are stuck in the legislature. In Vietnam the Higher Education Reform Agenda plans for greater autonomy and a comprehensive university charter. Already approved, implementation is only just starting.

a. Byun 2008.
b. World Bank 2007.
c. OECD 2008b.

---

gained three places, ranking 30th in the 2009 *THES*.

Finally, in Japan, while it is also quite early for a full assessment, since 2004, the year of governance reform (see box 5.4), the number of world-class universities has doubled from 5 to 11 in the *THES* ranking (see chapter 2).

Korea's situation, in which it continues to have highly centralized management structures for higher education but still manages to have a number of high-quality institutions, shows that centralization may also work. Given the huge private share, however, the government has to directly manage only 20 percent of the higher education system. Moreover, even then, that Korea's institutions are not as successful as technological and innovation partners for firms as they are in skill provision suggests that the governance model may not sufficiently encourage strategic vision, innovation, and flexibility.[14]

Two fundamental issues

This section reviews the two main issues with autonomy and accountability in low- and middle-income East Asia: (a) autonomy is incomplete, and (b) the accountability structure, while including some elements supportive of strong accountability to the government, rarely hits the mark in developing other lines of accountability. These two issues are worse among low-income countries, though they are present in middle-income countries as well.

Incomplete autonomy

The real push for decentralization of higher education management in East Asia came in the mid to late 1990s, beginning with Korea and Malaysia and followed by Indonesia and Thailand. A second wave of reforms came in the mid-2000s, when Japan and Singapore extended autonomy to their key higher education institutions (see box 5.4).

Autonomy for higher education institutions can be divided into two types: substantive and procedural[15] (table 5.1). Lack of alignment between the two is a problem because they need to work in a complementary fashion. For instance, innovation in substantive areas may require additional financial resources or higher-quality staff (often both), and this requires procedural autonomy.

Governments around the world vary in their levels of intervention in substantive and procedural issues, but they are generally letting autonomy rise (box 5.5).

In low- and middle-income Asian countries, both areas of higher education autonomy are still limited. The two policy areas where governments have extended autonomy furthest are (a) institutions' control over academic content and structure of programs and (b) at least in middle-income countries, the introduction of block grants. Significant limitations remain in other areas (table 5.2).[16] Box 5.6 highlights Japan's recent shift toward more substantive and procedural autonomy for its national universities.

Substantive autonomy

Academic autonomy is one area where several economies in the region have made some inroads, but this trend is clearer in upper-income economies, such as Hong Kong SAR, China, and Singapore, much of whose widespread academic autonomy predates the recent push for reform. Historically in East Asia, academic autonomy has been limited, and governments have often controlled academic content for both public and private universities. Even in Japan, where the National University Corporation Act of 2004 increased substantive autonomy across a range of areas, including human resource decisions and enrollment size, Japanese universities are still required to consult with the government when creating new departments and faculties. They are also required to secure government approval when modifying the number of students they enroll.

In middle-income countries, governments have extended some academic autonomy to higher education institutions in areas of academic structure and course content, but they continue to make enrollment decisions. In China, for example, institutions are required to get the approval of provincial and central authorities to introduce any new program. Certain course elements are mandatory, but institutions have some room to modify content. Admissions policy is based on a national exam and Chinese institutions are not allowed to accept students outside a set quota. A recent pilot project, however, is allowing some institutions to take in up to 5 percent of enrollment at their own discretion.[17]

Higher education institutions in Indonesia also have to meet certain mandatory requirements for course content, but beyond that, autonomous institutions have the freedom to develop content. In Malaysia autonomy over content is quite restricted. A university is allowed to modify up to 30 percent, but must gain approval from the Ministry of Higher Education for anything beyond this.[18]

Low-income countries have some autonomy in areas of academic structure and course content but little else. In the Lao People's Democratic Republic, the National

TABLE 5.1   **Substantive and procedural autonomy**

Substantive (academic)	Procedural (nonacademic)
Curriculum design	Budgeting
Research policy	Financing management
Entrance standards	Nonacademic staff appointments
Academic staff appointments	Purchasing
Awarding degrees	Entering into contracts

Source: Raza 2010.

BOX 5.5   Higher education autonomy outside East Asia

The United States has always had substantive autonomy for higher education institutions, but individual states vary on procedural autonomy. In Europe such institutions have been given substantial freedom to develop their own academic programs, with governments continuing to steer academic provision through a range of secondary tools, specifically, different forms of accreditation, licensing, or negotiating procedures. Areas in Europe that are still restricted include selection of students and, in some countries, staffing. Salaries for staff in most countries are set by institutions (with or without government intervention), and only in a few countries do governments directly determine salaries.[a]

In decentralized systems, faculty members are hired by the institution, which also sets salaries and hires under general contractual agreements.

In centralized systems, government authorities hire academics, often treating them as civil servants, and set salaries based on a government scale. In some systems, salaries are fully determined by the government.[b]

Many aspects of procedural autonomy are on the rise. A recent study shows that Europe is marking a trend toward allocating public funds in the form of block grants, usually attached to certain performance criteria.[c] European universities are increasingly allowed to collect fees from some of their student population, but the rules vary hugely.

a. Estermann and Nokkala 2009; De Weert 2001, cited in OECD 2008b.
b. Australia, Chile, and the United Kingdom are among many countries following a decentralized approach; countries such as Greece and Portugal follow a centralized approach.
c. Estermann and Nokkala 2009.

University of Laos is the only university that has acquired some autonomy. A decree in June 2000 stipulated its academic and administrative autonomy, specifically an increase in students admitted and changes to the curriculum. In Vietnam some autonomy over academic content is allowed. Higher education institutions there have also been given some autonomy over enrollment: they can take in fee-paying students once they have met the government's directives.

The other area where higher education institutions have some autonomy is staffing. In Hong Kong SAR, China, they have historically had such autonomy and can hire and fire faculty as well as set salaries. Japanese institutions, after the 2004 reforms, have been able to convert the status of university employees to non–civil servants and have committed to introduce fixed-term contracts. Korea, by contrast, continues to limit staffing autonomy in these institutions.

Middle-income countries' institutions seem to have partial autonomy on staffing, though it is quite restrictive. Institutions in Indonesia

that are self-financed can hire and fire faculty (which excludes most university staff, who continue to be paid by public funds). The Thai government no longer requires the 11 autonomous universities to offer faculty lifetime contracts and encourages pay to be incentivized through rewards.[19] It has made some attempt to convert university posts to non–civil service positions, case by case. For the most part, however, "public university employees are currently civil servants, which impose[s] higher costs and less flexibility in terms of hiring and firing staff."[20]

China and Malaysia seem to have more room to actually hire and fire. It is subject to contract in China, and in Malaysia, given that university staff are still civil servants, effective autonomy is not a given.

Low-income countries in the region have no or very limited staffing autonomy.

Procedural autonomy

Even more than for substantive autonomy, procedural—especially financial—autonomy differs widely between high-income economies and other categories.

TABLE 5.2   Autonomy among higher education institutions, East Asia

Economy	Institution type	Substantive autonomy			Procedural autonomy				
		Set academic structure/ course content	Employ and dismiss academic staff	Decide size of student enrollment	Own building and equipment	Borrow funds	Spend budgets to achieve objectives	Decide level of tuition fees	Set salaries
High income									
Japan	National	◐	●	●	●	●	●	◐	●
Singapore	National University of Singapore, Nanyang Technological University, and Singapore Management University	●	●	◐	○	○	●	●	●
Hong Kong SAR, China	Public	●	●	◐	◐	●	●	◐	●
Korea, Rep.	National/public	◐	◐	○	○	○	○	●	○
Middle income									
Malaysia	Public	◐	●	○	○	○	●	○	○
Thailand	Autonomous	●	◐	○	●	○	◐	○	◐
China	National and regional	◐	◐	◐	◐	◐	●	○	○
Indonesia	Autonomous	◐	◐	○	●	●	●	◐	◐
Philippines	Public	●	◐	●	○	○	◐	●	○
Low income									
Vietnam	Public	◐	○	◐	○	○	○	◐	○
Lao PDR	National University of Laos	◐	◐	○	○	○	◐	○	○
Cambodia	Public	◐	○	○	○	○	○	○	○

Source: Raza 2010, based on Expert Survey for this study.
Note: ○ has no autonomy; ● has autonomy; ◐ has autonomy in some respects.

In Japan after the 2004 reforms, national universities for the first time received none-armarked block grants to spend as they see fit. And although the Ministry of Education and Training sets the standard annual tuition fee, it allowed higher education institutions to increase fees 20 percent in 2007 (if they wanted to do so).[21]

Hong Kong SAR, China, has some financial autonomy across a range of areas. For example, its institutions can own and sell buildings that have been donated or have been self-financed. Universities can borrow funds from commercial banks and financial markets but cannot be publicly listed. Universities can set fees only for those programs that are self-funded.

After 2006 in Singapore, though the government remains committed to being the major funder in the sector, newly autonomous universities have been encouraged to seek out other sources of funding, particularly from industry. These universities have been given the freedom to set tuition fees and have been given full autonomy over human resources, including setting remuneration packages.

Korea, again, is different. Public universities remain constrained in areas of procedural autonomy despite a series of reforms after 1995.[22] Paradoxically, the reform process has led to an excessive focus on financial accountability in a negative way. Funding has become much more results focused and has produced a culture of excessive regulation

BOX 5.6 Autonomy in Japan's higher education before and after the National University Corporation Act of 2004

Japan's National University Corporation Act of 2004 greatly increased the institutional autonomy of its higher education institutions. The act incorporated national universities with their own governing boards. Under government supervision, universities moved from limited to extensive autonomy in both substantive and procedural autonomy (See table B5.6). These institutions were given more autonomy in managing their human resources and, for the first time, in admissions policies, building and equipment, long-term borrowing, and spending block grants. Faculty members were no longer civil servants, and universities had autonomy to set faculty salaries. But these institutions still had limited autonomy in setting their academic structure and content and had less autonomy in deciding tuition fees than they did before the act.

TABLE B5.6   Institutional autonomy of higher education institutions in Japan, 2003 and 2007

	Substantive autonomy			Procedural autonomy				
	Set academic structure/course content	Employ and dismiss academic staff	Decide size of student enrollment	Own their building and equipment	Borrow funds	Spend budgets to achieve objectives	Decide level of tuition fees	Set salaries
2003	◐	◐	○	○	○	○	●	○
2007	◐	●	●	●	●	●	◐	●

Source: Raza 2010.

Note: ○ has no autonomy; ● has autonomy; ◐ has autonomy in some respects.

Sources: Byun 2008; Newby and others 2009.

rather than "steering."[23] By contrast, private universities have seen their financial (and other) autonomy increase.

Governments in middle-income countries have granted some financial autonomy to selected universities. This has taken the form of transferring public funds as block grants, allowing some flexibility to set fees for selected programs, and in a few cases granting the ability to add to basic staff-remuneration packages. But even autonomous institutions are still restricted in borrowing funds commercially and in owning property.

In Thailand, the autonomous universities receive public funds through block grants and have autonomy to establish their own administrative structures or formulate rules on personnel and staffing.[24] These universities also have the authority to manage and use state property. Autonomous universities in Indonesia can also do that. Legislatively, Indonesia's autonomous universities have been given significant procedural autonomy, though this has not always translated into effective financial autonomy.[25] But Indonesia has been successful in introducing different types of competitive funds, going beyond its autonomous universities. Malaysian higher education institutions, too, receive their public funds through block grants.

Higher education institutions in low-income countries still have little procedural autonomy, but it is growing. In Vietnam they are shifting from relying only on the state budget and are being encouraged by the government to seek other sources of funding.[26] The number of fee-paying students has exceeded the number of students sponsored by government.[27] In Lao PDR the National University of Laos has been given some financial autonomy. A financial system allows the university to manage its own revenue under the supervision of the university council.[28]

With the exception of Hong Kong SAR, China, university branches or satellites (domestic or foreign) have very little academic and procedural autonomy.[29]

Incomplete accountability

Although decentralization is only incipient or incomplete in most low- and middle-income East Asian countries, the trend is still under way, and all countries therefore have to align their accountability systems with it. Current systems still fall short because of the limited development of accountability lines to nongovernment stakeholders (community, households, students, and academic and other staff) and some deficiencies in the design and implementation of accountability toward the central (government) level.

How does East Asia fare on the various mechanisms, relative to the rest of the world? The answer may be broken down into accountability to nongovernment stakeholders and to the government.

Accountability to nongovernment stakeholders

As higher education institutions receive more decision-making power, they need to increase their own institutional and management capacity. One important area is the governing board (box 5.7).

Like the rest of the world, East Asia is showing a trend toward establishing governing boards or university councils, but their powers and representativeness are still limited, even in upper-income East Asia (table 5.3). All economies except Korea have governing boards, but their functions are fairly limited in selecting the university leadership, and only in Singapore does the board select vice chancellors, presidents, and rectors. East Asian board heads are selected by the government, internal university bodies, the boards themselves, or a by a mixed approach (boards' members are generally selected by either the government or a mixed approach). Although most East Asian countries' external

stakeholders participate in boards, this is limited for students.

In Thailand the role of the university council has been strengthened in the autonomous universities,[30] though they remain heavily influenced by the Commission of Higher Education.[31] In Japan the authority of the university councils is second to that of the president of the university, which is unusual for both the region and world. The National University Corporation Act of 2004 centralized power under the presidents, far greater than in other OECD countries. In Indonesia autonomous universities are accountable to a board of trustees,[32] comprising representatives of ministries, the academic senate, and broader society, for example.

On other accountability mechanisms, most countries have a national career structure for academic staff, usually organized by career ranks.[33] The criteria for career advancement and tenure nearly always include qualifications and achievements in teaching and research,[34] though the importance of these criteria varies by country. (Seniority and personal connections are often more important than achievement.) In some countries, such as China,[35] achievement in research is more valued than teaching skills. But many institutions in Cambodia, Indonesia, and Mongolia, for example, have a weighting toward teaching.[36] Performance-pay management is still little used in the region, though growing. Box 5.8 provides examples of faculty performance programs in China.

Competition, the main mechanism to ensure exit, is constrained by lack of systemic financing and information mechanisms to support mobility across institutions. Competition is an effective tool to ensure client power (see figure 5.1), by allowing consumers who are unhappy with the provision of services to exit and opt for another provider. The fear of exit forces providers to be more accountable to consumers. Key elements for ensuring that this mechanism works include a strong and comparable alternative to existing higher education institutions (public or private), the option to exit, and information

---

BOX 5.7   Governing boards worldwide

Globally, there has been a trend toward establishing boards that favor a managerial model with a small number of external representatives.[a]

Universities and other higher education institutions in most countries worldwide are free to set their own internal academic structure, within a basic framework stipulated by the law. Both dual (board or council and senate) and unitary governance structures have been adopted, with a bit of an edge for dual structures. Alongside the external members who feature in a heavy majority of countries, boards are largely composed of academic staff, nonacademic staff, and students.

Typically, in OECD countries the governing board has responsibility for the mission and goals of the institution; approval of its policies and procedures; the appointment, review, and support of its president; oversight of its resources; and having an informed understanding of its programs and activities. In setting the strategy and direction of the institution, the board is a key actor in translating public policies and orientation in institutional practice and policy implementation. The board's functions tend to be strong on the role of presidents or rectors, who are usually appointed by the board and are thus accountable to it. The board's head tends to be elected (or appointed) by the board itself or by another internal university body.

These arrangements allow for some accountability of the institution to external stakeholders (such as private sector representatives) and for accountability of university leaders to their institution (through boards appointing the presidents or rectors and board heads appointed by the university).

a. Fielden and LaRocque 2008.

---

about the quality of provision so that consumers can make choices.

It is unclear how much private and public delivery compete, however. Most countries do not have academic credit transfers allowing students to move easily between institutions, and public information on the quality and relevance of institutions and their programs is patchy (table 5.4). Narrow use of demand-side financing, such as voucher schemes and government scholarships, for public and private sectors, also makes such mobility difficult.

Accountability to the government

While less involved in operational management, governments worldwide still have a leading role in strategic vision, monitoring and evaluation, and financing of the public sector. Various instruments governments need to manage a more autonomous public system are a strategic vision and higher education legislation, a quality assurance system, education management information systems, and performance-based financing (discussed in chapter 4).

In East Asia, most upper-income economies have a strategic vision as well as the necessary accompanying legislation.[37] Middle-income countries such as Indonesia, Malaysia, and Thailand are still transitioning and setting up the new systems, as are low-income countries.[38]

While academic autonomy is important to support a better fit between supply and demand for skills, core curriculum guidelines have to be set by the center. As part of their strategic vision for higher education, countries in lower- and middle-income East Asia will need to incorporate elements of a curriculum reform. Chapter 3 has pointed out that curricula are currently often outdated. Holding faculty and institutions accountable for better skill delivery will be greatly facilitated by a new curriculum approach (box 5.9).

All countries in the region have a quality assurance body and seem to be moving to a more outcome-based system, as seen in the widespread use of accreditation, audit, and assessments (see table 5.4). Upper-income economies have quality assurance approaches

TABLE 5.3   **University governance, East Asia**

Economy	Leadership of board selected by	Members of board selected by	Vice chancellors, presidents, rectors selected by	Senior management of universities selected by	Composition of board
High-income					
Japan	Governing board (public universities) Presidential selection committee (national universities)	Governing board	Internal selection	Appointed by vice chancellors, presidents, or rectors and internal selection	Academic staff, nonacademic staff, external stakeholders
Singapore	Governing board	Government	Governing board	—	Academic staff, nonacademic staff, external stakeholders
Hong Kong SAR, China	Government	Mixed[a]	Professional selection	Professional selection and appointed by vice-chancellors, presidents, or rectors	Academic staff, nonacademic staff, external stakeholders (2:1 ratio of external stakeholders to university members)
Korea, Rep.	Boards not allowed by law (in public universities)	n.a.	n.a.	n.a.	n.a.
Middle-income					
Malaysia	—	Mixed[b]	Government	Vice chancellors, presidents, rectors	Academic staff, nonacademic staff, external stakeholders
Thailand	Governing board	Mixed[c]	Professional selection	Professional selection	Academic staff, nonacademic staff, external stakeholders
China	Internal university bodies	Internal university bodies or government	Government	Professional selection	Academic staff, nonacademic staff, external stakeholders
Indonesia	Governing board	University senate	Internal selection[d]	Vice chancellors, presidents, rectors	Academic staff, nonacademic staff, external stakeholders
Philippines	Government	Mixed[e]	Internal selection	Vice chancellors, presidents, rectors	Mix of government officials and private citizens appointed by the president; students, and faculty
Low-income					
Vietnam	Government	Government	Professional selection	Professional selection	—
Lao PDR (National University of Laos)	Government	Government	Government	Government	—
Cambodia	Mixed[f]	Government	Mixed	Mixed	Academic staff, nonacademic staff, external stakeholders

Sources: Raza 2010 based on Expert Survey; OECD 2008b.
Note: Most institutions are public. — = not available; n.a. = not applicable.
a. Some members are selected by the chief executive (often the chancellor) of the university, and others are elected.
b. Members of the governing board are appointed by the government and the governing board.
c. Differs by institution.
d. Internal election involving the entire university community.
e. Members of the governing board are appointed by the government and university.
f. Appointed by the government (public) and the university owner (private).

that include accreditation, audit, and assessment, while low- and middle-income countries mainly use accreditation or audit.[39] Incentives for compliance appear to be generally strong: governments require public higher education institutions to undergo the quality assurance process, and apart from Hong Kong SAR, China, the same for private institutions (more on private institutions in the next chapter).

It is not clear yet, however, to what extent quality assurance is ready to take up the

BOX 5.8   Evaluating faculty performance in China

China has introduced over the years a number of faculty performance programs with positive effects that may be useful to other lower- and middle-income countries.

Teaching evaluation. The Chinese government formally established a teaching evaluation program of all regular higher education institutes in 2000. This evaluation involves a five-year cycle with the first round of outcomes made available to parents and the general public in 2003.

Under the auspices of the program, some institutions are making serious efforts to better assess their instructors' teaching effectiveness, using several tools. In some cases the teaching evaluation done at the university level consists of three parts, each conducted by a different group. Part 1 is teaching observation conducted by a "committee on teaching supervision" composed of senior teaching colleagues in an instructor's subject area (such as deans and professors). These supervisors have the right to attend any lecture for the purpose of assessing the instructor's teaching ability. Part 2 consists of teaching observations conducted by fellow colleagues. Part 3 is the use of student course evaluations, perceived by many instructors to be the most effective indicator of teaching performance, because student assessments affect the teachers' prestige in the faculty. Institutes applying these measures have improved their teaching facilities, increased their educational spending, and put extra emphasis on teaching quality.

Research and performance. Tianjin University considers papers published abroad and the frequency with which those papers are cited and quoted abroad. It has also moved to a system similar to merit pay in which instructors receive "work post subsidies" on the basis of their performance. Moreover, the Beijing University Teachers' Engagement and Promotions

System Reform Plan initiated at Beida (Beijing University) has been the precursor to personnel reform plans in other universities including Tianjin. The Beida reforms aim to make university hiring more competitive by giving existing lecturers a set number of years to be promoted; if their performances are not up to par, their contracts will not be renewed. As part of the reform, Beida institutions and departments are encouraged to not hire their own graduates, but instead to look for talent both domestically and abroad. Research outputs have increased in both Tianjin and Beijing universities.

Graduate employability. China faced both a serious decrease in teaching quality and an increase in unemployment rate among university graduates. While the rapid drop in educational quality was the focus of most faculty concern, the government was more concerned about graduates' unemployment. The government's response included graduate employment rate as a major indicator of program quality on the national "Assessment on the teaching standard of undergraduate programs in higher institutes." This focus on employment placed enormous pressure on university faculties to quickly address the problem or otherwise face consequences. If a specialization could not reach a graduate employment rate of 60 percent or above for a certain number of years, the specialization would then be eliminated. The government felt its actions had been largely successful when the Ministry of Education announced in 2006 that the new reforms resulted in an annual graduate employment rate of 70 percent. The recent crisis brought back unemployment issues but to a lesser extent.

Sources: Lai and Lo 2007; Li 2005; Y. Lin and others 2005; Postiglione 2006.

challenges of internationalization and distance education.[40] In particular, the internationalization of higher education offers tremendous opportunities but also some challenges (discussed in chapter 6).

Also noticeable is the fact that while the majority of countries' quality assurance bodies are independent or semi-independent,

this is not the case in Cambodia, Lao PDR, Vietnam, and Singapore. In the first three countries this underlines the early stages of the decentralization process; in Singapore the longer-term goal is to set up an independent quality assurance framework (the quality assurance body is currently based in the ministry of education). In Vietnam the lack of

TABLE 5.4 External quality assurance, East Asia

Economy	Type of body			Type of system			Body funding source			Requirement[a]		Disclosure		
	Independent body	Semi-autonomous body	Government-represented body	Accreditation	Audit	Assessment	Government	Institutions	Others	Mandatory	Voluntary	Complete	Limited	None
High-income														
Japan	X	X		X	X	X	X	X		X		X		
Singapore			X	X	X	X	X	X		X		X		
Hong Kong SAR, China[b]		X		X	X	X	X			X	X	X		
Korea, Rep.	X			X	X	X	X	X		X	X	X		
Middle-income														
Malaysia	X			X	X		X			X				X
Thailand	X			X	X		X			X		X		
China		X		X	X		X			X			X	
Indonesia	X			X			X			X		X		
Philippines	X			X				X		X			X	
Low-income														
Vietnam			X		X		X			X			X	
Lao PDR			X	X			X			X				X
Cambodia			X	X			X			X			X	

Sources: Raza 2010 based on Expert Survey, except Singapore, for which information taken from Ministry of Education, Singapore 2005.

a. This requirement is for public and private institutions, unless otherwise stated.

b. For Hong Kong SAR, China, quality assurance is mandatory for public universities and voluntary for private universities.

BOX 5.9   Curriculum reform for East Asia

For higher education systems in the region to be more relevant to labor market needs, curricula across disciplines must serve broader objectives than simply transmitting academic knowledge. Previous evidence has made clear that countries should place more emphasis on core behavioral skills that are particularly applicable to services, such as decision making, communication, and client-orientation skills, do a better job of incorporating in their curricula problem solving and creative thinking, and provide more relevant and practical technical and business skills for managers and professionals.

As a general pedagogical trend, multidisciplinary and transdisciplinary courses have become popular for equipping graduates to learn and think across a broad range of fields while also developing in-depth academic skills. These courses often follow a problem-centered approach and use case studies to understand complex systems. They do not require higher-qualified or more faculty. Indeed, if well developed and accompanied by adequate faculty training, problem-centered approaches enhance student independence and creativity, minimizing faculty supervision. These approaches could help improve the quality of teaching even within the current faculty constraints.

Universities in Europe, the United States, and Australia are instituting more of these courses. Following core national guidelines, the University of South Australia, for instance, has enumerated seven skills that it seeks to cultivate in its graduates and has reformed its pedagogical practices to achieve them:

- Technical skills within a given discipline in sufficient depth to begin professional practice
- The ability to undertake lifelong learning
- Problem-solving skills and critical thinking
- Teamwork skills
- Ethics and social responsibility
- Communication skills
- Skills to demonstrate international perspectives as a citizen and a professional

Sources: Hicks and George 1998; Kennedy and Lee 2008.

---

independence of the quality assurance body has also hampered the transition from a more traditional input approach to an outcome-based system of quality assurance, given that input control is the routine monitoring strategy.[41]

Few economies in East Asia have followed the international trend of separating operational management from national policy (including determining the scale and scope of the sector) at the central (government) level. Most governments continue to manage their higher education sectors through their ministries of education. The only exceptions are China, which divides the management of higher education between national and provincial authorities, and Hong Kong SAR, China, which has a buffer body.

Key functions are often delegated to such bodies, including quality assurance, standards review, and budget allocation (that is, operational functions). The central government maintains responsibility for mission, strategic planning, and the public budget. Buffer bodies have advantages and disadvantages. Ministries of education are wary that buffer bodies will become too powerful and will stand in the way of more far-reaching reforms. For their part, buffer bodies worry that the ministry may begin to interfere in the daily management of higher education, particularly when subjected to political pressure from lobbying groups.[42] Still, they generally help ensure less public interference in operational management, higher standards, and more time for strategic planning for the ministry.[43]

Finally, the lack of well-functioning and comprehensive education management information systems (including information not only on institutions but also on graduate employment and skills) in all countries is likely to weaken quality assurance by limiting information on outputs and outcomes.[44] This may also be why performance-based financing is still in its infancy.

Moving forward

All indicators suggest that the decision-making autonomy of higher education institutions is still limited in low- and middle-income East Asian countries. This explains at least part of the disconnect between institutions and firms in skills and research. Accountability lines to nongovernment stakeholders, including the role of boards, remain underdeveloped. Internal management processes are generally weak, with boards struggling (or even not having the power) to fulfill their fiduciary role.

The compact relationship (see figure 5.1) tends to be more developed, at least in terms of regulation and existence and the mandatory nature of quality-assurance mechanisms, and has been moving to some extent from an input-based to an output-based approach (from regulation to quality assurance). Yet performance measures on graduation, labor market outcomes, and research are rarely used for quality assurance and funding allocation, and performance standards are not set high.

Some of the main implications from this chapter are now given.

Autonomy

Increasing autonomy across income groups. While governments in middle-income countries may feel more urgency to increase autonomy than low-income ones (particularly China, which is the closest to the technology frontier), low-income countries should not lose time either, and they should aim at comprehensive and not piecemeal autonomy.

Increasing autonomy in staffing. Institutions should have full autonomy on hiring and firing (though adapting a decentralized hiring system in countries with centralized staffing may be difficult because of the civil service system).

Aligning substantive and procedural autonomy. Governments worldwide used to be more generous with substantive autonomy than procedural autonomy, though this is now changing. In East Asia, too, governments prioritize autonomy in substantive areas more than procedural areas. Governments need to conceive both types of autonomy as a whole, because many aspects of substantive autonomy can be undermined by the lack of procedural autonomy.

For example, within staffing policies, hiring and firing faculty will depend critically on the ability of institutions to set salaries. Diversifying funding is also an essential means of increasing autonomy.[45] Securing funding from the private sector is particularly important, because it is a critical mechanism of external efficiency. As higher education institutions continue to be mostly public bodies reliant on base funding, diversifying funding offers these institutions greater autonomy.

Accountability and system oversight

Strengthening accountability mechanisms. As they move to higher autonomy, all countries will need to align their accountability framework to this new setting. The most important step will be to strengthen accountability mechanisms to nongovernment stakeholders to ensure that autonomy translates into more socially efficient outcomes. This will require two main types of measures, both of which should be supported by the governments.

The first is strengthening and empowering governing boards. This should include the appointment of the board head by the board itself or internal bodies of universities as well as the capacity of the board to appoint the president or rector (as in most countries). Boards may need to receive extensive training, particularly in low-income countries. This move may also require keeping a limited number of members but preserving broad representativeness, which is essential to strengthen the client power relationship.[46]

The second is strengthening the exit option for students. This will entail steps to increase mobility and competition, including national qualification frameworks (box 5.10), disclosure and publication of information on institutional and graduate performance, and some demand-side financing.

More widely, the role of government, though changed, remains critical. As the power (and capacity) of boards increases, priority setting as well as monitoring and evaluation will become a shared responsibility. The challenge is how to make the various accountability relationships work in a complementary way, building on relative strengths.

Implementing successfully the compact relationship will require the capacity to hold institutions accountable on broad clear goals, while minimizing intrusions in daily management and protecting the capacity of institutions to fix many of their priorities. This will entail setting clear goals for the system as well as an effective quality assurance system focused on initial accreditation, audits, and outcome assessments. A semi-independent or independent system will be more credible. And the quality assurance system must address the challenges of internationalization (discussed in chapter 6).

Separating policy and operational management. Such separation at the central level would allow governments to maintain a distance from the regular lobbying in the sector to focus on policy[47] and help them articulate the sector's priorities with the broader overlapping labor market and education system. In most cases, East Asian governments have established separate departments within the ministry of education to be responsible for the sector, which may be better than entirely separate bodies for policy coordination but is insufficient to grant full policy coherence if the departments are too involved in the operational management of the sector.

Strengthening education management information systems. Alongside performance-based financing, governments should improve information to help enforce quality standards (with quality oversight provided by boards).

Creating an enabling environment

Several factors are important in creating an enabling environment for successful reform.

Generating ownership of the reform process. Successful outcomes are usually driven by domestic ownership of the reform process and by a political consensus that decentralizing higher education management is better for the economic needs of the country.[48] More emphasis needs to be placed on undertaking dialogue with key stakeholders,

---

BOX 5.10   National qualifications frameworks

Part of the broad quality assurance system, national qualifications frameworks help provide nationally consistent recognition of outcomes in postcompulsory education and thus are essential for student mobility between education and training institutions. While they can potentially address disconnects among skill providers (whether in a different or even in the same education level) and should therefore be supported, their design and implementation are complex. Challenges include developing standards-based on-the-job analysis, preparing new modular (competency-based) curricula, and designing assessment methods and new performance tests. These shifts have rarely been adopted in the region. Australia's national qualifications framework is the most accomplished. It was introduced in 1995 on a nationwide basis and was phased in over a period of five years, achieving full implementation by year 2000.

Sources: Australian Qualifications Framework Web site, www.aqf.edu.au; Johanson and Adams 2004.

particularly higher education institutions themselves, to ensure that they see the merits of how a decentralized system can potentially benefit them. Leadership at the government and higher education institution levels is also critical.

Building institutional capacity. Reforms often stumble because capacity is lacking within either government or higher education institutions, and this lack also makes governments wary of pursuing reform. Building capacity in areas such as financial management in higher education institutions or establishing an education management information system, for example, even before the reform formally starts, is essential. Given the limited capacity in institutions in low- and middle-income East Asian countries, the staggered approach to introducing autonomy that many countries have pursued makes some sense to address the issue of limited institutional capacity. By contrast, this slow pace has often led to reform stagnation or even reversal. A better option may therefore be to ensure that a minimum set of preconditions is in place and then start with far-reaching reform.

Prioritizing the legislative framework. Failure to adequately consider reform sequencing can slow the process, and prioritizing and getting the legislative framework right is key.[49] The legal focus in the region, rightly so, has prioritized the conversion of public higher education institutions into autonomous independent entities. What is equally important, however, is to ensure that the overall legislative framework is adequately reformed to accommodate the new autonomous role of these publicly owned institutions.[50]

Demonstrating success. One way to increase ownership and address opposition is providing autonomy only to top universities to generate a "demonstration" effect. (This is a stronger justification than lack of capacity for staggering reform.) This strategy could be useful in low-income countries where the domestic climate is yet not ready for reform or in middle-income countries where some top-performing universities are ready to take off.[51]

Notes

1. Definition of these relationships follows the *World Development Report (WDR) 2004* terminology (World Bank 2003).
2. Again, this follows *WDR 2004* terminology. The client power relationship can build on two main options: "participation," where communities have the mechanisms (such as councils and stakeholder associations) to express their preferences and hold the management of the institution accountable for results, or "exit," where students can leave nonperforming institutions (which requires competition among institutions).
3. Aghion and others 2007, 2008, and 2009.
4. OECD 2008b.
5. Raza 2010.
6. This was measured as the share of graduates in the 20- to 29-year-old age cohort.
7. Such accountability may occur, for example, through performance-based financing or by requiring the publication of employment information.
8. They can do so through competitive financing for research and broad-based university boards, for example. This latter point is discussed further below.
9. There is also a nearly complete lack of rigorous studies assessing the effects of autonomy on higher education in the region.
10. Doner, Intarakumnerd, and Ritchie 2010.
11. Postiglione 2011, as cited in Altbach and Salmi forthcoming.
12. Shik Rhee 2011, as cited in Altbach and Salmi forthcoming.
13. Altbach and Salmi forthcoming.
14. These are critical characteristics of excellence, according to Salmi 2009.
15. Berdahl 1971.
16. This information comes largely from an institutional survey applied to a group of regional experts (The Expert Group on New Skills for New Jobs) in 2010. Mongolia, not included in the survey, has a very centralized structure.
17. Raza 2010.
18. World Bank 2007.
19. Raza 2010.
20. World Bank 2009a, 84.
21. Byun 2008; Newby and others 2009.
22. Byun 2008.
23. Byun 2008.
24. World Bank 2009a.
25. In the areas of financing and staffing, effective autonomy has been undermined by the

lack of comprehensive reform in legislation, though a new law was passed in 2009, which seeks to cover some previous gaps in autonomy (World Bank 2010c).

26. World Bank 2009b.
27. UNESCO 2006.
28. UNESCO 2006.
29. Mok 2009.
30. Raza 2010.
31. World Bank 2009a.
32. World Bank 2005.
33. OECD 2008b.
34. Chapman 2010.
35. Wu 2010.
36. World Bank 2010c, 2010d, 2010e.
37. Raza 2010.
38. In Indonesia, for example, although the decision to make universities autonomous goes back to 1991, the strategic vision was only issued in 2003, the quality assurance system was put in place in 2008, and the legal framework for higher education was promulgated in 2009. In Malaysia the legal framework was in place as far back as 1996–97, but the strategic vision and quality assurance body were established only in 2007.
39. The push for more outcome-based accountability has evolved not only because of the changing relationship between government and universities, but also because of the increased focus on efficiency, value for money, and the globalization of education (Huisman and Currie 2004).
40. Distance education is a cheap and effective way to enroll students who under traditional modes would be unable to participate in the tertiary education system. The initial costs of distance education are high. Once the system is established, however, it can grow to scale at a relatively low cost. Distance education

represents between a fifth and a third of total higher education enrollment across China, Indonesia, Korea, and Thailand. But the emergence of distance learning in the region does pose new challenges that can threaten educational quality in countries with weaker regulatory capacity. The need to strengthen the capacity of national quality assurance systems must accompany the region's efforts to take advantage of these new opportunities.

41. World Bank 2008.
42. Fielden 2008.
43. By the same token, this may help address the disconnect between education levels by enhancing time and attention for strategic planning and public budget development across education levels within the ministry.
44. World Bank 2009a, 2009b.
45. Fielden and LaRocque 2008.
46. Empowering governing boards would also be instrumental in providing higher autonomy for satellites, by making them accountable to the boards.
47. Fielden and LaRocque 2008.
48. One reason why the Mongolia decentralization process did not succeed in the 1990s was that the process was imposed by international donors and lacked strong domestic roots (Steiner-Khamasi and Stolpe 2004).
49. An example is Indonesia, where the lack of a legislative framework has delayed the effective autonomy of institutions.
50. The recent approval of a university charter providing a clear framework for higher autonomy and the role of university councils is a good first step in Vietnam.
51. Vietnam is following this strategy with its special autonomy to some of its new model universities. It has worked in a few other countries, such as South Africa (Cloete 2002).

Providing Stewardship for Higher Education | 6

Effective management of public institutions will go a long way to address many of the disconnects—both in skills and research. But at the core of higher education systems are actors that do not operate directly under the responsibility of higher education departments: private higher education institutions (PHEIs; as skill and research providers), international skill providers, and firms (as skill and research users and providers), among others. This chapter discusses how countries can coordinate and handle these actors in ways that enhance skill and innovation outcomes (in other words, exercise appropriate stewardship of the overall system).

As seen previously, many disconnects are related to stewardship. While governments have less authority over PHEIs and international skill providers, they can go a long way to ensure that they fulfill their potential through effective policy decisions, helping address skill-related disconnects. And while firms are outside their sphere of day-to-day control, encouragement of effective university-industry links can provide the incentives for fruitful collaboration and interaction, helping address the disconnect between firms and providers in skills and research. (Interactions between institutions and research centers are

other important areas for support, briefly touched upon in this chapter.) Finally, better coordination among government bodies can go a long way to address several of the disconnects.

This chapter addresses the four critical challenges of providing effective coordination between higher education departments (or ministries) and the other education departments (or ministries), ministries of science and technology, and ministries of finance and labor; effective stewardship for private and international institutions with a focus on regulation and financing; and managing university-industry links.

The lack of an integrated and coordinated stewardship structure to guide the strategic development of tertiary education must be addressed. Countries will need to develop stronger capacity of coordination within their governments.

Private higher education (PHE) in all countries will play a large—or larger—role, given constraints on public funds. As the sector expands, though, the critical challenge will be to avoid sacrificing quality to quantity. Put another way, the quality of too many of the affordable demand-absorbing institutions is low in some countries, while the share of "semi-elite" institutions (usually more expensive but with stronger potential for innovation) is also low. The policy environment thus needs to encourage a move to both more and higher-quality institutions. But because policy makers and the public seem to have ruled out direct subsidies to PHE, policy makers and academics should consider the potential of indirect subsidies—from student loans to tax subsidies to competitive funds for research—in greater detail.

In managing their university-industry links, countries need to continue building capacity. As this will take many years, policy makers should start encouraging stronger links by assessing and gradually helping develop selected modalities. Approaches to be considered include better aligning university teaching with firms' skill demands through collaboration in curriculum development, encouraging entrepreneurship, setting up university incubators, and establishing technology licensing offices (TLOs) and spin-offs. Governments need to provide the incentives required to make such modalities work, including bringing in intermediaries and offering matching funds.

Finally, the globalization of higher education has the potential to address some of the disconnects constraining higher education. The final section of this chapter focuses on providing adequate stewardship of international skill providers. Governments need to manage the growing trends of international education in ways that promote quality and recognition, increase access and equity, encourage cost-effectiveness, and build capacity.

Providing effective coordination among government bodies

Some of the disconnects described in chapter 3 have been aggravated by poor coordination. Indeed, institutional segmentation and fragmentation appear to characterize many of the region's higher education systems.

In Vietnam, the planned transfer of decision-making authority to higher education institutes in recent years has been welcome, but it has also been accompanied by challenges related to the ambiguity of content, feasibility for implementation, comprehensiveness, and consistency between different regulations because of the lack of coordination between agencies responsible for administering higher education, science and technology, and university relationships with industry.[1]

In Mongolia, different agencies responsible for different roles in the technical and vocational education and training (TVET) system are working in silos without much coordination, interaction, or synergy.[2] The National Vocational Education and Training Methodology Center has 70 skill standards, but the National Council for Education Accreditation (located separately in the Ministry of Education) has yet to accredit any of these programs. And although there is evidence of collaboration with industry, such collaboration is still very limited to students' attachments, which range from 30 to 45 days. Any attachment beyond the stated duration is at the discretion of school directors, and the Ministry of Education has little initiative to forge closer collaboration with industry or employers. Recently, the Ministry of Foreign Affairs has been considering a special economic zone for small and medium enterprises. But neither the Ministry of Education nor the Ministry of Science and Technology has been part of this effort.

Most countries need to do a better job clearly articulating the direction and general action map for their higher education systems. Many governments have ambitious objectives for their higher education systems, but if decision making is fragmented and does not consider related issues and challenges, progress will be difficult. Without a bold, systematic, and comprehensive vision—and processes for implementing its reform—progress in most of East Asia will be much less substantial and systematic than expected. Indeed, overcoming the five disconnects will most likely involve coordination among entities spread over multiple places of decision making (ministries of education, science and technology, and labor, to name three). How can governments do a better job at coordinating across these agencies?

There are no obvious solutions for addressing this challenge. For instance, the integration of higher education within ministries of education can help solve the disconnects between education levels but may make the connections with science and technology more distant. And even within ministries, coordination between departments cannot be taken for granted. Overall, countries will need to dedicate more attention to these links, including developing stronger mechanisms for coordination within their governments.

While there are many different ways to coordinate the myriad actors in the higher education system, some countries may find it desirable to set up a national commission for tertiary education or similar body with broad representation from industry, key professions, and national and international academics. The commissions could be charged with the responsibility to set the strategic direction for tertiary education, coordinate the various actors, and monitor how higher education facilitates national and regional development. The commissions could also sponsor policy analysis and conduct strategic planning, but they have to be in very close contact with the ministry of education and its different departments (they could even be part of ministries of education). The Republic of Korea's Ministry of Education and Human Resources Development and the Korean Council for University Education have partnered to serve this function and mediate between the central government (including its different agencies), firms, and higher education institutions.[3]

Other countries outside the region have formal stewardship arrangements. In the United Kingdom the Commission on Higher Education helps set strategic direction by articulating five aims: enhancing excellence in learning and teaching; widening participation and fair access; promoting employer engagement and skills; enhancing excellence in research; and enhancing the contribution of higher education to the economy and society. New Zealand's Tertiary Education Commission, Te Amorangi Mātauranga Matua, steers the tertiary education system to achieve national objectives.[4] Its main function is to put into effect the tertiary education strategy and coordinate its implementation, which may be suboptimal for separating policy and operations in higher education. Still, in pursuing its directive, it works with several key government agencies, including the Ministry of Education; the New Zealand Qualifications Authority; and the Ministry of Research, Science, and Technology, as well as a range of private, education sector, and industry representative groups—a very positive feature.

Steering private delivery

East Asian countries face the challenge of managing their growing PHE sector in a way that maximizes its potential to deliver key outcomes. If handled well, PHEIs can increase the capacity of the higher education system to expand coverage, diversify, and provide many useful intermediate skills through quality college-level education (first disconnect). Adequate steering of private institutions can also improve the interrelationships among higher education institutions (fourth disconnect). This section reviews the main characteristics of private delivery in East Asia, assesses some of the critical issues, and concludes with some policy recommendations.

Characteristics of private delivery in East Asia

Across the world, PHE has developed as an alternative to public education with significant potential to increase coverage at low public cost and even provide skills and innovation that the public sector may not be providing (through, for instance, state-of-the-art pedagogy and facilities).

A review of the characteristics and potential of PHE is particularly relevant in the context of East Asia because it is not yet used to its full potential, either (more commonly) for quality or (less commonly) for quantity.

Private enrollment shares

PHE accounts for almost 30 percent of higher education enrollment in East Asia. This places East Asia behind only Latin America among the world's regions, ahead of South Asia and the United States and far ahead of Europe and Africa (figure 6.1).[5] Figure 6.2 provides the private share in terms of enrollment and institutions by economy. The enrollment share of PHE exceeds 50 percent in eight economies of the region and reaches 70–80 percent in Korea; Japan; Taiwan, China; and Indonesia.

Beyond the generally high private share, two characteristics are notable: (a) mainly higher shares for institutions than enrollment, highlighting the relatively small size of many private institutions, and (b) some substantial differences in shares across economies for enrollment. Enrollment shares vary from about 10 percent in Thailand and Vietnam to about 80 percent in Korea.

Upper-income economies have higher private enrollment shares, but there is no linear relationship between the private enrollment share and the country income level in low- and middle-income East Asia (table 6.1). The Lao People's Democratic Republic and

Vietnam have some of the lowest enrollment ratios, but Cambodia has a much higher share. Indonesia and the Philippines have shares coming close to those of Japan and Korea, while Malaysia and Thailand have lower or much lower shares. In general, East Asian countries with early PHE sectors (Japan, Korea, Indonesia, and the Philippines) have larger PHE shares than countries with middle (Malaysia, Thailand) and late (China and Southeast Asia) PHE sectors.

Demand-absorbing institutions

The lack of a tight income relationship is in part because the nonelite, demand-absorbing institution type is by far the largest in East Asia.[6] (As the name suggests, this type of institution has the potential to address unfulfilled overall demand and thus contribute to increased coverage, with minimum cost to governments—assuming it is entirely financed with private funds, the most common pattern.)

Strong, large public sectors long antedating PHE were rarely a reality at the time East Asian governments approved PHE. This may explain why in many countries the private sector expanded so swiftly with broad overall government support. Demand for higher education became powerful with postwar economic development and middle-class growth, and appeared all the more explosive because it came in the historic context of low cohort enrollment in higher education. Postwar development prioritized rural, primary, and then secondary education rather than higher education in the public sector. For higher education, the vehicle for growth in several large East Asian nations would be PHE, an important feature in the following assessment.

The demand-absorbing institution is also the basic type for forms of PHE that have other characteristics. For instance, Thailand shows a powerful correlation between family-owned PHEIs and demand-absorbing institutions.[7] Much of Chinese PHE involves institutions for adult studies, part-time status, and "self-study" to prepare for a national exam, and most of them are at the prebachelor's level.[8] Globally, the private share is

FIGURE 6.1   Private higher education enrollment share, by region or country

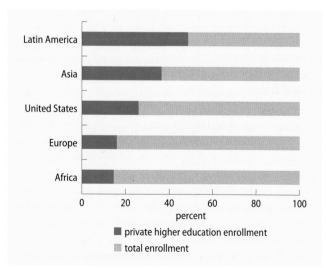

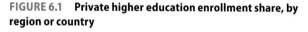

Source: PROPHE (Program for Research on Private Higher Education) International Databases, latest available year (2001–09).

FIGURE 6.2 Private higher education shares

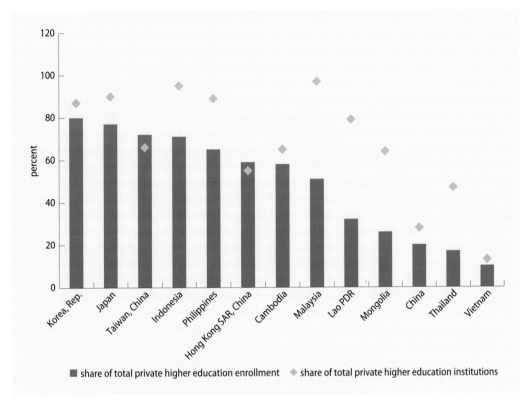

■ share of total private higher education enrollment ◆ share of total private higher education institutions

Sources: Based on Levy 2010; PROPHE International Databases, latest year available (2002–08); and WDI (World Development Indicators) database, 2007 data.
Note: Although data come from the most reliable (usually official) sources, criteria and inclusiveness vary greatly across countries, so comparisons should be made with caution. For example, the meaning of *higher education, university,* and *tertiary education* varies. In some databases, only accredited or at least licensed institutions may be counted; in others, the figures are more broadly inclusive. There are also differences in how enrollment and other variables are measured. Data years are the most recently available by country (generally 2006, 2007, or 2008).

TABLE 6.1 Private higher education shares and income groups

Private higher education share	Low-income economies	Middle-income economies	High-income economies
<33%	Lao PDR, Vietnam	China, Mongolia, Thailand	n.a.
33%–65%	Cambodia	Malaysia	n.a.
>65%	n.a.	Indonesia, Philippines	Hong Kong SAR, China; Japan; Korea, Rep.; Taiwan, China

Source: Authors' elaboration.
Note: n.a. = not applicable.

usually higher than the public share for nonuniversity enrollment, unlike university enrollment. In East Asia, this is particularly true for Malaysia, where the nonuniversity enrollment share is much larger than university enrollment for PHE, but all countries (including Japan and Thailand) show higher shares of nonuniversity enrollment in PHE than public higher education.

Demand-absorbing institutions make a significant contribution to the labor market particularly in the private market and can even make inroads into fields more expensive to offer, such as engineering and information technology (as recently documented by the Philippines[9] or even by some cases in China and Thailand).[10] However, the main demand-absorbing field remains business administration, with related studies in management, tourism, and the like.

Quantity-quality trade-off

The lack of a tight relationship with income levels also suggests gaps in the quality of some institutions, pointing to a quantity-quality trade-off in some countries: too much quantity can mean lower quality.

While data to compare the performance between public and private institutions are extremely scarce—starting with the impossibility of distinguishing people who have studied in public or private higher institutions in household and labor force surveys—skill surveys in Indonesia and the Philippines offer some clues.

In Indonesia graduates from public rather than private institutions seem to fare better across the board. The 2008 employer skill survey[11] shows that there are clearly more private than public universities performing

below average and that public technical institutes perform better than private ones (figure 6.3). Other sources confirm this evidence. BAN-PT's assessments generally show lower quality for private institutions.[12] Buchori and Malik (2004), too, noted that most PHEIs are of poor quality. They also state that private schools are often a prospective student's second choice.

Similarly, in the Philippines graduates from private institutions are less likely to be ranked "good" than those attending public universities or polytechnics (figure 6.3). Care needs to be taken in interpreting too narrowly these comparisons since, as is the case in Indonesia, "student sorting" (selection bias) between institutions may be common, with the best students preferring public to private institutions, which would help explain differences at graduation (though such sorting already suggests issues with PHE). Beyond these two countries, evidence from Cambodia indicates that private universities there may be of lower quality than public ones.[13] Some evidence also confirms that the research output is lower at private than at public institutions.[14]

FIGURE 6.3   **Rating of graduates from public and private tertiary institutions, Indonesia and the Philippines, 2008**

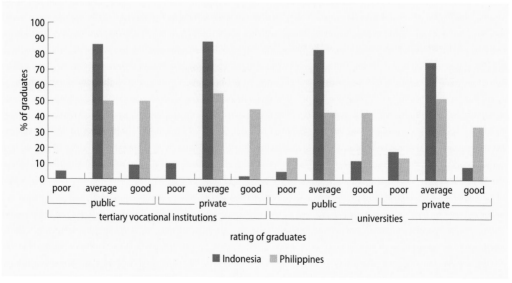

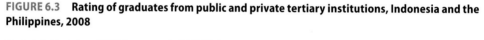

Sources: Indonesia and Philippines Skill Surveys 2008, as cited in di Gropello, Kruse, and Tandon 2011 and di Gropello, Tan, and Tandon 2010, respectively.
Note: Tertiary vocational institutions cover polytechnics only in the Philippines.

In some other countries, such as Korea, however, this quantity-quality trade-off is not visible, and, in fact, in East Asia there are many successful examples of private sector institutions, illustrating that there does not need to be a trade-off. In Malaysia, for example, PHEIs have pioneered in job-relevant fields, especially English, rarely available before, and some reports indicate that private institutions have better job-placement records.[15] A number of demand-absorbing PHEIs in China are accredited technical and vocational colleges that have made major efforts investing in infrastructure and equipment, enhancing curricula, establishing useful niche programs, and building links between graduates and employers. Similar to those in China, several demand-absorbing PHEIs in Thailand are fast-growing and successful specialized private institutions.

Semi-elite private universities
Like much of the world, East Asia is showing a rise in semi-elite universities.[16] These institutions, while not world-class in rankings or research, are high-status institutions within their countries with an objective of high-quality provision. They often compete with good public universities below the academic peak. They also sometimes compete with top-tier public universities in certain niche fields, above all business. They may also compete with the elite public universities for top students by paying more attention to teaching, though they lack the research capacity of top public universities.

In other words, they have the potential of providing very good academic, technical, and generic skills. Indeed, they can offer tough labor market competition to public institutions and, being entrepreneurial, can take the lead in innovative fields and fashion ties with businesses, nationally and internationally. They can even provide greater breadth of fields of study than public institutions by focusing on more costly but nonetheless essential fields of study,

such as science, technology, engineering, and mathematics.

Countries of late PHE development in East Asia tend to have a higher share of semi-elite institutions. Leading the way is, however, Korea, which has equal representation of private and public higher education institutions in the country's top-10 ranking and where semi-elite institutions have a strong presence in research and the sciences. Thailand's five semi-elite universities aim to produce graduates for business fields and technologically related industries networking with them. All these universities in Thailand are comprehensive in their programs but originally emphasized business-related fields, according to their founders.[17] Other countries also have their private semi-elite institutions: Japan's private sector is academically led by Waseda and Keio; the Philippines has its Ateneo de Manila, La Salle, and Santo Tomas;[18] Indonesia, Santa Dharma; and Vietnam, Phang Dong university.

While on the rise, semi-elite institutions are still relatively rare in most countries. Thailand, with as much as 40 percent of PHE enrollment in the semi-elite subsector,[19] appears to be an exception in middle-income East Asia. Even in the Philippines, the fact that only about 30 percent of private sector university graduates are considered good (against about 40 percent for the public sector) indicates that either the average quality of demand-absorbing institutions is still not good enough or that there is scope for more semi-elite institutions (or more enrollees in semi-elite institutions). In Indonesia the data suggest paucity of semi-elite private tertiary institutions.

Potential to expand and improve
private delivery
The clearest case of higher education expansion led by the private sector is in Korea, where the private gross enrollment ratio (GER) increased from less than 10 percent in the 1970s to almost 100 percent in 2008, alongside a massive expansion of PHE (figure 6.4). Indeed, Korea has built a strong higher education system based on

FIGURE 6.4   Higher education GER and enrollments, Republic of Korea, 1971–2008

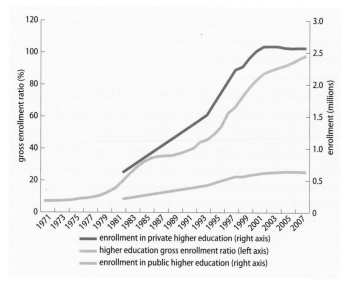

— enrollment in private higher education (right axis)
— higher education gross enrollment ratio (left axis)
— enrollment in public higher education (right axis)

Sources: PROPHE International Databases; WDI database.

some excellent PHEIs. Box 6.1 maps the growth of Korea's higher education system and the rise of private institutions to meet the demand for more access to higher education.

The growth of Japan's PHE is an early instance of demand absorption that led to high-quality private institutions.[20] Near the end of the 19th century, demand for higher education and the government's insufficient supply of public universities provided a market for PHE to fill the shortage. Private universities soon gained public approval because of their high-quality education. At the beginning of the 20th century, the government began to support PHE because of a desire to better link primary, secondary, and higher education; demand for more skilled workers in science and technology; support for a merit-based education system; and a new view that education could increase social opportunity. These factors led Japan to establish its University Code of 1918 to dramatically expand PHE and officially recognize current private institutions as accredited colleges and universities. By 1938 private institutions reached

their current level of supplying more than 70 percent of higher education enrollment.

Further down the income gradient, several low- and middle-income East Asian countries with low expansion or low quality of the private sector seem not to be using private delivery to its full potential. This failure has implications for their capacity to deliver skills and innovation. Some countries have much scope for further expansion, especially China, Lao PDR, Mongolia, and Vietnam.

In countries such as China and Vietnam, with less than 30 percent PHE enrollment, it is natural to assume that a further expansion of PHEIs would greatly help address coverage constraints or, conversely, that coverage may be currently constrained by low PHE shares. Indeed, in Malaysia the expansion of PHEIs was a particularly powerful complement to public institutions in rapidly expanding access. Malaysia had no PHEIs until 1992, when the number skyrocketed from 156 to 632 in 2000. This surge translated into an increase in the private enrollment share from about 10 percent in 1994 to about 40 percent in 2007 and, at the same time, an increase in the overall tertiary GER from about 15 percent in the mid-1990s to 30 percent in 2006.[21] By comparison, the private enrollment share (and the overall tertiary GER) has remained fairly stagnant in Thailand and Vietnam (figure 6.5).

Private delivery also has the potential to lead to system diversification and better provision of intermediate skills. In Mongolia, for instance, a stronger role for PHE may help support higher diversification of an otherwise homogeneous higher education sector, satisfying many skill needs. For its part, Thailand may have the potential to increase its PHE share to tackle issues of adult learning, for example.

Other countries have much scope for improving the quality of the private sector. The distinction between nonserious, demand-absorbing institutions (often called diploma mills) and serious demand-absorbing institutions is crucial. The former often accept students least prepared for higher education and provide them with little help or direction. The

BOX 6.1 Expanding private higher education in the Republic of Korea

In 1949 the new Republic of Korea announced a vision of universal primary education. The subsequent rise in primary-educated students led to increases in secondary enrollment, and eventually increasing demand for higher education (see figure B6.1). In 1995 a new deregulation policy eliminated higher education enrollment quotas, resulting in a boom of new universities and branch campuses. Altogether, the rising demand for higher education, the insufficient public higher education system, and the government's focus on primary and secondary education created a market for the private sector.[a] During the 1990s the higher education system experienced another boom, following the government's drive to build a market economy through privatization and competition. The government also implemented its Brain Korea 21 (BK21) project to increase innovation and promote a knowledge-based society focused on research and quality education for the 21st century. Among other initiatives, BK21 emphasized privatization, with more than half the

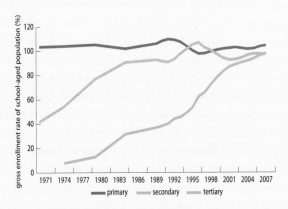

FIGURE B6.1 Enrollment by education level, Republic of Korea, 1971–2008

universities receiving BK21 funds being private universities.[b] Today, Korea's tertiary enrollment rate stands at 98 percent, with the private sector accommodating 80 percent of the students.[c]

Source: EdStats database.
a. Kim and Lee 2006.
b. Kim and Lee 2006; Ministry of Education and Human Resources Development, Republic of Korea 2010; Moon and Kim 2001.
c. EdStats database, 2008 data.

latter, by contrast, tend to orient themselves to the labor market, including tracking job-demand signals, providing counseling, engaging in joint initiatives with local businesses, and seeking feedback on job placements.

More generally, one can broadly differentiate institutions into those having problematic characteristics and of a poor quality and reputation ("garage"[22]) and those showing perseverance in job training ("serious"). Garage institutions typically are concerned with financial gain and focus on the short-cycle labor market (emphasizing low-cost fields), often through inferior resources, a lack of transparency, and overall low quality. Indonesia's ratings of PHE graduates appear to suggest that such garage institutions are quite common. Characteristics of

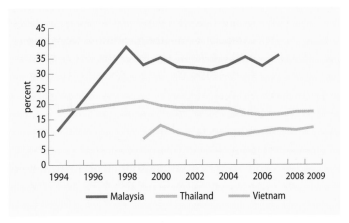

FIGURE 6.5 PHE enrollment share, Malaysia, Thailand, and Vietnam, 1994–2009

Sources: PROPHE International Databases; WDI database.

serious institutions include responsiveness to changing demands in the labor market, attraction of nontraditional students, effectiveness in management, and entrepreneurial orientation.

Looking ahead, the largest share of PHEIs will have to remain demand absorbing, given the higher cost of semi-elite institutions. But the current curriculum disconnects between institutions and the labor market, alongside the potential of semi-elite institutions, suggests that quality could also be improved by supporting a larger role for semi-elite institutions.

Main issues for private delivery in East Asia

Two main higher education issues face low- and middle-income East Asian countries: expansion (mainly in low-income and lower technology cluster countries but also in China and Thailand), and a quantity-quality trade-off (more visible in middle-income and middle technology cluster countries, notably Indonesia and the Philippines, but also in countries of the lower technology cluster where the private sector has been growing fast, such as Cambodia). Low PHE shares appear to stem largely from an earlier unfavorable policy stance or too restrictive regulation (or both), with insufficient resources playing a role as well. The quantity-quality trade-off may be an outcome of delayed or no regulation, leading to low-quality, demand-absorbing institutions, and limited resources and overregulation have no doubt hampered semi-elite institutions from gaining a higher share. The following review of policy stance and regulation, and of the financing framework, shows how these aspects affected quantity and quality of private delivery.

Policy stance and regulation

East Asian government policy has been mostly pro-private on enrollment expansion, though with notable differences among countries.[23] Government promotion following the demand-absorbing logic of encouraging more private supply to meet soaring demand has been particularly evident in countries with early PHE sectors (Indonesia, Japan, Korea, and the Philippines). Private demand absorption has, for instance, been very clear in Indonesia and the Philippines. Government stances were less clear-cut with private sectors that developed later (Malaysia and Thailand).

Malaysia's well-documented stance toward a more pro-private policy starting in the 1990s—with its impact visible in figure 6.5—is striking because it comes after the 1970s policy of "constraint" and then a 1980s policy of "controlled development."[24] The aim of access without public money became coupled with an approach to cut the brain drain of domestic students going abroad and to attract thousands of foreign students to Malaysia, specifically to Malaysian PHEIs. More long-standing, since the 1980s, have been twinning and related policies that have brought foreign institutions to Malaysia or sent Malaysian students abroad for part of their studies, though much of the thrust is now to avoid study abroad as too expensive.[25] The government is not fully pro-private, however, because it involves PHE in policy planning only to a limited extent.

Thailand is a slight aberration for its low and recently fallen share of PHE. The government does not proclaim goals for PHE shares and is attracted to expanding enrollment without a greater cost burden, but regulations remain quite restrictive. As a result, the private enrollment share has been stagnant since the early 1990s (see figure 6.5). The government itself seems to be divided at times on the issue, leaving it to the Commission on Higher Education to largely determine policy. PHE shares do not rise easily in the absence of public policy limits on public expansion.

The situation is different again in low-income or socialist-leaning economies where the private sector has been traditionally seen in less favorable terms, but the policy in these countries has been changing. China's policy stance, for instance, was for a long time unfavorable to the private sector. By 1994 it officially encouraged private growth (though less than wholeheartedly), and the stance really became unambiguous only in 2002. Since then the government has set goals for a growing private share (40 percent by 2020); has invited money from abroad and Hong Kong SAR, China; and is working on a long-term plan for PHE.[26]

Vietnam, too, has lately shown a more favorable stance, setting a goal in its Higher Education Agenda of higher education being 40 percent private by 2020. Its earlier goal of 30 percent by 2010 has, however, stalled, and regulations on private sector participation are ambiguous.[27] The private enrollment share is struggling to pick up (see figure 6.5).

Beyond the policy stance, regulations vary in nature, extent, and time of implementation across countries (table 6.2).[28] Cambodia, Malaysia, and Thailand are among countries

with laws to regulate PHE.[29] All these countries appear to have fairly tight regulations on PHE, but they were developed in different periods. Some evidence suggests that Chinese regulation is not extensive and instead allows ample competition.[30] In Indonesia autonomy from government seems to be high in practice, despite rules.[31]

This overview allows a few suggestions to be made on the role of the policy stance and regulation in East Asia in relation to expansion and the quantity-quality trade-off.

The relationship between the policy stance and the regulatory framework, and the growth of the PHE sector, is strong. The policy stance and regulatory framework have generally closely affected the development of

TABLE 6.2   Government regulations on private higher education, East Asia

Country	Policy or approach	Significance of the policy or approach
Malaysia	Private higher education act (1996)	Regulates PHE (tight control)
	For profit	Are explicitly permitted and extensive
	Purchasing power parity	Are mainly foreign universities and domestic colleges, with the former having some regulatory role over the latter, such as quality assurance
	Quality assurance	PHEIs have to obtain accreditation from the National Board of Accreditation; public universities have to carry out regular audits
Thailand	Private higher education act (1969)	Regulates PHE (comparatively restrictive)
	Ministerial regulations	Regulations and guidelines support the PHE act for procedural implementation of PHEIs (comparatively restrictive and detailed)
	Ambiguous for profit	For-profit institutions not allowed in higher education but "30 percent returns allowed" for licensees and investment encouraged
	Quality assurance and accreditation	PHEIs must be externally assessed and accredited by the Office for National Education Standards and Quality Assessment every five years; PHEIs and public universities use similar standards
China	Regulation (overall)	Not extensive and allows ample competition Varies by province and period
	Accreditation	Enhances autonomy and legitimacy (as well as quality), though most private higher education institutions have not earned it (620 have, 866 have not)
	Ambiguous for-profit	For-profit institutions not allowed in higher education but "reasonable returns" allowed and investment encouraged; for-profits allowed in training institutions
	Purchasing power parities	Are mainly public universities and private colleges, with the former having some regulatory role over the latter, such as quality assurance
	Governance: the Private Education Law (2002)	Requires a board of trustees for every private institution; stipulates that it consist of at least five people and that the institution's legal identity be with the chairperson of the board or the institution's president
Indonesia	Rules (overall)	Grant high autonomy from government in practice
	For profit	Are explicitly permitted and extensive
Philippines	For profit	Are explicitly permitted and extensive

Source: Levy 2010.
Note: The table is selective, and a policy shown in one country does not imply its lack in another.

the private sector in East Asia. In Indonesia, for instance, the expansion of the PHE sector was facilitated by a favorable policy stance combined with lax application of laws. China's PHE share is still low due to late take-off but has been increasing strongly[32] with the latest policy and regulatory steps. Vietnam's low share is due to the ambiguities of the regulatory framework (and policy stance), and Thailand's PHE share is hampered by the very tight legislation and generally unfavorable policy stance.

There is also a strong relationship between too laxly applied or "delayed" regulation and quality. Too lax or delayed regulation may have hampered (or be hampering) PHE quality in some countries with a high or growing PHE share. The regulations in Malaysia are likely to have helped maintain a minimum quality threshold in private institutions, thereby alleviating (or at least addressing) the quantity-quality trade-off.

Against this, the lax application of regulations in Indonesia is most likely a contributor to the poor quality of its PHE. Similarly, delayed regulation in the Philippines may also have played a role in the low quality of some institutions. While moving in the right direction, China needs to be careful to combine the higher level of autonomy given to private education with mechanisms of accountability. The fact that all Chinese private institutions need to have a board of trustees is, however, a fairly reassuring measure of accountability.[33] Lack of disclosure of higher education results in several countries has certainly contributed to some quality gaps.

These findings thus point to the need for the right regulation coupled with a favorable policy stance. The policy stance is critical because as long as it has been favorable, regulation has not necessarily hampered private sector growth in East Asia. The regulation applied in Korea (both before and after 1995), for instance, did not hamper the growth of the sector very much in the presence of a favorable general policy stance. A similar story holds for Malaysia (where the private share has continued to increase after the 1996 private higher education act), though,

consistently, to a lower level, given the more ambiguous policy stance.

By contrast, there is also a strong case against overregulation. While the pre-1995 regulations on Korea's PHE did not hamper growth, they may have hampered creativity and innovation because of their intrusive nature. This led to a relaxation of regulations in 1995, which then supported the growth and development of, for example, institutions such as Pohang University of Science and Technology (POSTECH).

It is also striking that specific regulations are sometimes tougher on private than public institutions. This is, for instance, the case in Malaysia, where only PHE needs to be accredited (and this decision may have contributed to a slowdown of private enrollment growth at the beginning of the new century—see figure 6.5). This duality can greatly constrain expansion.

Financing framework

The financing framework for PHE is generally sound in low- and middle-income East Asia, though there is scope to extend student loans to the PHE sector to support its demand-absorbing role and to further improve incentives to nontuition private funds to help establish more semi-elite institutions (and better demand-absorbing institutions). There may also be some scope to extend competitive research funding to the extent that competition between public and private institutions at the top can help spur innovation. Below is a brief review of the financing framework in East Asia, followed by an assessment of its soundness to address coverage and quality needs.

East Asia has for the most part followed the global rule: PHE is overwhelmingly funded through tuition. If anything, tuition dependence is especially marked in East Asia because PHE is concentrated in the demand-absorbing form, which, almost everywhere, is tuition dependent.[34] PHEIs in the Philippines get 85 percent of their income from tuition and in Vietnam, 82 percent,[35] and even in Japan[36] about 70 percent.[37] Overall, East Asia's tuition share accounts for more than

90 percent of operating costs, sometimes nearly the full load.[38] There are in most cases no fee caps, allowing fees to be higher—sometimes significantly so—than the public sector's.

There are also some nontuition sources of PHE income. Religious institutions may get funding from sponsoring or ownership organizations, or donated services. East Asian academics, sometimes retired, may offer their services. More important, wealth accumulation in East Asia has led to philanthropy (which shades into entrepreneurial investment), playing a larger role in PHE, as in the Philippines,[39] Singapore (the government matches private donations to higher education),[40] Japan (some families have used gains from their lower-education enterprises to donate to education corporations),[41] or Malaysia (businesses opened institutions or bought some set up by public university professor–entrepreneurs in the 1980s).[42]

Funding from abroad is another source of income, and of course arrangements vary greatly. In Vietnam, PHE started with foreign money, with domestic businesses following. Some Indonesian PHEIs maintain ties with institutions in the Netherlands.[43] The Chinese government has been wary of foreign ownership but has encouraged financial contributions, while Malaysia's twinning setups became substantial quickly.[44] Box 6.2 offers examples of resource diversification in China and Malaysia.

Direct government subsidies to PHEIs are very rare in East Asia, partly because of the numerical weight of the demand-absorbing subsector, globally the least likely to get such subsidies. Similarly, the recent nature of PHE in many East Asian countries plays a role because, internationally, older PHEIs are more likely to get government funding. Even in Japan, the share of private university income from that source is now only 10.5 percent. Nor does Korea offer a model for public subsidization of PHEIs: they get less than 2 percent of their income from the government.[45]

Indirect subsidies are more frequent, though not systematic. The three main indirect funding streams are student assistance, justified mostly on access and equity grounds; competitive research awards; and PHE hiring of public university teachers. (Donations

---

BOX 6.2   Resource diversification in China and Malaysia

China

- Funding comes from overseas Chinese and domestic businesses, with much initiative by professors and administrators from public universities.
- Family-owned and social group undertakings provide funds.
- Public universities provide initiatives for affiliated colleges.
- Partnerships exist between foreign institutions and Chinese private (or public) institutions.
- Recent change allows government loans for students in private institutions.
- Donations of land or buildings provide in-kind resources.

Malaysia

- Foreign funding is permitted for PHEIs.
- Business firms open their own institutions or buy institutions set up by individual proprietors.
- Various sorts of foreign financial and other participation are permitted for both higher education sectors.
- Foreign funds are prominent in private semi-elite institutions.
- Government pushes higher education to be a regional hub with a large, foreign student body paying tuition.
- Students enrolled in accredited programs in PHEIs are entitled to apply for government student loans.

Source: Levy 2010.

of land or buildings and favorable tax policies are other examples of indirect financing instruments.)

Student loans are still not systematically available to both the public and private sectors in East Asia, but policies are changing. Thailand has gone far enough that many of its PHEIs could be called "government dependent," given that student loans are their major income source.[46] Demand-absorbing Thai PHEIs rely on student loans the most because they need to keep fees reasonably affordable and tend to enroll poorer students than those at the semi-elite private universities (or public institutions). The semi-elite universities bank on student loans the least among PHEIs because they charge very high tuition and fees and enroll students with privileged backgrounds. They also get other sources of income. Until recently, China did not permit private students to access government loans—but that it does now is a significant change.

Competitive research funding is not yet systematically available to semi-elite universities. Very little research is undertaken in demand-absorbing institutions, making this subsidy route unlikely for this type of institution. One example of such funding for semi-elite institutions is Korea, where more than half the relevant government money goes to the top 10 of the 124 private institutions.[47]

Long seen in Latin America and now increasingly elsewhere is PHE hiring of professors from public universities who receive their main salary and benefits from the public institution. These professors are thus a public subsidy for PHE. This appears very common in East Asia. In China PHE use of public sector teachers has been facilitated by slack in the system, where some public professors had good benefits but did little research.

On the basis of the preceding review, the following assessment of the financing framework is offered.

The basic financing approach to PHE is reasonably sound. This is largely because there appear to be no strong grounds to support direct subsidies to the private sector.

Some arguments favor sector neutrality (subsidies provided to both public and private institutions);[48] others claim that it can dilute already scarce public funding and overburden the private sector with attached government regulation.[49] More important, private returns to tertiary education would seem to be high enough—overall and in the service sector—to provide an adequate incentive for private sector delivery and financing, especially in highly demanded "soft" sectors,[50] without public subsidies.

A case for direct subsidization can be made for semi-elite institutions—for instance, in science, technology, engineering, and mathematics—because of higher costs and (possibly) lower private returns, or larger externalities. But the evidence is missing that the private sector is more efficient than the public sector in providing these sorts of skills (and the private sector has shown itself to be capable of mobilizing sufficient funds to provide these types of skills). While it may therefore be useful to undertake further analysis to assess the cost-saving potential of subsidies for these "hard" fields, no strong case can be made for directly subsidizing the PHE sector generally.[51]

Indirect subsidies may still not be used sufficiently to support private sector expansion and quality. This is the case of student loans. Student loans have many rationales (reviewed in chapter 4). In Thailand student loans may explain why the disadvantaged have fairly good access to higher education, unlike in many other low- and middle-income countries where traditionally limited access to such loans in the private sector may have hampered equity and expansion. Middle-income countries such as China and Malaysia, having expanded loans to the private sector, may now be seeing the benefits of such a policy in coverage.

Competitive research funding could also be made more systematically available to semi-elite universities. Allowing them to compete for these grants may both strengthen them and spur healthy competition with the public sector. The Korean example is a case in point.

Finally, favorable tax policies, while they remain rare in the region (thus not discussed above), could have a positive effect on resource mobilization. The case for such policies is strong. They make sense for both private and public institutions. On the one side, there can be exemptions or partial exemptions from certain taxes; on the other, there can be tax breaks for individuals and businesses to donate, thus boosting philanthropy, which would have the potential to expand the semi-elite system.

Moving forward

Private education is clearly an integral part of the higher education system in East Asia, with about a third of the enrollment and with scope to continue growing.[52] In all countries PHE will continue playing or will have to play a large role, given constraints on public funds. This is particularly the case for demand-absorbing institutions that have a critical role in providing relatively low-cost but highly demanded fields. To the extent that more resources can be mobilized, semi-elite institutions can also have an important role in supporting innovative management and academic practices and in providing the public sector with high-level competition. Expansion will be all the more necessary in low-income countries where overall higher education coverage is still relatively low, and in countries with still low PHE participation.

As the sector expands, though, the critical challenge will be to avoid the quantity-quality trade-off dilemma that has appeared in some, mostly middle-income, countries. Addressing this trade-off and expansion requires policy and regulation, as well as a financing framework, to ensure that PHE is used to its full potential.

In low- and middle-income East Asia a proportion of demand-absorbing institutions (with high potential to provide affordable access to fields of study in high demand by the labor market) is of low quality, and the share of semi-elite institutions (more expensive but with higher potential for innovation and, to some extent, even hard sciences) is low. While

supporting a continued expansion of the PHE sector,[53] the policy environment thus also needs to encourage a move away from diploma mills to high-quality institutions to improve the quality and relevance of the private and overall higher education sector, notably through these two types of institutions.

Regulation (and information). Clear and efficient regulation is needed to provide clarity for private sector participation while restraining the development of low-quality demand-absorbing institutions. But excessive and undifferentiated regulation can greatly constrain participation—and even quality. Key aspects to be regulated are rules for use of public professors, the minimum curriculum, degree granting, licensing, examinations, and possibly board structures. Some pragmatism is needed to support the development of both serious demand-absorbing and semi-elite (or even elite) private institutions, which have different strengths and thus are both important to protect. This suggests that using the same standards (for instance, within an accreditation process) for public and private institutions may not be desirable, particularly when the private institutions are demand absorbing. Other levels of differentiation may include greater or lesser regulations for merely licensed institutions and for accredited ones, and for institutions receiving or not receiving public finance. Finally, the PHEI practice of voluntary accreditation should be supported.

Concrete incentives to performance will be more effective in supporting quality and relevance than strict and detailed bureaucratic rules. A clear example is allowing public and private higher education institutions to compete for research funds and to receive student loans. For both public and private institutions, regulation should as much as possible be outcome based rather than input based.

Similarly, various strategies should be devised to increase accountability to different stakeholders. Publication and dissemination of student performance in final exams, professional board licenses, and rules on board composition and responsibilities are all ways to ensure higher accountability for quality and relevance. Provision of information to all relevant stakeholders, including prospective students to allow them to make informed choices, will be particularly important. Information should include indicators of academic, research, and labor market performance of private sector institutions.

Financing. A strong case exists for public policy to encourage a variety of nontuition funding. This can help diversify the private sector (including supporting semi-elite institutions) and build a broader, more secure, and flexible base, from which welcome innovation springs. Tax policies more supportive to philanthropic and entrepreneurial funding with regulations favorable to foreign funds would help support a larger semi-elite sector.

At the same time, as tuition will remain the main income source for all types of East Asian PHE, and the overwhelming source for most PHEIs, public policy should be restrained in setting regulatory limits on it. Similar logic applies to restraint on imposing caps on enrollment at PHEIs.[54] The way to address equity issues and make PHE more affordable is rather through student loans and scholarships, offered by the institutions themselves or the government.

Direct subsidies of the government to PHEIs in East Asia are uncommon and should probably remain so given the limited available public funding and the associated risks of overregulation. Indirect subsidies— from competitive funds for research and student loans to tax subsidies—have much more potential, and low- and middle-income East Asia should make more use of them.

Encouraging effective university-industry links

While improved institutional management and coordination at the central level will go a long way toward strengthening links with firms, it will be insufficient unless it addresses other constraints. Some are related to capacity, but others can be tackled by smart choices in managing university-industry links. Policy makers across the region are looking at ways to make this link work.

Well-handled university-industry links can improve information flow between higher education and firms and the incentives to interact, enabling higher education institutions to meet skill and research demands of firms (first and second disconnects), and collaborate with other research providers (third disconnect). This section reviews the available modalities to build stronger links.

Although managing public and private institutions very much revolves around issues of autonomy and accountability, "reconnecting" the system—particularly the university-industry relationship—will also require other governance-related decisions to translate improved governance at the institutional level into stronger links for skills and research.

For university-industry links (also covering tertiary institutions generally), these governance-related elements include decisions on the modality of the links and the financing, fiscal, legal, and information-related incentives that may be needed to support them. These decisions will be all the more critical in the East Asian context where constraints to stronger university-industry links in research and technology are multiple (discussed in chapter 3).

The major hurdles in managing university-industry links are that firms in East Asia do not rank universities high either as sources of commercializable ideas and technical and commercial information or as fruitful collaborators. Additionally, risk-averse firms with little exposure to new technologies and a lack of technically skilled labor are often unwilling to bear the risks or put up the financing to bring new technologies to market.

Moving forward

Some of the deeper constraints related to limited research capability and lack of demand from the private sector will be addressed only with time, investment, smart governance, and economic reforms. Indeed, the success of university entrepreneurship will depend ultimately on the generation of significant ideas and findings and its reputation in providing high-quality education, so countries need to continue building capacity, step by step.

Not all countries have the same potential for university-industry links in research and technology. Countries from the lower technology cluster in particular see their potential very constrained by capacity gaps. They therefore need to continue strengthening their universities. Demand for innovation from their private sectors is also more limited. More selectivity, too, will be required for university-industry links: only a few first-tier universities in a country will ever have the potential to have strong formal interaction with firms.

While capacity is being built, policy makers can move to support stronger links (or at least put them in the right direction) in both skills and research.

The main modalities relevant to East Asia involve, in roughly descending order of importance, better aligning the teaching at university and firms' skill demands through collaboration in curriculum development, training firms' current workers, encouraging entrepreneurship, setting up university incubators, establishing TLOs and spin-offs, and developing extension and product development services. Bringing in intermediaries, providing matching funds, and pursuing greater sectoral and subsectoral selectivity will be instrumental in these modalities' success.

Encouraging university-industry collaboration in curriculum development. Aligning the skill demand of firms and instruction at university is probably the most urgent imperative, and stronger collaboration in curriculum development is necessary for meeting it. Among the most widely used (and most promising) modalities are appointing industrial practitioners on the staff of higher education institutions, establishing consultation mechanisms with industry, prioritizing student internships to encourage on-the-job learning and retrofit the curriculum, and including firm representatives on university boards.

In New Zealand, for example, the Tertiary Education Commission has funded "experts in residence" from industry to increase the relevance of curricula, financially supported student work placements, and developed a Business Links Fund to formalize industry input into curricular design.[55] France has enacted legislation (Law of August 2007 on the Freedom and Responsibility of Universities) to mandate that two representatives from industry or industrial associations serve on university governing boards.

Persuading tertiary institutions to play a more active role in training firms' current workers. Handled well, this modality has positive consequences for firms and curricula. For example, the University of the Philippines, Diliman, has partnered with the Department of Science and Technology to have engineering students and industrial plant workers undertake training at the university and at plant sites, partly under the direction of university instructors. Lessons learned during training are analyzed in the classroom, in line with theoretical and academic lessons, and then fed back to industry.[56] In Vietnam the Ho Chi Minh University of Technology has been active in training and skill development for local businesses.[57]

Encouraging entrepreneurship in tertiary institutions. Entrepreneurship training for faculty, students, managers, and workers is a very promising university-industry link for all countries. This will help boost weak management and leadership skills in low- and middle-income East Asia, indirectly lifting productivity. It should also help overcome the reluctance of some faculty members to get in touch with the business world—possibly because of a lack of business acumen and entrepreneurial drive—even if they have promising findings and new commercializable ideas. Deepening the pool of entrepreneurs can also complement research-promotion efforts.[58] Potter (2008) suggests various routes,[59] and the National University of Singapore has introduced several of these approaches in its entrepreneurship courses.

Setting up university incubators. This can help budding entrepreneurs commercialize ideas produced in a university. Universities in Taiwan, China, for example, are setting up incubation services to stimulate interactions with firms;[60] universities there run 81 percent of all incubators. But for incubators to launch viable start-ups, they should meet several conditions, in descending order: the university is a hotbed of ideas and a supportive promoter;[61] incubation facilities are networked with other incubators and firms;[62] and the university provides services facilitating the exit of firms from the university orbit.[63]

Establishing TLOs and spin-offs. Commercializing research and transferring technology by setting up TLOs and university-supported or sponsored spin-offs have good potential (box 6.3) but need to be well managed.

Among other things, TLOs can help universities address legal issues and deal with the "nitty-gritty" in reaching out to firms. Yet experience with university TLOs in the United States and Europe suggests that they often struggle to recruit and retain staff with the needed skills and that their incentive is to maximize revenue (inducing them to focus on the few most promising areas of research and to neglect other technologies with longer-term potential). Skills and university leadership are thus needed to support results. Separately, income generation through TLOs will probably remain small relative to total university income.[64]

The potential of spin-offs (start-ups) is possibly more for knowledge transfer than commercializing research. Spin-offs have become a lucrative source of revenue for many research institutions in China,[65] but only a handful are truly innovative; the bulk are regular firms that would be privately owned in other countries and just happen to be owned by universities in China.[66]

Start-up risks can be high. Even in more promising fields, such as biopharmaceuticals and nanotechnology, the payoff is uncertain.[67] And start-ups initiated by faculty "may lead productive faculty to leave the university, ultimately undermining the university's underlying capacity to generate new knowledge."[68] Spin-offs can, however, fulfill a role of knowledge and technology transfer, including joint research projects and assimilation of existing technology, and so offer some potential in countries of the middle and possibly lower technology clusters.

Reinforcing research and education policies through extension and product development services. Particularly to small and medium enterprises, such services can offer several benefits: providing a means of transferring valuable technical and problem-solving skills to industry; increasing the skill intensity of the subsector and encouraging research and development activity in firms that rarely engage in it; giving university graduates an opportunity to acquire practical experience and providing job opportunities; and partly neutralizing the disincentive effects of the recent global economic downturn for students contemplating a future in science and engineering or in research and development.[69]

The Fraunhofer Institutes in Germany,[70] the Technology Transfer from Research Institutes to Small and Medium Enterprises program in Sweden, the Advanced Technology Program in the United States,[71] and the

---

BOX 6.3   Technology licensing offices in three economies

Universities in Taiwan, China,[a] and in Hong Kong SAR, China, have set up TLOs to facilitate technology transfer and research collaboration.[b] Chinese universities are also collaborating increasingly with industry through contracts for technology services, patent licensing, and sales, and working through university-affiliated enterprises (unique to China). The two leading Beijing universities for commercializing ideas have established internal TLOs.

a. Mok 2010.
b. Mok 2010.

Technology Transfer Initiative (TTI) in Ireland (box 6.4) are successful models.

Bringing in intermediaries. Firms themselves should take the lead in initiating and organizing collaboration,[72] but this rarely happens because of credibility and communication gaps. Yet examples abound that intermediary groups or associations can help to bridge the university-industry gap. (Box 6.5 provides two—the first suitable to all countries, and the second more suitable to countries of the top technology cluster.)

While more unusual, local governments could also have an important role in relating universities to firms for both skill and technological development, as shown by the Ho Chi Minh City government in Vietnam. It encouraged links with local businesses by establishing a university council, which advised the government on how to promote training and innovation in universities linked to the city's development.[73]

Providing matching funds. Along the lines of providing more effective incentives, innovation funds may also support stronger links by providing matching funds to firms or universities to collaborate in adapting or developing technology. Such funds typically go further than competitive research funding by supporting the commercialization of research and tying up universities, research centers, and firms in collaborative research and technology projects. In a skill-provision role, applying the different university-industry link approaches may require some financial incentives. Additionally, training funds and dual-training programs to support internships and postemployment training could be explored further.[74]

Adopting greater selectivity. Skill-related university-industry links make sense in all sectors, but only a few first-tier universities will ever have the potential to have strong formal interactions with firms in research and development, and within these universities only a few departments representing specific sectors and subsectors may be able to pursue university-industry links. The priority sectors or subsectors should be the most dynamic and innovative parts of the economy.

BOX 6.4   **Creating university-industry links in Ireland**

The Technology Transfer Initiative is an innovative support structure for small and medium enterprises in some regions of Ireland. It emerged from an alliance of three regional universities. The TTI is cofunded by them and Enterprise Ireland, a state development agency focused on developing industry.

The role of the TTI is to act as a gateway for companies by facilitating access to the expertise and resources of the three universities. Its core aim is to encourage and assist Irish companies to become more innovative and thus more competitive and profitable. Essentially, the TTI aims to enhance technology transfer on an interindustry and interregional basis, increase innovation through research and development, and act as a single point of contact between expertise in the participating universities and local industry.

Companies request visits from TTI personnel who help identify potential research projects and topics to be addressed at specialist seminars with staff at universities. The TTI also organizes various innovation clubs between industry and academics. Companies meet regularly to discuss, present, and brainstorm new research areas, to share experience in new innovation, and to meet with academic researchers.

Feedback on the TTI from industry representatives suggests that it has been effective in giving small and medium enterprises access to in-depth knowledge of universities and that it has given university researchers a more practical look at the needs of industry.

Source: Technology Transfer Initiative; see http://www.biotechnologyireland.com/pooled/profiles/BF_COMP/view.asp?Q=BF_COMP_9249.

BOX 6.5   **Intermediary organizations**

TAMA association in Japan[a]

The aim of the TAMA (Technology Advanced Metropolitan Area) association is to improve the competitiveness of small and medium enterprises in the Tama region (northwest of Tokyo). The creation of the association was initially supported by the Kanto regional bureau of the Ministry of Economy, Trade, and Industry. Members of the association include small and medium enterprises, regional tertiary institutes, and banks.

The benefits of belonging to the association accrue mostly to those enterprises engaged in product innovation, rather than process innovation. So the first condition for this model (and other intermediary models) to have some utility is the existence of firms that are innovation driven, regardless of size.

Knowledge-integrating community[b]

A knowledge-integrating community supported by the Cambridge–MIT Institute (a collaboration between the University of Cambridge, United Kingdom, and the Massachusetts Institute of Technology, United States) may be a good model for government-industry-university collaboration.

One example is the Silent Aircraft knowledge-integrating community of the U.K. government. Because of the nature of the problem and the industry, collaboration among these three parties was seen as essential. A government body was needed to ensure compliance with existing regulations and potentially amending some of these. Industry partners (airlines) were involved because they are the end users. The analytical and research part was undertaken by a research institute. The involvement of banks helps address issues of capital.

a. T. Kodama 2008.
b. Acworth 2008.

High-tech subsectors offer potential for university-industry links—and in China, Thailand, and Vietnam particularly, in information technology and electronics. Yet other more medium-tech parts of an economy may offer scope for these links, such as the rubber industry in Thailand, which has shown promising collaboration, notably in testing and standards.[75] Some lower-value-added sectors dominated by small and medium enterprises may also offer such scope, to the extent that they are upgrading their technology, or some subsectors in agriculture.[76]

Stewardship of the internationalization of higher education

Over the past decade, higher education around the world has become more international: students enroll in full-time programs in foreign countries, faculty take up fellowships and posts in countries other than their own, and more and more students are using distance learning opportunities to take courses online in other countries. Providing effective stewardship of their higher education systems will mean that governments will have to confront the complex and growing trends of people mobility, program mobility, and institutional mobility in ways that promote quality and recognition, increase access and equity, encourage cost-effectiveness, and build capacity. Effective stewardship of the international dimensions of higher education can help higher education institutions meet skill and research demands of firms (the first and second disconnects) and collaborate with other skill and research providers (the third and fourth disconnects).

Characteristics of internationalized higher education in East Asia

Perhaps the biggest growing trend in internationalized higher education in East Asia is that of international "people mobility." Of all East Asian countries, China sends by far the greatest number of students to study in foreign countries. In 2007 more than 421,000 Chinese students were enrolled in tertiary education classes in a foreign country (figure 6.6). While the large disparity between China and other countries in the region on this indicator can likely be explained by population differences, the number of tertiary students studying abroad from other less populated countries in the region is not insignificant. More than 54,000 Japanese tertiary students were studying abroad in 2007, 45,000 Malaysian students, and more than 32,000 students from Hong Kong SAR, China. Among lower-income countries in the region, Vietnam sent about 27,000 tertiary students to study abroad in 2007.

The highest proportion of Asian tertiary students studying abroad in 2007 chose to study in the United States (33 percent; figure 6.7). About 13 percent chose to study in the United Kingdom, 12 percent in Australia, 10 percent in Japan, and 8 percent in Germany. This list of receiving countries is not surprising: the United States, the United Kingdom, Australia, Japan, and Germany account for almost 80 percent of foreign students worldwide and more than 76 percent of Asian students.[77]

Program mobility (which involves e-learning and face-to-face teaching in local partner institutions) is the second most popular form of cross-border higher education (box 6.6). Institutional mobility, where universities open campuses in foreign countries, is also an increasingly important, if novel to East Asia, feature of cross-border education.

Cross-border higher education can address several disconnects identified in chapter 3, and countries are pursuing opportunities to improve their higher education systems. The mobility of domestic and foreign students and staff often encourage political, cultural, and academic mutual understanding between

FIGURE 6.6   Tertiary students studying abroad, 2007

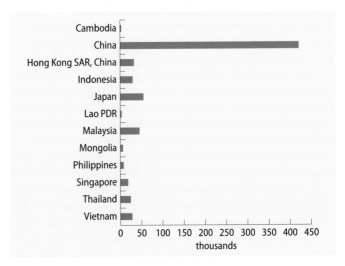

Source: UIS (UNESCO Institute for Statistics) Data Centre.

FIGURE 6.7   Asian students studying abroad in tertiary schools in the top-five receiving countries, 2007

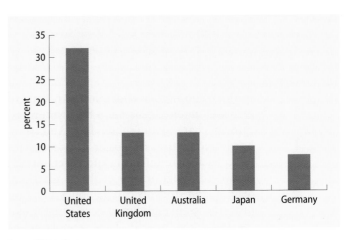

Source: UIS Data Centre.

institutions. Some countries see cross-border exchanges as skilled migration: the recruitment and retention of talented international students and faculty can pay large dividends for a host country's knowledge economy and make its higher education system more competitive and innovative. In this way, internationalization of higher education can help address the first and second disconnects. Moreover, giving more foreign students access

---

BOX 6.6   E-learning and virtual universities as instruments of internationalization

To increase accessibility to tertiary education, countries are turning with greater frequency to distance-learning centers and virtual universities. For many countries, this trend is attractive for three main reasons: it allows the sharing of resources, costs, and infrastructure to deliver e-learning; it provides a platform for competing with international providers; and it can reduce duplication among existing universities.

In most of the world, particularly East Asia, virtual universities are a novel activity. While enrollments are difficult to track, particularly in the region, the Organisation for Economic Co-operation and Development's Center for Educational Research and Innovation recently surveyed tertiary institutions offering e-learning modules to learn more about their activities. It found that many virtual universities are being used as instruments of internationalization. For example, the United Kingdom's Open University enrolls more than 25,000 international students, more than 15 percent of the total enrollment. Similarly, the Open University Catalunya's enrollment is more than 20 percent international. German and Mexican virtual universities reported similar international enrollment ratios.

As virtual universities become more popular, a central challenge will be to ensure quality and consumer protection for students and parents. National regulatory frameworks will have to take into account international benchmarks to ensure the comparability of degrees and easier comparison against international standards. With these efforts to enhance the international comparability of virtual learning, countries will need to improve the information available to prospective students so that they can make informed decisions about where to enroll. Institutional autonomy will also be important. Being able to partner with information technology institutions and providers to keep costs manageable will be a continuing challenge for virtual universities.

Source: OECD 2004.

---

to domestic higher education can lead to increased revenue generation for institutions, through charging full tuition fees. And cross-border education can offer opportunities for capacity building for sending countries: fellowship programs for civil servants, academics, and students can be policy-building instruments, in addition to developing teaching and research skills. These opportunities can help address the first and second disconnects, as well as the disconnects between higher education institutions themselves and higher education institutions and other skill providers (fourth disconnect).

In East Asia, the increasing cross-border participation appears to be demand driven: the growing internationalization of higher education is the result of skilled-worker migration (such as the recruitment of talented international students to work in the host country), revenue generation opportunities (as when foreign students generate income for institutions through entrepreneurship), and the need to develop a more skilled workforce (such as scholarship programs for domestic civil servants and academics to facilitate knowledge transfers between host and local institutions). Malaysia; Hong Kong SAR, China; China; and Singapore have been particularly active in cross-border education during the past decade.

Recent research confirms that the decisions to study abroad are often rooted in the labor market: students decide to enroll in tertiary education abroad to obtain a job in that country.[78] Indeed, greater numbers of students decide to pursue higher education in the United States from "lower skill-price" countries than from "higher skill-price" countries. Moreover, "higher skill-price" countries attract more foreign students than "lower skill-price countries."

Increasing the number of tertiary institutions in a sending country with a low skill-price increases outbound migration of tertiary students, whereas improving the quality of domestic tertiary institutions decreases student migration.[79] This is likely the result of the higher number of college graduates increasing the number of workers who would benefit from migrating to high skill-price countries. But higher quality retains students in country.

In East Asia, students who study abroad at the tertiary level tend to return to their home country in larger numbers than do students who study abroad from other regions.[80] But foreign-trained students from low-wage countries are less likely to return than foreign-trained students from high-income countries.

Moving forward

While the potential of the internationalization of higher education for East Asia is great, it must be managed carefully. How can it be handled in ways that promote quality and recognition, increase access and equity, encourage cost-effectiveness, build capacity, and best address the disconnects identified in chapter 3?

Lessons from the international experience suggest the following:[81]

- First, higher education policies in low-income countries and countries with low skill-prices need to be informed by the causes and consequences of the out-migration of students seeking higher-paying jobs.
- Second, as the global competition for skills intensifies, promoting consumer protection is paramount: students need transparent information about the quality and international validity of programs they wish to enroll in. This implies that quality assurance and accreditation systems need to cooperate at the international level and reference international benchmarks.
- Third, because student participation in cross-border education is largely financed by students, those of lower income and

educational backgrounds are less likely to participate. Financial support through targeted or means-tested scholarship programs and increased information about cross-border programs could narrow this equity gap. To help universities become more relevant, demand driven, entrepreneurial, and profitable, they need financial autonomy so that they can control the revenue they generate.
- Fourth, to build capacity, cross-border initiatives need to meet quality and skill needs of countries in ways that promote lifelong learning, while managing the risk of brain drain.

***

The previous parts of this study documented some of the main constraints that East Asia's higher education systems are facing. Five fundamental disconnects prevent the region's higher education systems from contributing to innovation and technological capability and from addressing the mismatches between the demand for and supply of skills.

These structural deficits result largely from country failures to implement coherent sets of policies to address the challenges and shape the directions of their higher education systems holistically. This lack of vision has led to inefficiencies throughout the system.

There is no magic formula for articulating and implementing a fully fledged vision for higher education, but success will depend on two key factors the previous chapters have examined: (a) setting the right incentives and (b) mobilizing and allocating resources efficiently and effectively. Effective financing policies will need to include a strategic framework that allows further resource mobilization while maximizing the effectiveness and efficiency of fund use and allocation. Improving the management of public institutions will require that countries reassess autonomy and accountability within their systems. And providing effective stewardship will require countries to better coordinate different government agencies, steer private higher education, encourage university-industry links, and navigate the increasing trend of cross-border education.

Two steps forward, one step back. East Asia's higher-income economies have made spectacular gains in higher education delivery over the past few decades, but the low- and middle-income economies are struggling to replicate the standard bearers' success. These final chapters have offered suggestions for how the higher education systems in low- and middle-income countries can close the gap with global leaders—some of which are their neighbors.

Notes

1. World Bank 2010f.
2. World Bank 2010d.
3. Mok 2010.
4. Tertiary Education Commission of New Zealand 2009.
5. This omits some Asian countries with older numbers.
6. Levy 2008b, 2010.
7. Praphamontripong 2010.
8. Although many Chinese PHEIs carry "university" in their name, there are officially no private universities (Yan 2010).
9. Valisno 2002.
10. Levy 2010.
11. Di Gropello, Kruse, and Tandon 2011.
12. BAN-PT (Indonesia's National Higher Education Accreditation Board) was established to introduce a quality-awareness and self-assessment tradition among public and private sector providers. It has also recently begun to reference international benchmarks in its accreditation processes.
13. World Bank 2010e.
14. In Vietnam in 2006, for example, average published articles per academic staff were only 0.01 percent for private universities but 0.45 percent for public universities (World Bank 2008).
15. Orbeta 2008; Yilmaz 2009.
16. Levy 2008a.
17. Doner, Intarakumnerd, and Ritchie 2010.
18. LaRocque 2002.
19. Semi-elite universities such as Bangkok University, Dhurakij Pundit University, and the University of the Thai Chamber of Commerce are individually much larger than the country's demand-absorbing institutions (Praphamontripong 2010).
20. Okada 2005.
21. Levy 2010.
22. Levy 2010.
23. The government policy stance mostly includes the existence of a supportive legal, strategic, and fiscal framework for PHE (PHE promotion laws and decrees, PHE growth targets, fiscal incentives) and decisions on public sector expansion.
24. M. Lee 1999.
25. Mei 2002.
26. Cao 2007; Deng 1997; J. Lin 1999.
27. World Bank 2009b.
28. The diagnostic of the regulatory environment across countries is constrained, however, by lack of systematic and fully comparable information across countries.
29. UNESCO 2006.
30. Cai and Yan 2009.
31. Sukamoto 2002.
32. The share of the private sector has been increasing rapidly in China from less than 9 percent in 2002 to about 20 percent now.
33. Lax regulation is more likely to be an issue where the internal management structure of a PHEI does not support accountability to the broader community.
34. Alternative (nontuition) private funding in East Asia, as elsewhere, is more common in semi-elite and religious or cultural subsectors.
35. Valisno 2002; World Bank 2008.
36. Japan is often taken as an example and benchmark in the advocacy of East Asian government subsidies to PHEIs.
37. Yonezawa and Baba 1998.
38. Levy 2010.
39. LaRocque 2002.
40. Bjarnason and others 2009.
41. Yonezawa and Baba 1998.
42. Mei 2002.
43. Bastiaens 2009.
44. M. Lee 2004.
45. Postiglione and Mak 1997.
46. Ziderman 2003, 2006.
47. S. H. Lee 1998.
48. Arguments include fairness to the private sector, expansion of PHE, improvement of PHE, increased competition between the public and private sectors, that higher education provides externalities and so merits public subsidies, and that a vulnerable private sector

can lead to a proportional shift that burdens the public sector.

49. Chapman and Drysdale 2008.

50. These are typically business, finance, languages, and various social sciences.

51. Limited subsidies have not prevented the sector from expanding (or moving to higher quality) in Korea, for example.

52. Notwithstanding the proportional decline in a couple of countries.

53. In this respect, Malaysia, Thailand, and Vietnam may want to change their policy stance. They might also consider making the impact on PHE one element in their deliberations on public expansion.

54. As seen in Taiwan, China.

55. OECD 2008b.

56. Tansisin 2007.

57. Ca 2006.

58. Audretsch 2008.

59. These approaches include classroom lectures, business plans, case studies, entrepreneurs as guest speakers, student business start-ups, business games, student entrepreneur clubs and networks, placements with small firms, feasibility studies, communication training, consulting for small and medium enterprises, support for graduate student start-ups following the course, universitywide entrepreneurship education, specialist entrepreneurship degrees, distance education programs, external partnerships, and courses for entrepreneurship teachers.

60. Mok 2010.

61. Patton, Warren, and Bream 2009.

62. Hansen and others 2000.

63. Potter 2008.

64. Perhaps no more than five universities in the United States derive significant income from licensing of research findings or from royalties (Geiger and Sa 2008).

65. Wu 2010.

66. Chen and Kenney 2007.

67. Chinese universities are also discovering the downside of start-ups and are distancing themselves from direct ownership and responsibilities (Zhou 2008).

68. Miner and others 2001.

69. Bramwell and Wolfe 2008; Lundvall 2007.

70. Yusuf and Nabeshima 2009.

71. Darby, Zucker, and Wang 2004.

72. As Seagate did in Thailand in the late 1990s (Doner, Intarakumnerd, and Ritchie 2010).

73. Ca 2006.

74. In East Asia the case of the dual-training program in the Philippines is a good example of government, firm, and institution collaboration in training (di Gropello, Tan, and Tandon 2010).

75. Doner, Intarakumnerd, and Ritchie 2010.

76. See, for example, Brimble and Doner (2007) and Kruss and Lorentzen (2007) on the shrimp industry in Thailand and the wine industry in South Africa, respectively.

77. Rosenzweig 2009.

78. Rosenzweig 2009.

79. Rosenzweig 2009.

80. Rosenzweig 2009.

81. OECD 2004; UNESCO 2006.

Appendixes

Appendix A

Number and Type of Higher Education Institutions in East Asia

TABLE A.1   **Number and type of higher education institutions in East Asia**

Economy	Types of higher education institutions
Cambodia	**Public:** 34 institutions **Private:** 57 institutions **Other:** higher education includes universities, institutes or technical institutes, and a royal academy
China	**Public:** 1,079 four-year institutions, 1,184 three-year vocational or technical institutions, 400 adult higher education institutions **Private:** 218 Minban higher education, 322 independent colleges and universities **Other:** self-study programs provided by distance-education universities
Indonesia	**Public:** 48 universities, 7 institutes, 2 colleges (Sekolah Tinggi), 26 polytechnics **Private:** 372 universities, 42 institutes, 1,249 colleges (Sekolah Tinggi), 985 academies, 118 polytechnics **Other:** 52 Islamic universities
Korea, Rep.	**Public:** 26 universities, 15 junior colleges, 11 University of Education, 8 industrial universities, 1 open university **Private:** 145 universities, 143 junior colleges, 10 industrial universities, 1 technical university, 17 cyber universities, 1 corporate university, 28 grad school universities, 5 miscellaneous schools
Lao PDR	**Public:** 22 institutions **Private:** 77 institutions **Others:** higher education includes universities, institutes, or technical institutes
Malaysia	**Public:** 20 universities **Private:** 487 total (20 universities, 21 university colleges, 398 colleges, 5 foreign branch campuses, open universities, virtual universities) **Other:** 24 polytechnics, 37 community colleges
Mongolia	**Public:** 49 institutions **Private:** 131 institutions **Other:** colleges award diplomas (three years) and bachelor's degrees (four years); institutions may also provide master's (1.5 to 2 years); universities offer all degrees including doctoral (three to five years)
Philippines	**Public:** 110 state universities and colleges with 424 satellite campuses,[a] 1 Commission on Higher Education–supervised institutions, 93 local universities and colleges, and 15 other government schools and special higher education institutions **Private:** 334 sectarian institutions (religious, private nonprofit) and 1,270 nonsectarian institutions (private for profit)
Singapore	**Public:** 5 autonomous universities **Private:** 9 universities/institutions **Other:** 13 junior colleges (two to three years), 1 centralized institute (three years), 5 polytechnics, 1 Institute of Technical Education (one to two years), 2 arts institutions
Thailand	**Public:** 66 selective-admissions universities, 2 open-admissions universities, 11 autonomous universities, 19 two-year community colleges **Private:** 39 universities, 25 colleges, 7 private institutions **Other:** 1–4 years for vocational diploma with two to three years for bachelor's degree, 2 autonomous Buddhist universities
Vietnam	**Public:** 306 institutions **Private:** 80 nonpublic institutions **Other:** four- to six-year universities, three-year colleges, one- to three-year master's degrees, two- to four-year doctorate (after master's), vocational college, vocational secondary, vocational training center, in-service higher education

Source: Authors' elaboration.
a. Satellite campuses include state universities and college extension campuses and external study center.

Appendix B

Economic Indicators

TABLE B.1   GDP growth of upper-income East Asian economies
average annual percent

Economy	1990–99	2000–09
Singapore	7.6	5.6
Hong Kong SAR, China	3.6	5.0[a]
Korea, Rep.	6.3	4.4
Taiwan, China	6.5	3.6[a]
Japan	1.5	0.7

Source: World Development Indicators (WDI) database.
a. Average for 2000–08.

TABLE B.2   Savings and investment of upper-income East Asian economies
average percentage of GDP

Economy	Gross domestic savings		Gross capital formation	
	1990–99	2000–09	1990–99	2000–09
Singapore	48.3	45.7[a]	35.2	23.2[a]
Korea, Rep.	36.3	31.6	35.4	29.5
Hong Kong SAR, China	31.9	31.5[a]	29.4	22.6[a]
Taiwan, China	26.8	25.9[a]	24.4	20.7[a]
Japan	30.6	24.6	29.0	23.4

Source: WDI database.
a. Average for 2000–08.

TABLE B.3   Exports of upper-income East Asian economies
average percentage of GDP

Economy	1990–99	2000–09
Singapore	—	215.0[a]
Hong Kong SAR, China	133.3	179.7[b]
Taiwan, China	45.7	62.1[b]
Korea, Rep.	30.8	40.7
Japan	9.9	13.6

Source: WDI database.
Note: — not available.
a. Average for 2001–08.
b. Average for 2000–08.

TABLE B.4   **Leading export sectors, upper-income East Asian economies**
percentage of total exports

Economy	1995	2007
Japan		
Engineering products	26.5	25.7
Automotive products	18.0	23.3
Electronic and electrical products	28.1	17.6
Process industry	7.1	9.0
Korea, Rep.		
Electronic and electrical products	29.5	26.9
Engineering products	15.1	18.3
Automotive products	7.4	13.2
Other resource-based products	4.4	10.5
Taiwan, China[a]		
Electronic and electrical products	36.0	35.5
Other low-technology products	16.1	13.5
Process industry	8.6	12.0
Engineering products	13.7	11.3
Singapore		
Electronic and electrical products	52.5	38.4
Other resource-based products	9.7	19.4
Engineering products	14.5	18.7
Process industry	4.6	6.2

Source: World Integrated Trade Solution (WITS) database.
Note: Data are not available for Hong Kong SAR, China.
a. Data for initial year are from 1997.

TABLE B.5   **GDP growth of middle-income East Asian economies**
average annual percentage

Economy	1990–99	2000–09
China	10.0	10.3
Mongolia	−0.3	5.9
Indonesia	4.8	5.1
Malaysia	7.2	4.8
Philippines	2.8	4.6
Thailand	5.3	4.1

Source: WDI database.

TABLE B.6   **Exports of middle-income East Asian economies**
average percentage of GDP

Economy	1990–99	2000–09
Malaysia	91.2	110.5
Thailand	43.0	69.9
Mongolia	50.5	59.8
Philippines	38.1	46.1
Indonesia	30.1	32.4
China	19.6	31.1

Source: WDI database.

TABLE B.7   Savings and investment of middle-income East Asian economies
average percentage of GDP

Economy	Gross domestic savings		Gross capital formation	
	1990–99	2000–09	1990–99	2000–09
China	41.2	45.8	39.1	41.2
Malaysia	40.7	42.2	36.3	21.8
Thailand	35.3	31.7	36.3	25.9
Indonesia	30.2	30.5	27.6	25.0
Mongolia	18.7	25.4	31.2	35.3
Philippines	16.2	14.9	22.4	16.6

Source: WDI database.

TABLE B.8   Leading export sectors, middle-income East Asian economies
percentage of total exports

Economy	1995	2007
China		
Electronic and electrical products	10.8	30.1
Textiles, garments, and footwear	30.9	16.5
Engineering	10.6	15.3
Other low-technology products	15.8	14.8
Indonesia		
Primary products	36.0	35.4
Agro-based products	18.6	17.6
Other resource-based products	8.3	12.5
Textiles, garments, and footwear	15.9	9.4
Malaysia		
Electronic and electrical products	38.7	39.3
Primary products	10.9	15.3
Agro-based products	15.2	11.4
Engineering products	15.4	9.6
Philippines		
Electronic and electrical products	49.0	47.9
Primary products	7.3	9.9
Agro-based products	7.3	9.0
Other resource-based products	3.0	7.3
Thailand		
Electronic and electrical products	23.0	23.2
Engineering products	10.1	13.6
Primary products	16.9	11.4
Other low-technology products	11.1	10.2

Source: WITS database.
Note: Data are not available for Mongolia.

TABLE B.9   GDP growth of lower-income East Asian economies
average annual percentage

Economy	1990–99	2000–09
Cambodia	7.2[a]	8.1
Vietnam	7.4	7.3
Lao PDR	6.3	6.7

Source: WDI database.
a. Cambodia average for 1994–99.

TABLE B.10   **Exports of lower-income East Asian economies**
average percentage of GDP

Economy	1990–99	2000–09
Vietnam	37.6	65.8
Cambodia	29.1[a]	60.1
Lao PDR	23.0	31.4[b]

Source: WDI database.
a. Cambodia average for 1993–99.
b. Lao PDR average for 2000–08.

TABLE B.11   **Savings and investment of lower-income East Asian economies**
average percentage of GDP

Economy	Gross domestic savings		Gross capital formation	
	1990–99	2000–09	1990–99	2000–09
Vietnam	16.0	28.3	23.5	35.8
Lao PDR	—	19.9[a]	—	31.4[a]
Cambodia	−0.6[b]	11.5	13.8[b]	19.1

Source: WDI database.
Note: — not available.
a. Lao PDR averages for 2000–08.
b. Cambodia averages for 1993–99.

TABLE B.12   **Leading export sectors, lower-income East Asian economies**
percentage of total exports

Economy	2000	2007
Vietnam		
Primary products	51.6	40.6
Textiles, garments, and footwear	26.6	27.3
Other low-tech products	4.6	10.4
Engineering products	2.9	5.6
Cambodia		
Textiles, garments, and footwear	72.8	72.9
Other low-tech products	20.3	23.1
Primary products	1.3	2.3
Agro-based products	4.5	0.6

Source: WITS database.
Note: Data are not available for Lao PDR.

Appendix C

Trends in Returns to Skill and Share of Skilled Workers, by Sector

FIGURE C.1 **Return to skill by sector over time (tertiary and above), Indonesia**

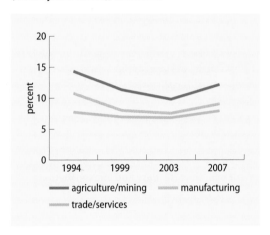

Source: di Gropello and Sakellariou 2010, based on labor and household surveys (various years).

FIGURE C.2 **Proportion of skilled workers by sector over time (tertiary and above), Indonesia**

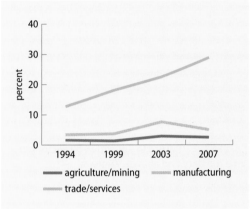

Source: di Gropello and Sakellariou 2010, based on labor and household surveys (various years).

FIGURE C.3 **Return to education by sector over time (tertiary and above), Philippines**

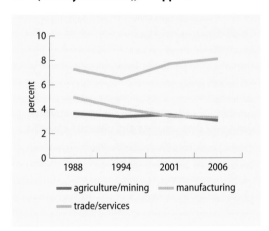

Source: di Gropello and Sakellariou 2010, based on labor and household surveys (various years).

FIGURE C.4 **Proportion of educated workers by sector over time (tertiary and above), Philippines**

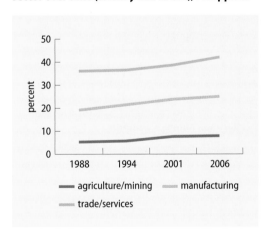

Source: di Gropello and Sakellariou 2010, based on labor and household surveys (various years).

FIGURE C.5 **Return to skill by sector over time (tertiary and above), Thailand**

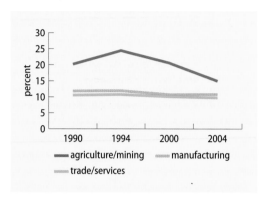

Source: di Gropello and Sakellariou 2010, based on labor and household surveys (various years).

FIGURE C.6 **Proportion of skilled workers by sector over time (tertiary and above), Thailand**

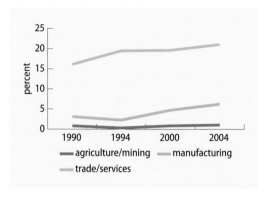

Source: di Gropello and Sakellariou 2010, based on labor and household surveys (various years).

FIGURE C.7 **Return to education by sector over time (tertiary and above), Vietnam**

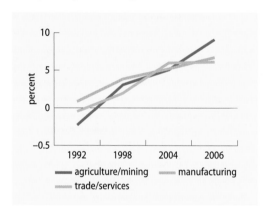

Source: di Gropello and Sakellariou 2010, based on labor and household surveys (various years).

FIGURE C.8 **Proportion of educated workers by sector over time (tertiary and above), Vietnam**

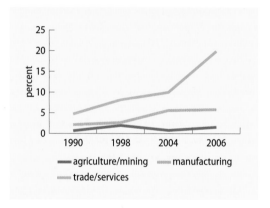

Source: di Gropello and Sakellariou 2010, based on labor and household surveys (various years).

FIGURE C.9 **Return to skill by sector over time (tertiary and above), Cambodia**

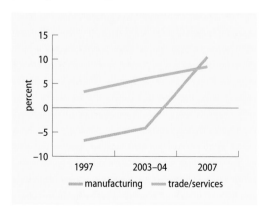

Source: di Gropello and Sakellariou 2010, based on labor and household surveys (various years).

FIGURE C.10 **Proportion of skilled workers by sector over time (tertiary and above), Cambodia**

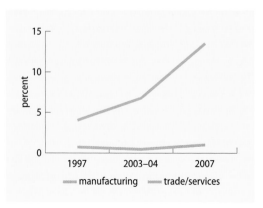

Source: di Gropello and Sakellariou 2010, based on labor and household surveys (various years).

FIGURE C.11   Return to skill by sector over time (tertiary and above), China

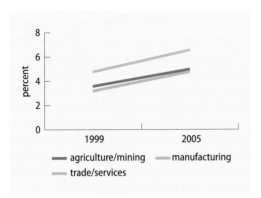

Source: di Gropello and Sakellariou 2010, based on labor and household surveys (various years).

FIGURE C.12   Proportion of skilled labor by sector over time (tertiary and above), China

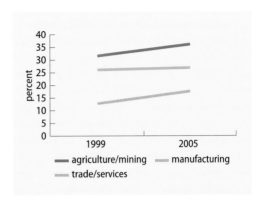

Source: di Gropello and Sakellariou 2010, based on labor and household surveys (various years).

FIGURE C.13   Return to skill by sector over time (tertiary and above), Mongolia

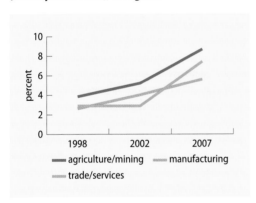

Source: di Gropello and Sakellariou 2010, based on labor and household surveys (various years).

FIGURE C.14   Proportion of skilled labor by sector over time (tertiary and above), Mongolia

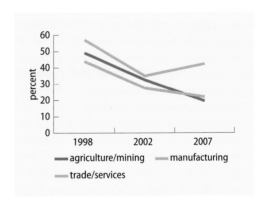

Source: di Gropello and Sakellariou 2010, based on labor and household surveys (various years).

Appendix D

Changes in Wage and Industry Education Premiums, by Subsector

FIGURE D.1   **Change in unstandardized weighted industry and skill premiums by sector, Indonesia, 1996–2007**

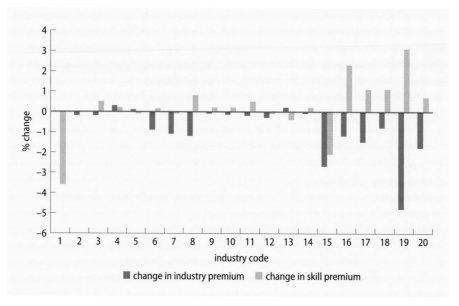

Source: di Gropello and Sakellariou 2010.
Note: The numbers on the *x* axis refer to these industries: 1. agriculture; 2. forestry; 3. fishery; 4. mining/minerals; 5. metal ore/other mining; 6. food/beverage/tobacco; 7. textile; 8. timber and furniture; 9. paper and printing; 10. chemicals; 11. nonmetallic production; 12. metal industry; 13. other industry; 14. utilities; 15. construction; 16. wholesale trade; 17. retail trade; 18. transportation/communications; 19. finance/real estate; 20. public administration/health/other services.

FIGURE D.2 **Change in unstandardized weighted industry and skill premiums by sector, Philippines, 1988–2006**

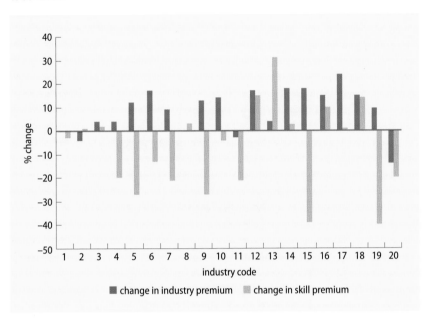

Source: di Gropello and Sakellariou 2010.
Note: The numbers on the *x* axis refer to these industries: 1. growing crops; 2. fishing; 3. nonmetal mining; 4. food/beverages/tobacco; 5. textiles; 6. wood/furniture; 7. paper products; 8. chemicals; 9. utilities; 10. construction; 11. wholesale trade; 12. retail trade; 13. hotels/restaurants; 14. transportation; 15. financial services; 16. business services; 17. public administration; 18. education; 19. health and social work; 20. private household employment.

FIGURE D.3 **Change in unstandardized weighted industry and skill premiums by sector, Indonesia, 1990–2004**

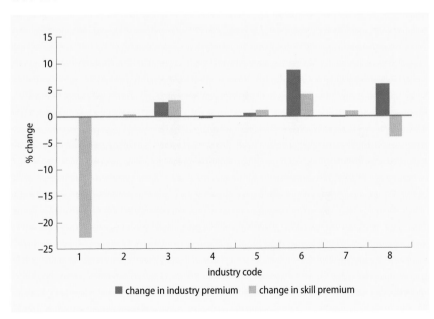

Source: di Gropello and Sakellariou 2010.
Note: The numbers on the *x* axis refer to these industries: 1. agriculture; 2. mining; 3. manufacturing; 4. utilities; 5. construction; 6. trade; 7. transportation; 8. other services.

FIGURE D.4   Change in unstandardized weighted industry and skill premiums by sector, Vietnam, 1992–2006

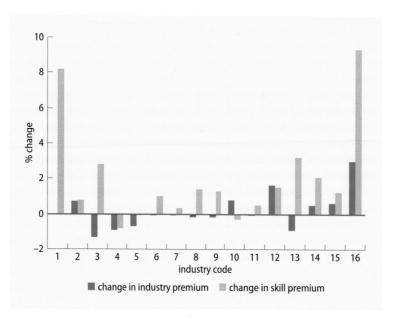

Source: di Gropello and Sakellariou 2010.
Note: The numbers on the x axis refer to these industries: 1. agriculture; 2. mining; 3. food/beverage/tobacco; 4. textiles; 5. wood/furniture; 6. paper; 7. chemicals; 8. nonmetal mining products; 9. metal; 10. other manufacturing; 11. utilities; 12. construction; 13. trade; 14. transport/communications; 15. finance/business; 16. other services.

FIGURE D.5   Change in unstandardized weighted industry and skill premiums by sector, Cambodia, 1997–2007

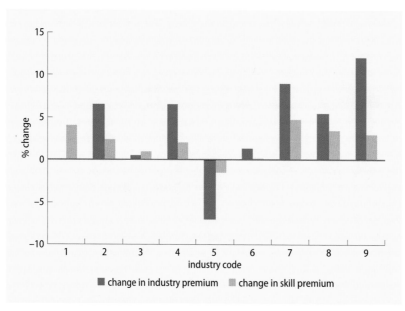

Source: di Gropello and Sakellariou 2010.
Note: The numbers on the x axis refer to these industries: 1. agriculture/mining; 2. manufacturing; 3. utilities; 4. construction; 5. trade; 6. transportation/communications; 7. finance/business; 8. public administration; 9. other services.

FIGURE D.6   Change in unstandardized weighted industry and skill premiums by sector, China, 1995–2005

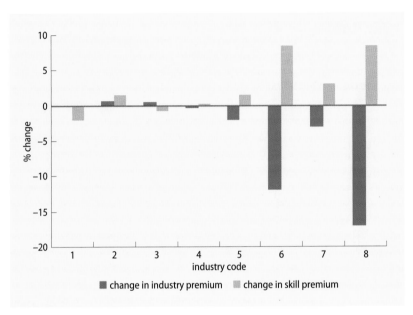

Source: di Gropello and Sakellariou 2010.
Note: The numbers on the x axis refer to these industries: 1. agriculture/mining; 2. manufacturing; 3. utilities; 4. construction; 5. transportation/communications; 6. trade; 7. public administration; 8. other services (including finance and business and others).

FIGURE D.7   Change in unstandardized weighted industry and skill premiums by sector, Mongolia, 1998–2007

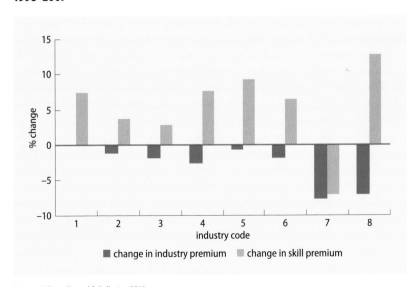

Source: di Gropello and Sakellariou 2010.
Note: The numbers on the x axis refer to these industries: 1. agriculture/mining; 2. manufacturing; 3. utilities; 4. construction; 5. transportation/communications; 6. trade; 7. public administration; 8. other services (including finance and business and others).

Appendix E

Openness, Technology, and Demand for Tertiary Graduates, Regression Tables

TABLE E.1 Openness, technological innovation, and the demand for skills

Variable	(1)	(2)	(3)	(4)	(5)	(6)	(7)
Exporter	−0.177***	0.043	0.041	−0.017	−0.019	−0.029	−0.058
	[0.0350]	[0.0350]	[0.0359]	[0.0389]	[0.0388]	[0.0387]	[0.0388]
Foreign ownership	0.429***	0.358***	0.354***	0.283***	0.278***	0.262***	0.211***
	[0.0386]	[0.0374]	[0.0381]	[0.0395]	[0.0394]	[0.0393]	[0.0394]
Technological innnovation					0.246***	0.230***	0.226***
					[0.0316]	[0.0316]	[0.0318]
Age of firm	−0.00907***	−0.00320***	−0.00377***	−0.00719***	−0.00706***	−0.00713***	−0.00672***
	[0.00130]	[0.00121]	[0.00121]	[0.00127]	[0.00127]	[0.00125]	[0.00124]
Public ownership	0.261***	0.268***	0.291***	0.274***	0.267***	0.260***	0.256***
	[0.0486]	[0.0449]	[0.0454]	[0.0486]	[0.0484]	[0.0482]	[0.0483]
Managerial postsecondary education						0.745***	0.696***
						[0.0877]	[0.0911]
Sales per employee (log)							0.0447***
							[0.00814]
Industry fixed effects?	No	Yes	No	No	No	No	No
Country fixed effects?	Yes	Yes	No	No	No	No	No
Country-industry fixed effects?	No	No	Yes	No	No	No	No
Country-industry-size fixed effects?	No	No	No	Yes	Yes	Yes	Yes
Observations	8,087	8,087	8,087	8,087	8,047	8,047	7,746
R-squared	0.09	0.23	0.25	0.32	0.33	0.34	0.34

Source: Almeida 2009b, based on World Bank Investment Climate Survey database.
Note: Dependent variable is share of workers in the firm with more than secondary education (12 years of schooling). Standard deviation shown in brackets.
Significance level: *** = 1 percent.

TABLE E.2 Openness, technological innovation, and the demand for skills: Robustness to technological variables

Variable	(1)	(2)	(4)	(5)	(6)
Exporter	−0.0634	−0.135***	−0.137***	−0.228***	0.00842
	[0.0415]	[0.0467]	[0.0469]	[0.0647]	[0.0429]
Foreign ownership	0.208***	0.247***	0.232***	0.0691	0.142***
	[0.0411]	[0.0473]	[0.0474]	[0.0606]	[0.0442]
Technological innovation	0.199***	0.204***	0.244***	0.264***	0.0616
	[0.0341]	[0.0410]	[0.0405]	[0.0469]	[0.0376]
ISO certificate	0.267***				
	[0.0381]				
R&D		0.295***			
		[0.0424]			
R&D/sales			0.00603***		
			[0.00214]		

(continued next page)

TABLE E.2 **(continued)**

Variable	(1)	(2)	(4)	(5)	(6)
Use of computers				0.642*** [0.0543]	
Use of e-mail and Internet					0.558*** [0.0434]
Baseline firm characteristics?	Yes	Yes	Yes	Yes	Yes
Country-sector-size effects?	Yes	Yes	Yes	Yes	Yes
Observations	7,208	5,069	5,069	4,059	4,928
R-squared	0.346	0.302	0.297	0.394	0.385

Source: Almeida 2009b, based on World Bank Investment Climate Survey database.
Note: Dependent variable is share of workers in the firm with more than secondary education (12 years of schooling). Standard deviation shown in brackets.
Significance level: *** = 1 percent.

TABLE E.3 **Openness, technological innovation, and the demand for skills: Robustness to alternative samples**

Variable	Cambodia (1)	China (2)	Indonesia (3)	Korea, Rep. (6)	Malaysia (4)	Philippines (5)	Thailand (7)	Vietnam (8)
Panel A: Excluding one country at a time								
Exporter	−0.0683* [0.0386]	0.118*** [0.0426]	−0.0888** [0.0397]	−0.061 [0.0393]	−0.0725* [0.0393]	−0.056 [0.0395]	−0.130*** [0.0475]	−0.0776* [0.0455]
Foreign ownership	0.201*** [0.0393]	0.186*** [0.0448]	0.234*** [0.0405]	0.208*** [0.0401]	0.216*** [0.0411]	0.229*** [0.0402]	0.255*** [0.0474]	0.0969** [0.0441]
Technological innovation	0.240*** [0.0322]	0.123*** [0.0379]	0.227*** [0.0326]	0.232*** [0.0322]	0.234*** [0.0326]	0.205*** [0.0324]	0.251*** [0.0363]	0.250*** [0.0364]
Baseline firm characteristics?	Yes	Yes	Yes	Yes	Yes	Yes	Yes	Yes
Country-sector-size effects?	Yes	Yes	Yes	Yes	Yes	Yes	Yes	Yes
Observations	7,443	4,931	7,270	7,261	7,427	7,255	6,451	6,184
R-squared	0.313	0.36	0.333	0.332	0.343	0.351	0.344	0.355
Panel B: Including one country at a time								
Exporter	1.531*** [0.542]	−0.406*** [0.0755]	0.388** [0.159]	0.015 [0.210]	0.336 [0.228]	−0.028 [0.166]	0.142** [0.0562]	−0.050 [0.0665]
Foreign ownership	0.628 [0.422]	0.191*** [0.0705]	−0.118 [0.178]	0.419*** [0.156]	0.131 [0.138]	−0.231 [0.198]	0.012 [0.0618]	0.400*** [0.0797]
Technological innovation	−0.161 [0.179]	0.342*** [0.0555]	0.247* [0.139]	0.051 [0.168]	0.007 [0.135]	0.497*** [0.142]	0.134** [0.0564]	0.055 [0.0592]
Baseline firm characteristics?	Yes	Yes	Yes	Yes	Yes	Yes	Yes	Yes
Country-sector-size effects?	Yes	Yes	Yes	Yes	Yes	Yes	Yes	Yes
Observations	303	2,815	476	485	319	491	1,295	1,562
R-squared	0.366	0.344	0.303	0.383	0.172	0.246	0.22	0.259

Source: Almeida 2009b, based on World Bank Investment Climate Survey database.
Note: Dependent variable is share of workers in the firm with more than secondary education (12 years of schooling). Panel A excludes from the sample one country at a time. Panel B restricts the sample to one country at a time. Standard deviation shown in brackets.
Significance level: * = 10 percent; ** = 5 percent; *** = 1 percent.

TABLE E.4   **Openness, technological innovation, and the demand for skills: Robustness to alternative samples**

Variable	Low-income countries	Low-middle-income countries	Middle-income countries	Excluding capital city
	(1)	(2)	(3)	(4)
Exporter	0.00159	−0.115**	−0.0958**	−0.0728*
	[0.0746]	[0.0489]	[0.0474]	[0.0425]
Foreign ownership	0.459***	0.0721	0.0785	0.182***
	[0.0933]	[0.0512]	[0.0486]	[0.0426]
Technological innovation	0.015	0.297***	0.280***	0.225***
	[0.0589]	[0.0395]	[0.0380]	[0.0345]
Baseline firm characteristics?	Yes	Yes	Yes	Yes
Country-sector-size effects?	Yes	Yes	Yes	Yes
Observations	1,865	5,077	5,396	6,635

Source: Almeida 2009b, based on World Bank Investment Climate Survey database.
Note: Dependent variable is share of workers in the firm with more than secondary education (12 years of schooling). Standard deviation shown in brackets. Significance level: * = 10 percent; ** = 5 percent; *** = 1 percent.

Appendix F

Demand for Job-Specific and Generic Skills in East Asia

FIGURE F.1 **Key job-specific and generic skills in a sample of East Asian economies (according to employers)**

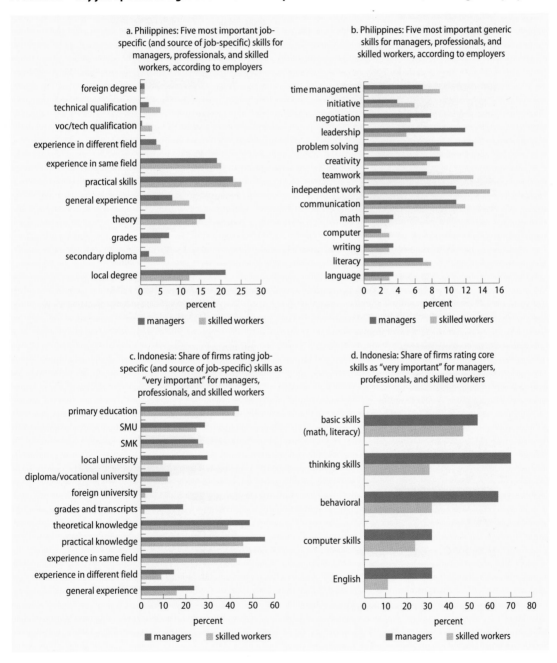

(continued next page)

FIGURE F.1 (continued)

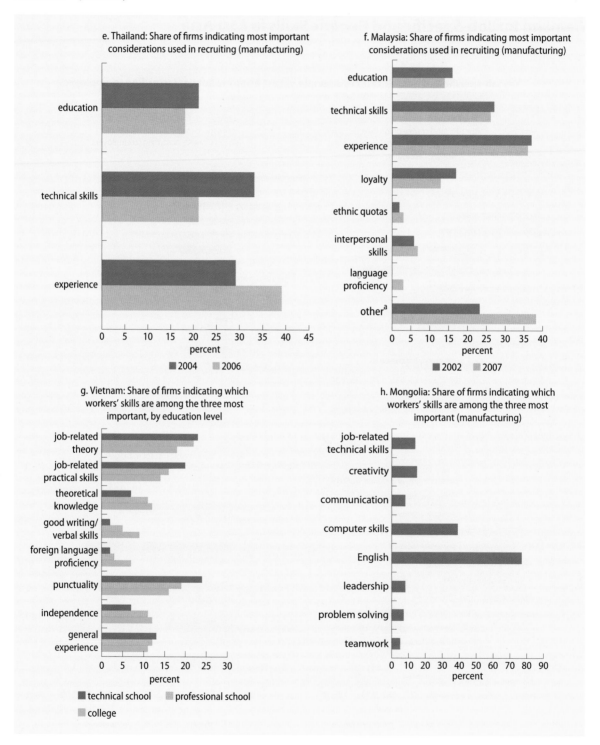

e. Thailand: Share of firms indicating most important considerations used in recruiting (manufacturing)

f. Malaysia: Share of firms indicating most important considerations used in recruiting (manufacturing)

g. Vietnam: Share of firms indicating which workers' skills are among the three most important, by education level

h. Mongolia: Share of firms indicating which workers' skills are among the three most important (manufacturing)

(continued next page)

FIGURE F.1 **(continued)**

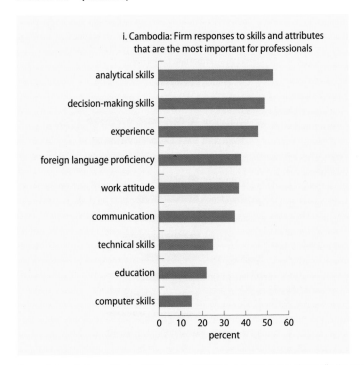

i. Cambodia: Firm responses to skills and attributes
that are the most important for professionals

Sources: di Gropello, Tan, and Tandon 2010, based on 2008 Philippines Skills Survey; di Gropello, Kruse, and Tandon 2011, based on 2008 Indonesia Skills Survey; Thailand World Bank Investment Climate Survey 2004 and 2006; Malaysia World Bank Investment Climate Survey 2002 and 2007; World Bank 2008, based on 2003 Vietnam MOLISA-ADB survey on labor market; Mongolia World Bank Investment Climate Survey 2010; HRINC. 2010, based on Cambodian Federation of Employers and Business Associations Youth and Employment Study (BDLINK Cambodia Co. 2008).
a. "Other" includes thinking and problem-solving skills among other factors.

FIGURE F.2 **Key skills in a sample of East Asian economies (according to employees)**

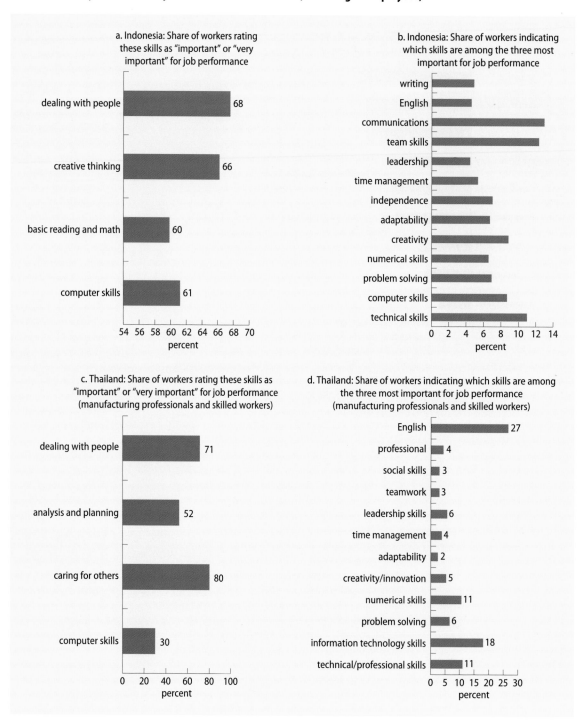

(continued next page)

FIGURE F.2   **(continued)**

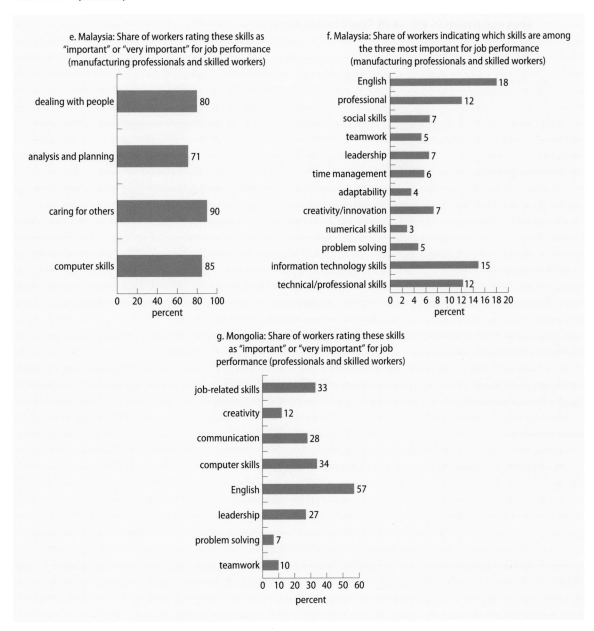

e. Malaysia: Share of workers rating these skills as "important" or "very important" for job performance (manufacturing professionals and skilled workers)

f. Malaysia: Share of workers indicating which skills are among the three most important for job performance (manufacturing professionals and skilled workers)

g. Mongolia: Share of workers rating these skills as "important" or "very important" for job performance (professionals and skilled workers)

Source: di Gropello, Kruse, and Tandon 2011, based on 2008 Indonesia Skills Survey; Thailand World Bank Investment Climate Survey 2004; Malaysia World Bank Investment Climate Survey 2002; Mongolia World Bank Investment Climate Survey 2010.

Appendix G

Determinants of Skill Gap Indicators

TABLE G.1 Determinants of time to fill skilled vacancies

Variable	(1)	(2)	(3)	(4)	(5)
Technological innovation	0.114	0.083	0.077	0.082	0.073
	0.025*	0.026***	0.027***	0.026***	0.026***
Open	0.129	0.084	0.082	0.084	0.069
	0.026*	0.028***	0.029***	0.028***	0.028**
Small enterprise		0.063	0.119	0.074	0.078
		0.050	0.047**	0.049	0.048
Medium enterprise		0.138	0.189	0.155	0.158
		0.057**	0.055***	0.056***	0.055***
Large enterprise		0.155	0.190	0.175	0.195
		0.057***	0.055***	0.056***	0.056***
Very large enterprise		0.231	0.241	0.256	0.261
		0.057***	0.054***	0.056***	0.055***
Public ownership		0.011	0.002	0.010	0.030
		0.051	0.054	0.051	0.051
Age of firm > 2 years and < 4 years		−0.142	−0.136	−0.137	−0.094
		0.794	0.792	0.784	0.792
Age of firm > 4 years and < 6 years		−0.192	−0.187	−0.191	−0.144
		0.793	0.792	0.784	0.792
Age of firm > 6 years		−0.247	−0.242	−0.245	−0.196
		0.793	0.7912	0.783	0.791
Average years of schooling of workforce			0.005		
Share of skilled workers				0.158	0.142
				0.060***	0.058**
Basic firm-level controls included?	Yes	Yes	Yes	Yes	Yes
Industry fixed effects?	Yes	Yes	Yes	Yes	No
Country fixed effects?	Yes	Yes	Yes	Yes	Yes
Country-industry fixed effects?	No	No	No	No	Yes
Observations	4,351	4,226	3,705	4,214	4,214
R-squared	0.098	0.102	0.094	0.103	0.107

Source: Almeida 2009a, based on World Bank Investment Climate (IC) Surveys database.
Note: Dependent variable is a dummy variable that assumes the value 1 if the firm fills skilled vacancies. Table reports the marginal effects (at mean values) on the firm's propensity to fill skilled vacancies from probit regressions. Microfirms (with fewer than than 10 employees) are the omitted size group.
Significance level: * = 10 percent; ** = 5 percent; *** = 1 percent.

TABLE G.2 Determinants of managerial perceptions of skills and education of East Asian workforce

Variable	(1)	(2)	(3)	(4)	(5)
Technological innovation	0.046	0.036	0.033	0.035	0.033
	0.010***	0.010***	0.011***	0.010***	0.010***
Open	0.043	0.028	0.026	0.030	0.032
	0.010***	0.010***	0.011**	0.010***	0.011***
Small enterprise (10–49 employees)		0.038	0.026	0.048	0.051
		0.021*	0.025	0.022**	0.023**
Medium enterprise (50–99 employees)		0.090	0.077	0.105	0.107
		0.026***	0.030***	0.028***	0.029***

(continued next page)

TABLE G.2   **(continued)**

Variable	(1)	(2)	(3)	(4)	(5)
Large enterprise (100–249 employees)		0.094	0.076	0.109	0.112
		0.027***	0.030***	0.028***	0.029***
Very large enterprise (+250 employees)		0.087	0.066	0.104	0.109
		0.026***	0.029**	0.027***	0.029***
Public ownership		0.021	0.036	0.017	0.018
		0.017	0.018**	0.017	0.017
Age of firm > 2 years and < 4 years		−0.065	−0.064	−0.068	−0.069
		0.036	0.043	0.036*	0.036*
Age of firm > 4 years and < 6 years		−0.074	−0.074	−0.077	−0.078
		0.035*	0.042	0.035**	0.035*
Age of firm > 6 years		−0.103	−0.099	−0.105	−0.106
		0.048**	0.057*	0.048**	0.049**
Average years of schooling of workforce			0.001		
			0.002		
Share of skilled workers				0.068	0.079
				0.022***	0.023***
Industry fixed effects?	Yes	Yes	Yes	Yes	No
Country fixed effects?	Yes	Yes	Yes	Yes	Yes
Country-industry fixed effects?	No	No	No	No	Yes
Observations	8,099	7,961	6,737	7,864	7,726

Source: Almeida 2009a, based on World Bank IC Surveys database.
Note: Dependent variable is a dummy variable equal to 1 where firms rate skills and education of workforce as a major or very severe obstacle to growth.
Significance level: * = 10 percent; ** = 5 percent; *** = 1 percent.

TABLE G.3   **Determinants of managerial perceptions of skills of workforce: Robustness to additional variables**

Variable	(1)	(2)	(4)	(5)	(6)
Technological innovation	0.034	0.018	0.030	0.038	0.029
	0.011***	0.014	0.014**	0.010***	0.016*
Open	0.026	0.043	0.032	0.020	0.030
	0.011**	0.023*	0.014**	0.012*	0.016*
ISO certificate	0.003				
	0.012				
Research and development		0.050			
		0.015***			
tech_R~g			0.0002		
			0.001		
Use of e-mail and Internet				0.032	
				0.011***	
Use of computers					0.054
					0.016***
Industry fixed effects?	Yes	Yes	Yes	Yes	Yes
Country fixed effects?	Yes	Yes	Yes	Yes	Yes
Country-industry fixed effects?	No	No	No	No	No
Observations	7,266	4,608	4,704	6,363	3,324

Source: Almeida 2009b, based on World Bank IC Surveys database.
Note: Dependent variable is a dummy variable equal to 1 where firms rate skills and education of workforce as a major or very severe obstacle to growth. ISO = International Organization for Standardization.
Significance level: * = 10 percent; ** = 5 percent; *** = 1 percent.

TABLE G.4 **Determinants of time to fill skilled vacancies: Robustness to additional variables**

Variable	(1)	(2)	(3)	(4)	(5)
Technological innovation	0.093	0.016	0.033	0.077	0.175
	0.027***	0.028	0.027	0.029***	0.052***
Open	0.079	0.079	0.081	0.015	0.213
	0.028***	0.030***	0.030***	0.034	0.051***
ISO certificate	1.076				
	0.782				
Research and development (R&D)		0.099			
		0.031***			
Percentage of R&D/sales			−0.0004		
			0.001		
Internet use				0.177	
				0.033***	
Computer use					0.180
					0.059***
Basic firm-level controls included?	Yes	Yes	Yes	Yes	Yes
Industry fixed effects?	Yes	Yes	Yes	Yes	Yes
Country fixed effects?	Yes	Yes	Yes	Yes	Yes
Observations	3,970	2,893	2,893	3,455	1,434
R-squared	0.112	0.041	0.039	0.119	0.134

Source: Almeida 2009b, based on World Bank IC Surveys database.
Note: Dependent variable is a dummy variable that assumes the value 1 if the firm fills skilled vacancies. Table reports the marginal effects (at mean values) on the firm's propensity to fill skilled vacancies from probit regressions. Microfirms (with fewer than 10 employees) are the omitted size group.
Significance level: *** = 1 percent.

TABLE G.5 Determinants of managerial perceptions of skills of workforce: Robustness to different geographical areas

Variable	Cambodia (1)	China (2)	Indonesia (3)	Lao PDR (4)	Malaysia (5)	Mongolia (6)	Philippines (7)	Korea, Rep. (8)	Thailand (9)	Vietnam (10)
Panel a. Excluding one country at a time										
Technological innovation	0.037	0.041	0.032	0.036	0.033	0.036	0.032	0.034	0.040	0.031
	0.011***	0.010***	0.010***	0.010***	0.010***	0.010***	0.011***	0.011***	0.011***	0.012***
Open	0.032	0.028	0.030	0.032	0.034	0.031	0.027	0.029	0.027	0.033
	0.011***	0.011**	0.011***	0.011***	0.011***	0.010***	0.011**	0.011***	0.011**	0.012***
Industry fixed effects?	Yes	Yes	Yes	Yes	Yes	Yes	Yes	Yes	Yes	Yes
Country fixed effects?	Yes	Yes	Yes	Yes	Yes	Yes	Yes	Yes	Yes	Yes
Observations	7,393	6,434	7,182	7,621	7,141	7,672	7,247	7,342	6,480	6,244
Panel b. Restricting sample to only one country										
Technological innovation	−0.001	0.003	0.066	0.013	0.063	−0.044	0.062	0.025	0.017	0.046
	0.029	0.029	0.033**	0.033	0.036*	0.077	0.026**	0.024	0.028	0.020**
Open	−0.017	0.042	0.026	−0.014	−0.005	−0.008	0.089	0.045	0.048	0.026
	0.037	0.028	0.038	0.045	0.035	0.090	0.033***	0.033	0.029*	0.022
Industry fixed effects?	Yes	Yes	Yes	Yes	Yes	Yes	Yes	Yes	Yes	Yes
Country fixed effects?	Yes	Yes	Yes	Yes	Yes	Yes	Yes	Yes	Yes	Yes
Observations	407	1,421	678	240	723	188	616	470	1,384	1,577

Source: Almeida 2009b, based on World Bank IC Surveys database.
Note: Dependent variable is a dummy variable equal to 1 where firms rate skills and education of workforce as a major or very severe obstacle to growth.
Significance level: * = 10 percent; ** = 5 percent; *** = 1 percent.

TABLE G.6   Determinants of managerial perceptions of skills of workforce: Robustness to different geographic areas, by income levels

Variable	Low income (2)	Low-middle income (3)	Middle income (4)	Excluding capital city (5)
Technology innovation	0.032	0.031	0.035	0.040
	0.014**	0.016**	0.014**	0.011***
Openness	0.012	0.044	0.037	0.032
	0.017	0.015***	0.014***	0.011***
Industry fixed effects?	Yes	Yes	Yes	Yes
Country fixed effects?	Yes	Yes	Yes	Yes
Observations	2,505	4,102	4,825	6,436

Source: Almeida 2009b, based on World Bank IC Surveys database.
Note: Dependent variable is a dummy variable equal to 1 where firms rate skills and education of workforce as a major or very severe obstacle to growth.
Significance level: ** = 5 percent; *** = 1 percent.

TABLE G.7   Determinants of time to fill skilled vacancies: Robustness to different geographical areas

Variable	China (1)	Indonesia (2)	Malaysia (3)	Korea, Rep. (4)	Thailand (5)	Vietnam (6)
Panel a: Excluding one country at a time						
Technology innovation	0.098	0.029	0.094	0.098	0.088	0.086
	0.029***	0.026	0.028***	0.028***	0.031***	0.028***
Openness	0.058	0.051	0.111	0.099	0.089	0.084
	0.033*	0.028*	0.029***	0.030***	0.034***	0.030***
Basic firm-level controls included?	Yes	Yes	Yes	Yes	Yes	Yes
Industry fixed effects?	Yes	Yes	Yes	Yes	Yes	Yes
Country fixed effects?	Yes	Yes	Yes	Yes	Yes	Yes
Observations	3,460	3,534	3,565	3,755	2,916	3,840
R-squared	0.115	0.031	0.117	0.107	0.117	0.105
Panel b. Restricting sample to only one country						
Technology innovation	−0.006	0.457	0.018	−0.040	0.081	0.050
	0.054	0.113***	0.068	0.057	0.048*	0.049
Openness	0.121	0.284	−0.082	−0.096	0.065	0.091
	0.052**	0.129**	0.076	0.082	0.049	0.066
Basic firm-level controls included?	Yes	Yes	Yes	Yes	Yes	Yes
Industry fixed effects?	Yes	Yes	Yes	Yes	Yes	Yes
Country fixed effects?	Yes	Yes	Yes	Yes	Yes	Yes
Observations	754	680	649	459	1,298	374
R-squared	0.026	0.068	0.040	0.081	0.019	0.088

Source: Almeida 2009b, based on World Bank IC Surveys database.
Note: Dependent variable is a dummy variable that assumes the value 1 if the firm fills skilled vacancies. Table reports the marginal effects (at mean values) on the firm's propensity to fill skilled vacancies from probit regressions. Microfirms (with fewer than 10 employees) are the omitted size group.
Significance level: * = 10 percent; ** = 5 percent; *** = 1 percent.

TABLE G.8   Determinants of time to fill skilled vacancies: Robustness to different geographical areas, by income levels

Variable	High income (1)	Low income (2)	Low-middle Income (3)	Middle income (4)	Excluding capital city (5)
Technology innovation	−0.040	0.050	0.131	0.104	0.086
	0.057	0.049	0.035***	0.031***	0.029***
Openness	−0.096	0.091	0.144	0.105	0.066
	0.082	0.066	0.035***	0.032***	0.032**
Basic firm-level controls included?	Yes	Yes	Yes	Yes	Yes
Industry fixed effects?	Yes	Yes	Yes	Yes	Yes
Country fixed effects?	Yes	Yes	Yes	Yes	Yes
Observations	459	374	2,732	3,381	3,509
R-squared	0.081	0.088	0.125	0.109	0.109

Source: Almeida 2009 b, based on World Bank IC Surveys database.
Note: Dependent variable is a dummy variable that assumes the value 1 if the firm fills skilled vacancies. Table reports the marginal effects (at mean values) on the firm's propensity to fill skilled vacancies from probit regressions. Microfirms (with fewer than 10 employees) is the omitted size group.
Significance level: ** = 5 percent; *** = 1 percent.

Appendix H

Reasons for Skill Shortages in East Asia

FIGURE H.1 **Reasons for skill shortages, by sector, Philippines**

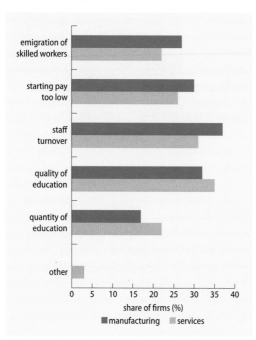

Source: di Gropello, Tan, and Tandon 2010, based on 2008 Philippines Skills Survey.

FIGURE H.2 **Reasons for skill shortages, by sector, Indonesia**

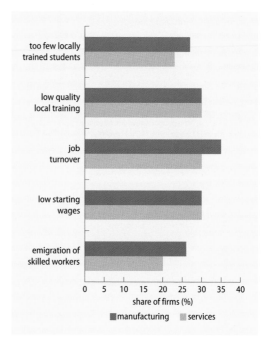

Source: di Gropello, Kruse, and Tandon 2011, based on 2008 Indonesia Skills Survey.

FIGURE H.3   Three main causes of vacancies in manufacturing in Thailand identified by firms

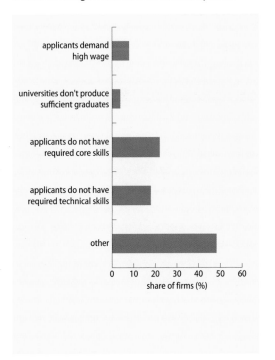

Source: World Bank IC Surveys database: Thailand 2006.

FIGURE H.4   Three main causes of vacancies in manufacturing in Malaysia identified by firms

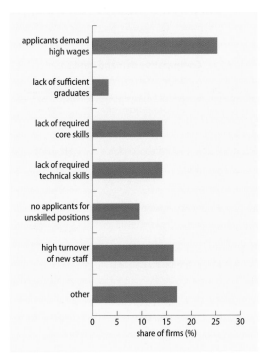

Source: World Bank IC Surveys database: Malaysia 2007.

FIGURE H.5   Main obstacles for recruiting, Vietnam

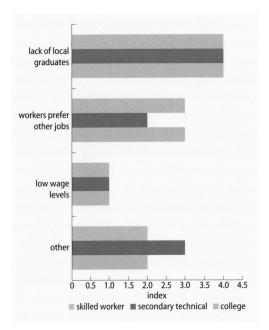

Source: World Bank 2008, based on 2003 MOLISA-ADB survey on labor market.
Note: Ranking of reasons for difficulties.

FIGURE H.6   Most important reasons for vacancies in manufacturing in Mongolia

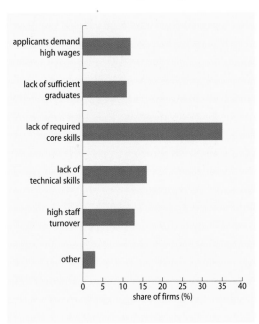

Source: World Bank IC Surveys database: Mongolia 2010.

Appendix I

Comparative Demand- and Supply-Side Indicators

TABLE I.1   Comparative demand- and supply-side indicators, by country

Indicator	Vietnam	Cambodia	Mongolia	China
Trends in tertiary education premium (increase vis-à-vis secondary and below)	Increase	Sharp increase	Increase	Increase
Trends in tertiary-educated workforce	Sharp increase	Sharp increase	Decrease	Slight increase
Trends in tertiary premium across generations	No impact	Increases	No impact	—
Tertiary education premium (increase vis-à-vis secondary and below), most recent available year (%)	55	90	70	60
Tertiary-educated workforce (%)	13	3.40	33	24
Weeks to fill professional vacancies (year)	2.5 (2005)	4 (2007)	4.5 (2003); 6 (2009)	About 5 (2003)
Trends in unemployment rate of tertiary graduates	Slight increase	Decrease	Slight decrease	—
Unemployment of tertiary graduates, most recent available year (%)	1.22	2.11	6.70	6.86
Percentage employed as professionals or managers, most r ecent available year (%)	84	52	69	—

(continued next page)

TABLE I.1   (continued)

Indicator	Indonesia	Philippines	Malaysia	Thailand
Trends in tertiary education premium (increase vis-à-vis secondary and below)	Stable/slightly decreasing	Stable/slightly increasing	—	Stable/slightly increasing
Trends in tertiary-educated workforce	Sharp increase	Increase	—	Increase
Trends in tertiary premium across generations	No impact for youth Increase for 35–49	No impact for youth Increase for 35–49	—	Decrease
Tertiary education premium (increase vis-à-vis secondary and below), most recent available year (%)	84	70	—	120
Tertiary-educated workforce (%)	21	27	—	21
Weeks to fill professional vacancies (year)	About 2 (ICS 2003) About 3 (SS 2008)	About 3 (ICS 2003) About 5 (SS 2008)	Almost 6 (2002) Almost 5 (2007)	About 6 (2004) 7.5 (2006)
Trends in unemployment rate of tertiary graduates	Slight decrease	Slight increase	—	Slight decrease
Unemployment of tertiary graduates, most recent available year (%)	8.55	11.55	—	2.11
Percentage employed as professionals or managers, most r ecent available year (%)	45	59	—	68

Sources: Author elaboration on the basis of *WDI database;* Sakellariou 2010a, 2010b; di Gropello and Sakellariou 2010; World Bank IC Surveys database; di Gropello, Kruse, and Tandon 2011; di Gropello, Tan, and Tandon 2010.
Note: — = not available; ICS = Investment Climate Survey; SS = Skill Survey.

Appendix J

Skill Gaps in East Asia

FIGURE J.1   **Skill gaps identified by employers**

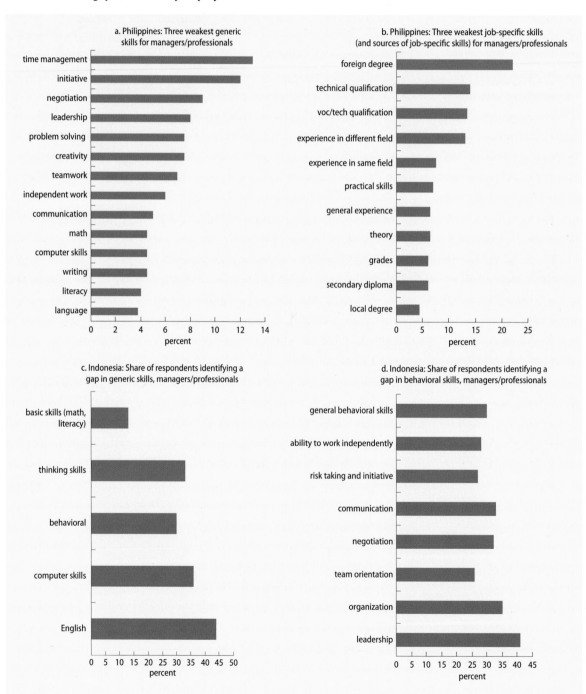

(continued next page)

FIGURE J.1 **(continued)**

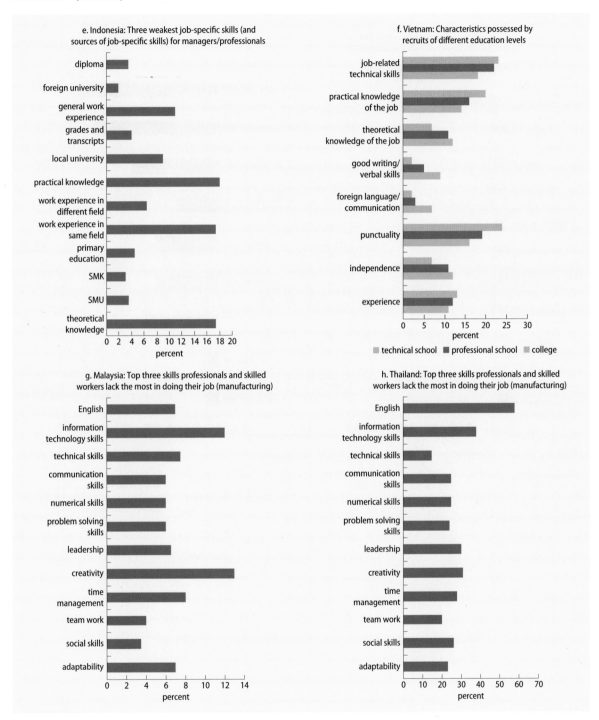

e. Indonesia: Three weakest job-specific skills (and sources of job-specific skills) for managers/professionals

f. Vietnam: Characteristics possessed by recruits of different education levels

g. Malaysia: Top three skills professionals and skilled workers lack the most in doing their job (manufacturing)

h. Thailand: Top three skills professionals and skilled workers lack the most in doing their job (manufacturing)

(continued next page)

FIGURE J.1 **(continued)**

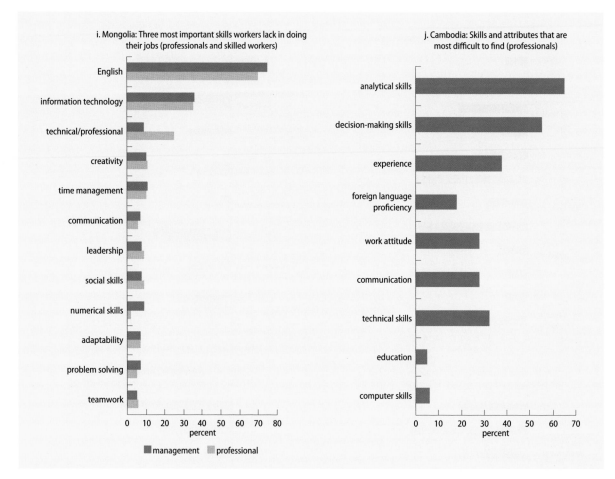

i. Mongolia: Three most important skills workers lack in doing their jobs (professionals and skilled workers)

j. Cambodia: Skills and attributes that are most difficult to find (professionals)

Sources: di Gropello, Tan, and Tandon 2010, based on 2008 Philippines Skills Survey; di Gropello, Kruse, and Tandon 2011, based on 2008 Indonesia Skills Survey; World Bank 2008, based on 2003 Vietnam MOLISA-ADB survey on labor market; World Bank IC Surveys database: Malaysia 2007; World Bank IC Surveys database: Thailand 2004; World Bank IC Surveys database: Mongolia 2010; HRINC 2010, based on Cambodian Federation of Employers and Business Associations Youth and Employment Study (BDLINK Cambodia Co. 2008).
Note: SMK = vocational secondary schools (Indonesia); SMU = general secondary schools (Indonesia).

FIGURE J.2 **Skill gaps according to employees**

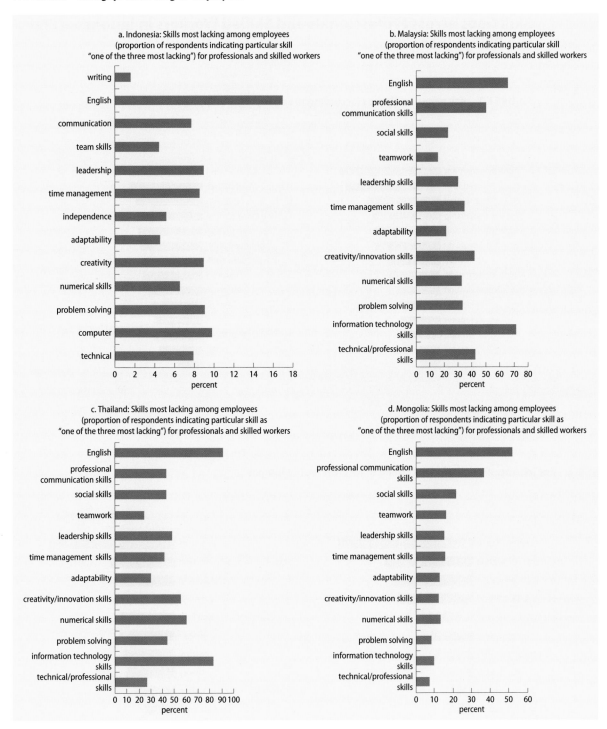

Sources: di Gropello, Kruse, and Tandon 2010, based on 2008 Indonesia Skills Survey; World Bank IC Surveys database: Malaysia 2007; World Bank IC Surveys database: Thailand 2004; World Bank IC Surveys database: Mongolia 2010.

Appendix K

Skill Gaps across Professionals and Skilled Workers in Indonesia and the Philippines

FIGURE K.1 **Key generic skill gaps (according to employers), Philippines**

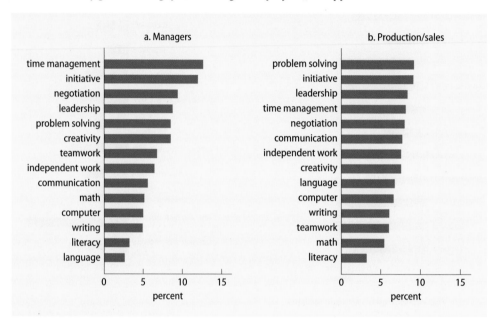

Source: di Gropello, Tan, and Tandon 2010, based on 2008 Philippines Skills Survey.

FIGURE K.2 **Key job-specific skill gaps (according to employers), Philippines**

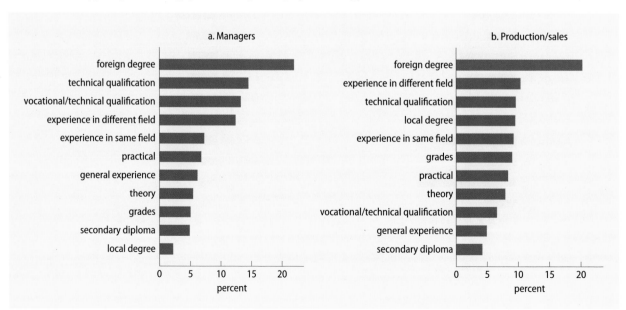

Source: di Gropello, Tan, and Tandon 2010, based on 2008 Philippines Skills Survey.

FIGURE K.3   Share of respondents identifying a gap in generic skills, Indonesia

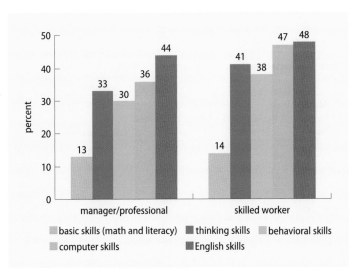

Source: di Gropello, Kruse, and Tandon 2011, based on 2008 Indonesia Skills Survey.

FIGURE K.4   Share of respondents identifying a gap in behavioral skills, Indonesia

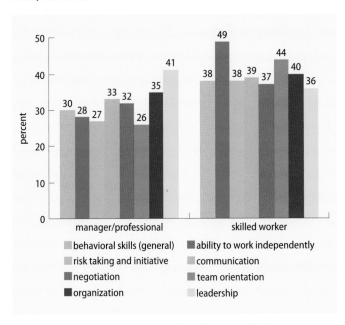

Source: di Gropello, Kruse, and Tandon 2011, based on 2008 Indonesia Skills Survey.

Appendix L

Doctoral Degrees Earned in Science and Engineering

TABLE L.1   Science and engineering doctoral degrees earned in selected regions and locations, by field (2000 or most recent year)

Region and location	All doctoral degrees	All S&E	Natural sciences[a]	Math/ computer sciences	Agricultural sciences	Social/behavioral sciences	Engineering	Non-S&E
All regions	207,383	114,337	46,715	7,389	7,761	20,054	32,418	93,046
Asia[b]	47,489	24,409	8,658	373	3,085	1,467	10,826	23,080
China (2001)	13,001	8,153	2,655	—	536	621	4,341	4,848
India (1997)	10,408	4,764	3,498	—	968	—	298	5,644
Japan[c] (2001)	16,078	7,401	1,586	—	1,241	610	3,964	8,677
Kyrgyz Republic	396	256	161	19	8	20	48	140
Korea, Rep.	6,143	2,865	614	247	242	108	1,654	3,278
Taiwan, China (2001)	1,463	970	144	107	90	108	521	493
Middle East[b]	5,759	2,902	1,307	241	265	495	594	2,857
Sub-Saharan Africa[b]	2,064	679	253	0	142	143	141	1,385
Europe[b]	97,840	53,119	23,567	4,412	2,577	8,927	13,636	44,721
America[b]	50,544	31,198	12,015	2,188	1,512	8,738	6,745	19,346
North America	46,475	28,590	10,824	2,095	1,039	8,421	6,211	17,885
South America	4,069	2,608	1,191	93	473	317	534	1,461

Sources: Chapman 2010; National Science Board, Science & Engineering Indicators 2004, http://www.nsf.gov/statistics/seind04/c2/c2s5.htm.
Note: S&E = science and engineering; — = not available.
Data for doctoral degrees use the International Standard Classification of Education (1997) 6 level. S&E data do not include health fields.
a. Includes physical, biological, earth, atmospheric, and ocean sciences.
b. Includes only those locations for which relatively recent data are available.
c. Includes thesis doctorates, called *ronbun hakase*, earned by employees in industry.

Appendix M

Simulations for Financing Higher Education

The simulation model presented in chapter 4 has been built so that it computes the projected intake, enrollment, and flow rates for an individual country's higher education system (figure M.1). These estimates are based on population data and are adapted to enrollment and quality-related policy options (such as increasing the number of classrooms, constructing new laboratories, recruiting new instructors, providing faculty fellowships, providing bursaries to students, and so on). The ensuing number of enrollments by level and type of education, combined with the current and future modalities of resource utilization (teaching staff, equipment, infrastructure, and so on), provide estimates of future requirements of teachers, nonteaching staff, instructional materials, and educational facilities. These projected requirements, together with cost-related data and parameters, can give an estimate of financial requirements and possible financing gaps.

FIGURE M.1   Architecture of the simulation model

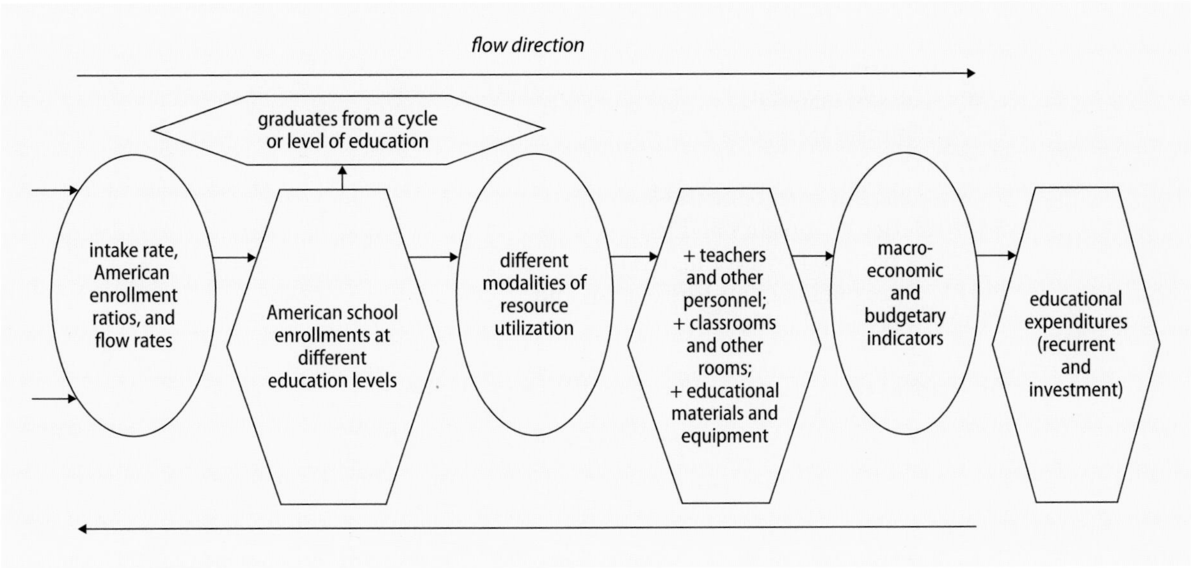

Source: Adapted from UNESCO 2005.

Designed in this way, the model can provide simulations of both capital and recurrent expenditures over time. Total costs are given by the following equation

$$C_d^t = RC_d^t + I_d^t$$

where

    t = year
    d = level of education
    C_d^t = total costs
    RC_d^t = total recurrent costs, and
    I_d^t = investment.

Recurrent costs are derived by the following equations

$$RC_d^t = CT_d^t + CM_d^t + CA_d^t + CO_d^t$$

$$CT_d^t = \sum_{i=1}^{n} \sum_{j+1}^{k} T_{dij}^t w_{dij}$$

$$CM_d^t = E_d^t \times CMPS_d$$

$$CA_d^t = E_d^t \times CAPS_d$$

$$CO_d^t = E_d^t \times COPS_d$$

where

    CT_d^t = teachers' costs
    CM_d^t = costs of materials
    CA_d^t = administrative costs
    CO_d^t = other costs
    T_{dij}^t = teachers by category i and level j
    w_{dij}^t = salaries by category and level
    $CMPS_d$ = per pupil cost for materials
    $CAPS_d$ = per pupil administrative cost, and
    $COPS_d$ = per pupil other costs.

And capital costs are derived by the following equation

$$I_d^t = CBPS \times \left[E_d^t - (1-a) \times E_d^{t-1} \right]$$

where

    $CBPS_d$ = per pupil building cost,
    E_d^t = enrollment, and
    a = replacement rate of buildings.

References

Acworth, E. B. 2008. "University-Industry Engagement: The Formation of the Knowledge Integration Community (KIC) Model at the Cambridge-MIT Institute." *Research Policy* 37 (8): 1241–54.

Aghion, P., M. Dewatripont, C. Hoxby, A. Mas-Colell, and A. Sapir. 2007. "Why Reform Europe's Universities?" Bruegel Policy Brief 2007/04, Bruegel, Brussels.

———. 2008. *Higher Aspirations: An Agenda for Reforming European Universities.* Bruegel Blueprint 5. Brussels: Bruegel.

———. 2009. "The Governance and Performance of Research Universities: Evidence from Europe and the U.S." NBER Working Paper Series 14851, National Bureau of Economic Research, Cambridge, MA.

Allen, M. 1996. "Research Productivity and Positive Teaching Evaluations: Examining the Relationship Using Meta-Analysis." *Journal of the Association for Communication Administration* 2: 77–96.

Almeida, R. 2009a. "Does the Workforce in East Asia Have the Right Skills? Evidence from Firm-Level Surveys." Background paper prepared for Regional Study on Skills in East Asia, World Bank, Washington, DC.

———. 2009b. "Innovation and Openness in East Asia: Are They Increasing the Demand for Educated Workers?" Background paper prepared for Regional Study on Skills in East Asia, World Bank, Washington, DC.

Altbach, P. G., and J. Salmi, eds. Forthcoming. *The Road to Academic Excellence: The Making of World-Class Research Universities.* Washington, DC: World Bank.

AmCham-China (American Chamber of Commerce in the People's Republic of China). 2010. "2010 Business Climate Survey Report." Beijing: AmCham-China. http://www.amcham china.org/businessclimate2010.

Asia Business Council. 2009. *Asia Business Council Annual Survey 2009.* Hong Kong: Asia Business Council.

Askling, B., M. Bauer, and S. Marton. 1999. "Swedish Universities towards Self-Regulation: A New Look at Institutional Autonomy." *Tertiary Education and Management* 5 (2): 173–93.

Audretsch, D. B. 2008. *The Entrepreneurial Society.* New York: Oxford University Press.

Autor, D. H., F. Levy, and R. J. Murnane. 2001. "The Skill Content of Recent Technological Change: An Empirical Exploration." NBER Working Paper Series 8337, National Bureau of Economic Research, Cambridge, MA.

Barr, N. 2008. "Financing Higher Education." In *Annual World Bank Conference on Development Economics—Regional, 2008: Higher Education and Development,* ed. Justin Yifu Lin and Boris Pleskovic, 143–74. Washington, DC: World Bank.

Barro, R. J., and X. Sala-i-Martin. 1995. *Economic Growth.* New York: McGraw-Hill.

Bastiaens, J. 2009. *International Assistance and State-University Relations (Studies in Higher Education)*. New York: Routledge.

Baum, S., and K. Payea. 2005. *Education Pays 2004: The Benefits of Higher Education for Individuals and Society*. New York: College Board Publications.

BDLINK Cambodia Co. 2008. *Youth and Employment: Bridging the Gap*. Youth Employment and Social Dialogue Project. Cambodia Federation of Employers and Business Associations, Phnom Penh.

Berdahl, R. O. 1971. *Statewide Coordination of Higher Education*. Washington, DC: American Council on Education.

Berman, E., J. Bound, and S. Machin. 1998. "Implications of Skill-Biased Technological Change: International Evidence." *Quarterly Journal of Economics* 113 (4): 1245–80.

Berry, C. R., and E. L. Glaeser. 2005. "The Divergence of Human Capital Levels across Cities." NBER Working Paper Series 11617, National Bureau of Economic Research, Cambridge, MA.

Bertschy, K., M. A. Cattaneo, and S. C. Wolter. 2009. "PISA and the Transition into the Labor Market." *LABOUR: Review of Labour Economics and Industrial Relations* 23 (Special Issue): 111–37.

Bjarnason, S., K. M. Cheng, J. Fielden, M. J. Lemaitre, and D. Levy. 2009. *A New Dynamic: Private Higher Education*. Paris: United Nations Educational, Scientific and Cultural Organization (UNESCO).

Bladh, A. 2007. "Institutional Autonomy with Increasing Dependency on Outside Actors." *Higher Education Policy* 20: 243–59.

Bloom, D., M. Hartley, and H. Rosovsky. 2004. "Beyond Private Gain: The Public Benefits of Higher Education." In *International Handbook of Higher Education*, vol. 18, I, ed. J.J.F. Forest and P. Altbach, 293–308. Oxford: Oxford University Press.

Borghans, L., A. L. Duckworth, J. J. Heckman, and B. ter Weel. 2008. "The Economics and Psychology of Personality Traits." *Journal of Human Resources* 43 (4): 972–1059.

Boudard, E. 2001. *Literacy Proficiency, Earnings and Recurrent Training: A Ten Country Comparative Study*. Stockholm: Institute of International Education, Stockholm University.

BPS (Badan Pusat Statistik). 1994, 1996, 1999, 2001, 2003, 2005, 2006. *Indonesia National Labor Force Survey (SAKERNAS)*. Jakarta, Indonesia.

———. 1998, 2007, 2009. *Indonesia National Socioeconomic Survey (SUSENAS)*. Jakarta, Indonesia.

Bramwell, A., and D. A. Wolfe. 2008. "Universities and Regional Economic Development: The Entrepreneurial University of Waterloo." *Research Policy* 37 (8): 1175–87.

Brimble, P., and R. F. Doner. 2007. "University-Industry Links and Economic Development: The Case of Thailand." *World Development* 35 (6): 1021–36.

Buchori, M., and A. Malik. 2004. "Higher Education in Indonesia." In *Asian Universities: Historical Perspectives and Contemporary Challenges,* ed. P. Altbach and T. Umakoshi, 249–78. Baltimore: Johns Hopkins University Press.

Byun, K. 2008. "New Public Management in Korean Higher Education: Is It Reality or Another Fad?" *Asia Pacific Education Review* 9 (2): 190–205.

Ca, T. N. 2006. "Universities as Drivers of the Urban Economies in Asia: The Case of Vietnam." Policy Research Working Paper Series 3949, World Bank, Washington, DC.

Cai, Y., and F. Yan. 2009. "The Responses of Private Higher Education Institutions to Market-Oriented Environments in China—an Institutional Approach." Paper presented at the 22nd CHER (Consortium of Higher Education Researchers) conference, Porto, Portugal, September 10–12.

Cao, Y. 2007. "Chinese Private Colleges and the Labor Market." PhD diss., Educational Administration and Policy Studies, University at Albany, State University of New York.

Carney, R. W., and L. Y. Zheng. 2009. "Institutional Incentives to Innovate: An Explanation for Singapore's Innovation Gap." *Journal of East Asian Studies* (May–August).

CASS-IPS (Institute for Population Studies at the Chinese Academy of Social Sciences). 1999, 2005. China Urban Labor Survey (CULS). CASS-IPS, Beijing, China.

Castellacci, F., and D. Archibugi. 2008. "The Technology Clubs: The Distribution of Knowledge across Nations." *Research Policy* 37 (10): 1659–73.

Chapman, B., and P. Drysdale. 2008. "Financing Higher Education in East Asia." *East Asian Bureau of Economic Research Newsletter* (August). http://www.eaber.org/intranet/publish/Public/newsletters.php.

Chapman, D. W. 2010. "Higher Education Faculty in East Asia." Background paper prepared for World Bank 2011, University of Minnesota. http://siteresources.worldbank.org/INTEAST ASIAPACIFIC/Resources/EastAsia-Higher EducationFaculty.pdf.

Chen, K., and M. Kenney. 2007. "Universities/ Research Institutes and Regional Innovation Systems: The Cases of Beijing and Shenzhen." *World Development* 35 (6): 1056–74.

Cloete, N. 2002. "South African Higher Education and Social Transformation." *Higher Education Digest Supplement* (Autumn).

Cohn, E., S.L.W. Rhine, and M. C. Santos. 1989. "Institutions of Higher Education as Multi-Product Firms: Economies of Scale and Scope." *Review of Economics and Statistics* 71 (2): 284–90.

Cornford, F. M. 1908. *Microcosmographia Academica: Being a Guide for the Young Academic Politician*. Cambridge: Bowes & Bowes.

Darby, M. R., L. G. Zucker, and A. Wang. 2004. "Universities, Joint Ventures and Success in the Advanced Technology Program." *Contemporary Economic Policy* 22 (2): 145–61.

Deng, P. 1997. *Private Education in Modern China*. Westport, CT: Praeger.

di Gropello, E. 2006. *Meeting the Challenges of Secondary Education in Latin America and East Asia: Improving Efficiency and Resource Mobilization*. Directions in Development Series. Washington, DC: World Bank.

di Gropello, E., A. Kruse, and P. Tandon. 2011. *Skills for the Labor Market in Indonesia: Trends in Skills Demand, Gaps, and Supply*. Directions in Development Series. Washington, DC: World Bank.

di Gropello, E., and C. Sakellariou. 2010. "Industry and Skill Wage Premiums in East Asia." Policy Research Working Paper Series 5379, World Bank, Washington, DC.

di Gropello, E., H. Tan, and P. Tandon. 2010. *Skills for the Labor Market in the Philippines*. Directions in Development Series. Washington, DC: World Bank.

Directorate General for Higher Education, Ministry of National Education. 2009. *Directorate General for Higher Education Annual Report 2009*. Indonesia.

Doner, R. F., P. Intarakumnerd, and B. K. Ritchie. 2010. "Higher Education and Thailand's National Innovation System." Background paper prepared for World Bank 2011, World Bank, Washington, DC. http://siteresources .worldbank.org/INTEASTASIAPACIFIC/ Resources/Thailand-HENationalInnovation System.pdf

Dowrick, S. 2003. "Ideas and Education: Level or Growth Effects?" NBER Working Paper Series 9709, National Bureau of Economic Research, Cambridge, MA.

EdStats (Education Statistics) (database). World dataBank, World Bank, Washington, DC. http://databank.worldbank.org.

Estermann, T., and T. Nokkala. 2009. *University Autonomy in Europe I: Exploratory Study*. Brussels: European University Association.

The Expert Group on New Skills for New Jobs. 2010. "New Skills for New Jobs: Action Now." A report prepared for the European Commission, European Union, Brussels.

Fajnzylber, P., and A. M. Fernandes. 2004. "International Economic Activities and the Demand for Skilled Labor: Evidence from Brazil and China." Policy Research Working Paper Series 3426, World Bank, Washington, DC.

Farrell, D., and A. J. Grant. 2005. "China's Looming Skilled Labor Shortage," *McKinsey Quarterly* (November). http://mkqpreview1.qdweb .net/article_page.aspx?ar=1685.

Feenstra, R. C., and G. H. Hanson. 1997. "Foreign Direct Investment and Relative Wages: Evidence from Mexico's Maquiladoras." *Journal of International Economics* 42 (3–4): 371–94.

Feldman, K. 1987. "Research Productivity and Scholarly Accomplishment of College Teachers as Related to Their Instructional Effectiveness: A Review and Exploration." *Research in Higher Education* 26 (3): 227–98.

Fielden, J. 2008. "Global Trends in University Governance." World Bank Education Paper Series, World Bank, Washington, DC. http:// siteresources.worldbank.org/EDUCATION/ Resources/278200-1099079877269/547664-1099079956815/Global_Trends_University _Governance_webversion.pdf.

Fielden, J., and N. LaRocque. 2008. "The Evolving Regulatory Context for Private Education in Emerging Economies." Education Working Paper Series 14, International Finance Corporation and World Bank, Washington, DC.

Fry, R. 2004. "Latino Youth Finishing College: The Role of Selective Pathways." Pew Hispanic Center Report, Washington, DC.

Geiger, R., and C. Sa. 2008 *Tapping the Riches of Science: Universities and the Promise of Economic Growth*. Cambridge, MA: Harvard University Press.

Gittleman, M., and E. N. Wolff. 1993. "International Comparisons of Inter-industry Wage Differentials." *Review of Income and Wealth* 39 (3): 295–312.

Glaeser, E. L. 2007. "Entrepreneurship and the City." NBER Working Papers Series 13551, National Bureau of Economic Research, Cambridge, MA.

Goldberg, P. K., and N. Pavcnik. 2005. "Trade, Wages, and the Political Economy of Trade Protection: Evidence from the Colombian Trade Reforms." *Journal of International Economics* 66 (1): 75–105.

Gonzales, P., J. C. Guzman, L. Partelow, E. Pahlke, L. Jocelyn, D. Kastberg, and T. Williams. 2004. *Highlights from the Trends in International Mathematics and Science Study (TIMSS) 2003.* Washington, DC: National Center for Education Statistics.

Gonzales, P., T. Williams, L. Jocelyn, S. Roey, D. Kastberg, and S. Brenwald. 2008. *Highlights from TIMSS 2007: Mathematics and Science Achievement of U.S. Fourth- and Eighth-Grade Students in an International Context.* Washington, DC: National Center for Education Statistics.

Government of the Philippines. 2007. *Comments of the National Economic and Development Authority on the Joint Resolution Creating a Congressional Commission to Review and Assess the State of Competitiveness of Science and Technology.* Manila: Government of the Philippines.

GSO (General Statistics Office) [Vietnam]. 1992, 1998, 2004. *Vietnam Living Standards Survey (VLSS).* Hanoi, Vietnam: General Statistics Office

———. 2006. *Result of the Viet Nam Household Living Standards Survey* [VHLSS] *2006.* Hanoi, Vietnam: General Statistics Office.

———. 2008. *Result of the Survey on Household Living Standards* [VHLSS] *2008.* Hanoi, Vietnam: General Statistics Office.

Guan, J. C., R. C. Yam, and C. K. Mok. 2005. "Collaboration between Industry and Research Institutes/Universities on Industrial Innovation in Beijing." *Technology Analysis and Strategic Management* 17 (3): 339–53.

Hansen, M. T., H. W. Chesbrough, N. Nohria, and D. N. Sull. 2000. "Networked Incubators: Hothouses of the New Economy." *Harvard Business Review* 78 (5): 74–84.

Hanushek, E. A., and L. Wößmann. 2007. *Education Quality and Economic Growth.* Washington, DC: World Bank.

Hashimoto, K., and E. Cohn. 1997. "Economies of Scale and Scope in Japanese Private Universities." *Education Economics* 5 (2): 107–15.

Hattie, J., and H. W. Marsh. 1996. "The Relationship between Research and Teaching: A Meta-Analysis. *Review of Educational Research* 66 (4): 507–42.

Heckman, J. J., J. Stixrud, and S. Urzua. 2006. "The Effects of Cognitive and Noncognitive Abilities on Labor Market Outcomes and Social Behavior." *Journal of Labor Economics* 24 (3): 411–82.

Hicks, M., and George, R. 1998. "Approaches to Improving Student Learning at the University of South Australia." Presentation at the HERDSA annual conference "Transformation in Higher Education," Auckland, New Zealand, July 7–10.

Hill, H., and P. Tandon. 2010. "Innovation and Technological Capability in Indonesia." Background paper prepared for World Bank 2011, World Bank, Washington, DC.

Hoachlander, G., A. C. Sikora, and L. Horn. 2003. *Community College Students: Goals, Academic Preparation, and Outcomes.* NCES 2003-164, National Center for Education Statistics. Washington, DC: U.S. Department of Education.

HRINC. 2010. "Higher Education and Skills for the Labor Market in Cambodia." Background paper prepared for World Bank 2011, HRINC, Phnom Penh, Cambodia.

Huisman, J., and J. Currie. 2004. "Accountability in Higher Education: Bridge over Troubled Water?" *Higher Education* 48 (4): 529–51.

IMF (International Monetary Fund). 2006. *World Economic Outlook 2006: Financial Systems and Economic Cycles.* Washington, DC: IMF.

Information Office of the State Council of the People's Republic of China. 2005. "Regional Autonomy for Ethnic Minorities in China." White Paper on Ethnic Minorities, Information Office of the State Council of the People's Republic of China, Beijing. http://www.china.org.cn/e-white/20050301/index.htm.

Ingles, S. J., J. A. Owings, P. Kaufman, M. N. Alt, and X. Chen. 2002. *Coming of Age in the 1990s: The Eighth-Grade Class of 1988 12 Years Later.* Washington, DC: U.S. Department of Education, Institute of Education Sciences, National Center for Education Statistics.

Jakubowski, M., H. A. Patrinos, E. Porta, and J. Wisniewski. 2010. "The Impact of the 1999 Education Reform in Poland." Policy Research Working Paper Series 5263, World Bank, Washington, DC.

Jenkins, A., T. Vlackman, R. Lindsay, and R. Paton-Salzburg. 1998. "Teaching and Research: Student Perspectives and Policy Implications." *Studies in Higher Education* 23 (2): 127–41.

Johanson, R. K., and A. V. Adams. 2004. *Skills Development in Sub-Saharan Africa*. Washington, DC: World Bank.

Johnson, G. 1994 *University Politics: F.M. Cornford's Cambridge and His Advice to the Young Academic Politician*. Cambridge: Cambridge University Press.

Johnstone, B. D. 2004. "The Economics and Politics of Cost Sharing in Higher Education: Comparative Perspectives." *Economics of Education Review* 23 (4): 403–10.

KAM (Knowledge Assessment Methodology) (data tool). World Bank, Washington, DC. https://www.worldbank.org/kam.

Kapur, D., and M. Crowley. 2008. "Beyond the ABCs: Higher Education and Developing Countries." Working Paper Series 139, Center for Global Development, Washington, DC.

Kennedy, K. J., and Z. Lee. 2008. *The Changing Role of Schools in Asian Societies: Schools for the Knowledge Society*. London: Routledge.

Kim, A., and Y. Lee. 2008. *Student Loan Schemes in the Republic of Korea: Review and Recommendations*. Bangkok, Thailand: UNESCO.

Kim, S., and J.-H. Lee. 2006. "Changing Facets of Korean Higher Education: Market Competition and the Role of the State." *Higher Education* 52 (3): 557–87.

Kirsch, I. S., A. Jungeblut, L. Jenkins, and A. Kolstad. 1993. *Adult Literacy in America: A First Look at the Results of the National Adult Literacy Survey*. Princeton, NJ: Educational Testing Service.

Kodama, F., and J. Suzuki. 2007. "How Japanese Companies Have Used Scientific Advances to Restructure Their Business: The Receiver-Active National System of Innovation." *World Development* 35 (6): 976–90.

Kodama, T. 2008. "The Role of Intermediation and Absorptive Capacity in Facilitating University-Industry Linkages—an Empirical Study of TAMA in Japan." *Research Policy* 37 (8): 1224–40.

Koshal, R. K., and M. Koshal. 1999. "Economies of Scale and Scope in Higher Education: A Case of Comprehensive Universities." *Economics of Education Review* 18 (2): 269–77.

Kruss, G., and J. Lorentzen. 2007. "University-Industry Links for Development: The Case of Western Cape Province, South Africa." World Bank, Washington, DC.

Lai, M., and L.N.K. Lo. 2007. "The Changing Work Lives of Academics: The Experience of a Regional University in the Chinese Mainland." *Higher Education Policy* 20 (20): 145–67.

Lane, K., and F. Pollner. 2008. "How to Address China's Growing Talent Shortage," *McKinsey Quarterly* (July). http://www.mckinseyquarterly.com/How_to_address_Chinas_growing_talent_shortage_2156.

LaRocque, N. 2002. *Private Education in the Philippines: A Market and Regulatory Survey*. Manila: Asian Development Bank.

Laursen, K., and A. Salter. 2004. "Searching High and Low: What Types of Firms Use Universities as a Source of Innovation?" *Research Policy* 33: 1201–15.

Lederman, D., and W. F. Maloney. 2003. "R&D and Development." Policy Research Working Paper 3024, World Bank, Washington, DC.

Lee, M. 1999. "Corporatization, Privatization, and Internationalization of Higher Education in Malaysia." In *Private Prometheus: Private Higher Education and Development in the 21st Century*, ed. P. Altbach, 137–61. Westport, CT: Greenwood Press.

———. 2004. "Malaysian Universities: Toward Equality, Accessibility, and Quality." In *Asian Universities: Historical Perspectives and Contemporary Challenges*, ed. P. Altbach and T. Umakoshi, 221–46. Baltimore, MD: Johns Hopkins University Press.

Lee, S. H. 1998. "Korean Private Higher Education Faces Economic Crisis." *International Higher Education* 13: 9–20.

Levy, D. 2008a. "Exploring the Viability of a Semi-Elite Category." Paper presented at the 33rd Annual Conference of the Association for the Study of Higher Education (ASHE), International Division, Jacksonville, Florida, November 5–8.

———. 2008b. "Private Higher Education's Global Surge: Emulating U.S. Patterns?" Paper presented at Privatization in Higher Education Conference, Samuel Nieman Institute for Advanced Studies in Science and Technology, Technion, Haifa, Israel, January 6–8.

———. 2010. "East Asian Private Higher Education: Reality and Policy." Background paper prepared for World Bank 2011, University of Albany, State University of New York.

Li, C., ed. 2005. *Bridging Minds across the Pacific: U.S.-China Educational Exchanges, 1978–2003*. New York: Lexington Books.

Lin, J. 1999. *Social Transformation and Private Education in China*. Westport, CT: Praeger.

Lin, T.-C. 2004. "The Role of Higher Education in Economic Development: An Empirical Study of Taiwan Case." *Journal of Asian Economics* 15 (2): 355–71.

Lin, Y., Y. Xia, L. Feixuai, L. Jing, H. Weilie, and W. Junyong. 2005. "The Beida Reform Triggers Chain Reactions." *Chinese Education and Society* 38 (1): 49–61.

Linh, V. H., L. V. Thuy, and G. T. Long. 2010. "Equity and Access to Tertiary Education: The Case of Vietnam." Background paper prepared for World Bank 2011, Indochina Research & Consulting (IRC) and National Economics University, Hanoi.

Loyalka, P. K. 2009. "Is Aid Reaching Poor Students? The Distribution of Student Financial Aid across Chinese Higher Education System." Paper presented at the 2009 International Academic Symposium on Higher Education Finance, Beijing, November 7.

Luan, Z. 2007. "Exploration of the Problem of Equal Access to Higher Education in Shangdong Province." Unpublished master's thesis, Shangdong Normal University, China.

Lundvall, B.-Å. 2007. "National Innovation Systems: Analytical Concept and Development Tool." *Industry and Innovation* 14 (1): 95–119.

Ma, W. 2010. "Equity and Access to Tertiary Education: Case Study—China." Background paper prepared for World Bank 2011. http://site resources.worldbank.org/EASTASIAPACIFIC EXT/Resources/226300-1279680449418/ HigherEd_ChinaEquityStudy.pdf.

Macerinskiene, I., and Vaiksnoraite, B. 2006. "The Role of Higher Education to Economic Development." *Vadyba (Management)* 2 (11): 82–90.

Martinez, M., and S. Klopott. 2005. *The Link between High School Reform and College Access and Success for Low-Income and Minority Youth*. Washington, DC: American Youth Policy Forum and Pathways to College Network.

Marton, S. 2000. *The Mind of the State: The Politics of University Autonomy in Sweden, 1968–1998*. Göteborg: BAS Publishers.

Mei, T. A. 2002. *Malaysian Private Higher Education: Globalization, Privatization, Transformation and Marketplaces*. London: ASEAN Academic Press.

Michaelowa, K. 2007. "The Impact of Primary and Secondary Education on Higher Education Quality." *Quality Assurance in Education* 15 (2): 215–36.

Miner, A. S., D. T. Eesley, M. Devaughn, and T. Rura-Polley. 2001. "The Magic Beanstalk Vision: Commercializing University Inventions and Research." In *The Entrepreneurship Dynamic: Origins of Entrepreneurship and the Evolution of Industries*, ed. C.B. Schoonhoven and E. Romanelli, 109–46. Palo Alto, CA: Stanford University Press.

Mingat, A., B. Ledoux, and R. Rakotomalala. 2010. *Developing Post-Primary Education in Sub-Saharan Africa: Assessing the Financial Sustainability of Alternative Pathways*. Africa Human Development Series. World Bank: Washington, DC.

Ministry of Education, Singapore. 2005. "Education in Singapore: Corporate Brochure." Singapore.

Ministry of Education and Human Resources Development, Republic of Korea. 2010. "Brain Korea 21, a Project for Nurturing Highly Qualified Human Resources for the 21st Century Knowledge-Based Society." Ministry of Education, Seoul. http://unpan1.un.org/ intradoc/groups/public/documents/apcity/ unpan015416.pdf.

Mitchell, J. E., and D. S. Rebne. 1995. "Nonlinear Effects of Teaching and Consulting on Academic Research Productivity." *Socio-Economic Planning Sciences* 29 (1): 47–57.

Moeliodihardjo, B. Y. 2010. "Equity and Access in Higher Education: The Case of Indonesia." Background paper prepared for World Bank 2011, Fakultas Ilmu Komputer Universitas Indonesia, Indonesia.

MOET (Ministry of Education and Training), Vietnam. 2005, 2010. University Survey. Hanoi, Vietnam.

Mok, K. H. 2009. "The Quest for Regional Hub of Education: Searching for New Governance and Regulatory Regimes in Singapore, Hong Kong and Malaysia." Paper prepared for the East-West Senior Seminar on Quality Issues in the Emerging Knowledge Society. Kuala Lumpur, Malaysia, October.

———. 2010. "Innovation and Higher Education: A Comparative Study of Five Asian Societies." Background paper prepared for World Bank 2011, Hong Kong Institute of Education, Hong Kong.

Moon, M., and K. Kim. 2001. "A Case of Korean Higher Education Reform: The Brain Korea 21

Project." *Asia Pacific Education Review* 2 (2): 96–105.

Motohashi, K. 2005. "University-Industry Collaborations in Japan: The Role of New Technology-Based Firms in Transforming the National Innovation System." *Research Policy* 34 (5): 583–94.

Mukherjee, H. 2010. "Access to and Equity in Higher Education: Malaysia." Background paper prepared for World Bank 2011, World Bank, Washington, DC.

Mullis, I., M. Martin, E. Gonzalez, K. Gregory, R. Garden, K. O'Connor, S. Chrostowski, and T. Smith. 2000. *TIMSS 1999 International Mathematics Report: Findings from IEA's Repeat of the Third International Mathematics and Science Study at the Eighth Grade.* Chestnut Hill, MA: Boston College.

National Science Board. 2008. *Science and Engineering Indicators 2008.* Arlington, VA: National Science Foundation.

National Statistical Office of Mongolia. 1998, 2002, 2007, 2010. *Living Standards Measurement Survey (LSMS).* Ulaanbaatar, Mongolia: National Statistical Office. http://www.nso.mn.

Neave, G., and F. A. van Vught, eds. 1994. *Government and Higher Education Relationships across Three Continents: The Winds of Change.* Oxford: Pergamon.

Nelson, R. 1987. *Understanding Technical Change as an Evolutionary Process.* Amsterdam: Elsevier Science.

Newman, J. H. 1976 [1st ed. 1852]. *The Idea of a University.* Oxford: Clarendon Press.

NIS (National Institute of Statistics). 1997, 1999, 2003, 2007, 2009. *Cambodia Socio-Economic Survey (CSES).* National Institute of Statistics. Phnom Penh, Cambodia.

NSO Philippines (National Statistics Office, Republic of the Philippines). 2000a, 2006a. *Family Income and Expenditure Survey (FIES).* Manila, Philippines: National Statistics Office.

———. 1988, 1991, 1994, 1997, 2000b, 2001, 2004, 2006b. *Labor Force Survey (LFS).* Manila, Philippines: National Statistics Office.

NSO Thailand (National Statistical Office Thailand). 1990, 1992, 1994, 1996, 1998, 2000, 2002, 2004, 2006. *Thailand Socio-Economic Survey (SES).* Bangkok, Thailand: National Statistical Office.

OECD (Organisation for Economic Co-operation and Development). 2004. "The Internationalisation of Higher Education." OECD Policy Brief (August), OECD, Paris.

———. 2005. *Learning a Living: First Results of the Adult Literacy and Life Skills Survey.* Paris: OECD.

———. 2007a. *OECD Education at a Glance 2007.* Paris: OECD.

———. 2007b. *Program for International Student Assessment 2006.* Paris: OECD.

———. 2008a. *The Internationalisation of Business R&D: Evidence, Impact and Implications.* Paris: OECD.

———. 2008b. *Tertiary Education for the Knowledge Economy.* Paris: OECD.

———. 2009a. *OECD Reviews of Tertiary Education: China 2009.* Paris: OECD.

———. 2009b. *OECD Reviews of Tertiary Education: Korea 2009.* Paris: OECD.

———. 2009c. *OECD Reviews of Tertiary Education: Japan.* Paris: OECD.

———. 2010a. *PISA 2009 Results: Overcoming Social Background: Equity in Learning Opportunities and Outcomes.* Volume II. Paris: OECD.

———. 2010b. *PISA 2009 Results: What Students Know and Can Do: Student Performance in Reading, Mathematics and Science.* Volume I. Paris: OECD.

Okada, A. 2005. "A History of the Japanese University." In *The "Big Bang" in Japanese Higher Education: The 2004 Reforms and the Dynamics of Change,* ed. J. G. Eades, R. Goodman, and Y. Hada, 32–51. Melbourne: Trans Pacific Press.

Orbeta, A. C., Jr. 2008. "Higher Education in the Philippines." World Bank, Washington, DC. Background paper prepared for di Gropello, Tan, and Tandon. 2010, World Bank, Washington, DC.

Patton, D., L. Warren, and D. Bream. 2009. "Elements That Underpin High-Tech Business Incubation Processes." *Journal of Technology Transfer* 34 (6): 621–36.

Permani, R. 2009. "The Role of Education in Economic Growth in East Asia: A Survey." *Asian-Pacific Economic Literature* 23 (1): 1–20.

Ping Chung, Y. 2007. *The Student Loans Scheme in Hong Kong.* Bangkok, Thailand: UNESCO Bangkok; Paris: International Institute of Educational Planning. http://ddp-ext.world bank.org/EdStats/CHNpub03.pdf.

Postiglione, G. 2006. "Higher Education in China: Perils and Promises for a New Century." *Harvard China Review* 5 (2): 138–43.

Postiglione, G., and G. Mak, eds. 1997. *Asian Higher Education: An International Handbook and Reference Guide*. Westport, CT: Greenwood Press.

Potter, J. 2008. "Entrepreneurship and Higher Education: Future Policy Directions." In *Entrepreneurship and Higher Education*, ed. J. Potter, chapter 14. Paris: OECD Local Economic and Employment Programme.

Praphamontripong, P. 2010. "Intra-Sectoral Diversity: A Political Economy of Thai Private Higher Education." PhD diss., Educational Administration and Policy Studies, University at Albany, State University of New York.

PROPHE (Program for Research on Private Higher Education) International Databases. Private and Public Higher Education Shares. University of Albany, State University of New York. http://www.albany.edu/dept/eaps/prophe/data/international.html. Accessed October 2010.

Przirembel, C. 2005. "Transplanting Industries: The ICAR Project: Embedding the Automotive Industry in South Carolina." Paper presented at MIT's "1st International Conference on Local Innovation Systems," Cambridge, MA, December 13.

Raza, R. 2010. "Higher Education Governance in East Asia." Background paper prepared for World Bank 2011, World Bank, Washington, DC. http://siteresources.worldbank.org/INTEASTASIAPACIFIC/Resources/HigherEducationGovernance.pdf.

Rosenzweig, M. 2009. "Higher Education and International Migration in Asia: Brain Circulation." In *Annual World Bank Conference on Development Economics 2008, Regional: Higher Education and Development*, ed. J. Y. Lin and B. Pleskovic, 59–84. Washington, DC: World Bank.

Round, A. 2003. "Higher Education and 'Skills' in ICT Disciplines: A Partial Review of the Literature." Produced for the Council of Professors and Heads of Computing (CPHC), Swindon, United Kingdom.

Rumbley, L., I. Pacheco, and P. Altbach. 2008. *International Comparison of Academic Salaries*. Boston: Boston College, Center for International Higher Education.

Sakellariou, C. 2010a. "Access to and Equity of Higher Education in East Asia." Background paper prepared for World Bank 2011, World Bank, Washington, DC.

———. 2010b. "Labor Market Outcomes of Higher Education in East Asia." Background paper prepared for World Bank 2011, World Bank, Washington, DC.

Salmi, J. 2007. "Autonomy from the State vs. Responsiveness to Markets." *Higher Education Policy* 20 (3): 223–42.

———. 2009. *The Challenge of Establishing World-Class Universities*. Washington, DC: World Bank.

Salmi, J., and A. M. Hauptman. 2006. "Innovations in Tertiary Education Financing: A Comparative Evaluation of Allocation Mechanisms." Education Working Paper Series 4, World Bank, Washington, DC.

Salmi, J., and A. Saroyan. 2007. "League Tables as Policy Instruments: Uses and Misuses." *Higher Education Management and Policy* 19 (2): 24–62.

Schiller, D., and P. Brimble. 2009. "Capacity Building for University-Industry Linkages in Developing Countries: The Case of the Thai Higher Education Development Project." *Science, Technology and Society* 14 (1): 59–92.

Schott, P. K. 2006. "The Relative Sophistication of Chinese Exports." NBER Working Paper 12173, National Bureau of Economic Research, Cambridge, MA.

Scotchmer, S. 2004. *Innovation and Incentives*. Cambridge, MA: MIT Press.

Senker, J. 1995. "Tacit Knowledge and Models of Innovation." *Industrial and Corporate Change* 4 (2): 425–47.

Sianesi, B., and J. van Reenen. 2003. "The Returns to Education: Macroeconomics." *Journal of Economic Surveys* 17: 157–200.

SJTU (Shanghai Jiao Tong University) Academic Ranking of World Universities (ARWU). http://www.arwu.org/.

Smeaton, B., and M. Hughes. 2003. "A Basis for Skills: Investigating Intermediate Skills." Learning Skills and Development Agency, London.

Smeby, J.-C. 1998. "Knowledge Production and Knowledge Transmission: The Interaction between Research and Teaching at Universities." *Teaching in Higher Education* 3 (1): 7–20.

Sohn, D.-W., and M. Kenney. 2007. "Universities, Clusters, and Innovation Systems: The Case of Seoul, Korea." *World Development* 35 (6): 991–1004.

Sorensen, C. W. 1994. "Success and Education in South Korea." *Comparative Education* 38: 10–35.

Steiner-Khamasi, G., and I. Stolpe. 2004. "Decentralization and Recentralization Reform in

Mongolia: Tracing the Swing of the Pendulum." *Comparative Education* 40: 29–53.

Sukamoto. 2002. "Private Higher Education in Indonesia." In *The Report of the Second Regional Seminar on Private Higher Education: Its Role in Human Resource Development in a Globalised Knowledge Society*, ed. UNESCO PROAP and SEAMEO RIHED, 39–46. Bangkok, Thailand: UNESCO-RIHED.

Sutton Trust. 2004. "Select Government Fund Matching Programmes: An Examination of Characteristics and Effectiveness." CASE Europe, London.

Tan, E. A. 2010. "The State of the Philippines' National Innovation System." Background paper prepared for World Bank 2011, University of the Philippines, Manila. http://site resources.worldbank.org/INTEASTASIA PACIFIC/Resources/philippine-national-innovation-system.pdf.

Tangkitvanich, S., and A. Manasboonphempool. 2010. "Evaluating the Student Loan Fund of Thailand." *Economics of Education Review* 29: 710–21.

Tansinsin, L. 2007. "Filipino Experience in Fostering University-Industry Partnership." World Intellectual Property Organization, Geneva, Switzerland.

Tertiary Education Commission of New Zealand. 2009. *Tertiary Education Commission Statement of Intent 2009–2012*. New Zealand: Tertiary Education Commission.

THE (Times Higher Education) World University Rankings. http://www.timeshighereducation .co.uk/.

TIMSS (Trends in International Mathematics and Science Study) (database). U.S. Deparment of Education, Institute of Education Sciences (IES), National Center for Education Statistics, Washington, DC. http://nces.ed .gov/timss/.

Tybout, J. 2000. "Manufacturing Firms in Developing Countries: How Well Do They Do and Why?" *Journal of Economic Literature* 38: 11–44.

UNESCO (United Nations Educational, Scientific and Cultural Organization). 2005. *Education Policy and Strategy Simulation Model EPSSim Version 2.1*. Paris: UNESCO.

———. 2006. *Higher Education in South-East Asia*. Bangkok: UNESCO Asia and Pacific Regional Bureau for Education.

UNESCO (United Nations Educational, Scientific and Cultural Organization) Asia Pacific Quality Network. 2006. *Regulating the Quality of Cross-Border Education*. Bangkok: UNESCO Asia and Pacific Regional Bureau for Education.

UIS (UNESCO Institute for Statistics) Data Centre. Montreal, Canada. http://www.uis .unesco.org/Pages/default.aspx.

UIS. 2009. *Global Education Digest 2009: Comparing Education Statistics across the World*. Montreal, Canada: UIS.

Usher, A. 2005. *A Little Knowledge Is a Dangerous Thing: How Perceptions of Costs and Benefits Affect Access to Education*. Toronto, ON: Educational Policy Institute.

Valisno, M. D. 2002. "Private Higher Education in Philippines." In *The Report of the Second Regional Seminar on Private Higher Education: Its Role in Human Resource Development in a Globalised Knowledge Society*, ed. UNESCO PROAP and SEAMEO RIHED, 75–118. Bangkok, Thailand: UNESCO-RIHED.

van der Sluis, J., M. van Praag, and W. Vijverberg. 2008. "Education and Entrepreneurship Selection and Performance: A Review of the Empirical Literature." *Journal of Economic Surveys* 22 (5): 795–841.

Vandenbussche, J., P. Aghion, and C. Meghir. 2006. "Growth, Distance to Frontier and Composition of Human Capital." *Journal of Economic Growth* 11 (2): 97–127.

VCCI (Vietnam Chamber of Commerce and Industry). 2009. *Vietnam Business Annual Report 2008*. Hanoi, Vietnam: National Political Publishing House.

Wadhwa, V., G. Gereffi, B. Rising, and R. Ong. 2007. "Where the Engineers Are." *Issues in Science and Technology* Spring: 73–84.

WIPO (World Intellecutal Property Organization). 2009. *World Intellectual Property Indicators 2009*. Geneva: WIPO.

World Bank. 1997. *China: Higher Education Reform*. World Bank: Washington, DC.

———. 2003. *World Development Report 2004: Making Services Work for Poor People*. Washington, DC: World Bank and Oxford University Press.

———. 2005. "Project Appraisal Document: Managing Higher Education for Relevance and Efficiency Project." Report Series 31644-ID. Washington, DC: World Bank.

———. 2007. *Malaysia and the Knowledge Economy: Building a World-Class Higher Education System*. Washington, DC: World Bank.

———. 2008. *Vietnam: Higher Education and Skills for Growth*. Washington, DC: World Bank.

———. 2009a. *Thailand Social Monitor: Towards a Competitive Higher Education System in a Global Economy.* Bangkok, Thailand: World Bank.

———. 2009b. *Vietnam Knowledge Report Revised.* Washington, DC: World Bank.

———. 2010a. "Assessing the Quality of Education in Shanghai, China, Using PISA 2009." World Bank, Washington, DC.

———. 2010b. "Emerging Stronger from the Crisis." *East Asia and Pacific Economic Update, Volume 1.* Washington, DC: World Bank.

———. 2010c. "Indonesia: Higher Education Financing." World Bank, Washington, DC.

———. 2010d. "Mongolia Policy Note. Tertiary Education in Mongolia: Meeting the Challenges of the Global Economy." Report No. 52925–MN. World Bank, Washington, DC.

———. 2010e. "Program Appraisal Document for a Higher Education Quality and Capacity Improvement Project in Cambodia." Washington, DC: World Bank.

———. 2010f. "Program Document for a Higher Education Development Policy Credit to Vietnam." Washington, DC: World Bank.

———. 2010g. "Vietnam High Quality Education for All by 2020." World Bank, Washington, DC.

———. 2011. *Putting Higher Education to Work: Skills and Research for Growth in East Asia.* Washington, DC: World Bank.

World Bank IC (Investment Climate) Surveys (database). World Bank, Washington, DC. https://www.enterprisesurveys.org.

World Development Indicators (WDI) database. World dataBank, World Bank, Washington, DC. http://databank.worldbank.org.

World Integrated Trade Solution (WITS) (data tool). World Bank, Washington, DC. https://wits.worldbank.org

Wright, M., B. Clarysse, A. Lockett, and M. Knockaert. 2008. "Mid-Range Universities' Links with Industry: Knowledge Types and the Role of Intermediaries." *Research Policy* 37 (8): 1205–23.

Wu, W. 2010. "Higher Education Innovation in China." Background paper prepared for World Bank 2011, Virginia Commonwealth University, Richmond, VA.

Yan, F. 2010. "The Academic Profession in China in the Context of Social Transition: An Institutional Perspective." *European Review* 18 (supplement 1): S117–39.

Yilmaz, Y. 2009. "Skills Development in East Asia: A Comparative Study of Supply of Education and Training Systems." Background paper prepared for Regional Study on Skills in East Asia, World Bank, Washington, DC.

———. 2010. "Higher Education Institutions in Thailand and Malaysia: Can They Deliver?" Background paper prepared for World Bank 2011, World Bank, Washington, DC.

Yonezawa, A., and M. Baba. 1998. "The Market Structure for Private Universities in Japan." *Tertiary Education and Management* 4 (2): 145–52.

Yusuf, S. 2003. *Innovative East Asia: the Future of Growth.* Washington, DC: World Bank.

Yusuf, S., and K. Nabeshima. 2009. *Tiger Economies under Threat: Comparative Analysis of Malaysia's Industrial Prospects and Policy Options.* Washington, DC: World Bank.

———. 2010. "From Technological Mastery to Innovation." Background paper prepared for World Bank 2011, World Bank, Washington, DC.

Zaman, M. Q. 2004. *Review of the Academic Evidence on the Relationship between Teaching and Research in Higher Education.* London: Department for Education and Skills Publications.

Zhou, Y. 2008. *The Inside Story of China's High-Tech Industry: Making Silicon Valley in Beijing.* New York: Rowman & Littlefield Publishers.

Ziderman, A. 2003. *Student Loans in Thailand: Are They Effective, Equitable, Sustainable?* Policy Research and Dialogue Student Loans Schemes in Asia Series, vol. 1, no. 1. Bangkok: United Nations Educational, Scientific and Cultural Organization and International Institute for Educational Planning.

———. 2004. *Policy Options for Student Loan Schemes: Lessons from Five Asian Case Studies.* Policy Research and Dialogue Student Loans Schemes in Asia Series, vol. 1, no. 6. Bangkok: United Nations Educational, Scientific and Cultural Organization and International Institute for Educational Planning.

———. 2006. "Student Loans in Thailand: From Social Targeting to Cost Sharing." *International Higher Education* 42: 6–8.